IN THE EVENT

IN THE EVENT
Toward an Anthropology of Generic Moments

Edited by

Lotte Meinert and Bruce Kapferer

berghahn
NEW YORK · OXFORD
www.berghahnbooks.com

First published in 2015 by

Berghahn Books

www.berghahnbooks.com

© 2015 Berghahn Books

Originally published as a special issue of *Social Analysis*, volume 54, issue 3.

Library of Congress Cataloging-in-Publication Data

In the event : toward an anthropology of generic moments / edited by
    Lotte Meinert and Bruce Kapferer.
        pages cm
    Originally published as a special issue of Social analysis (volume 54,
    issue 3).
    Includes bibliographical references and index.
    ISBN 978-1-78238-889-0 (pbk. : alk. paper)—ISBN 978-1-78238-890-6 (ebook)
        1. Ethnology—Philosophy. 2. Ethnology—Methodology. 3. Symbolic
    anthropology. 4. Experience. 5. Life change events. I. Meinert, Lotte,
    editor. II. Kapferer, Bruce. III. Social analysis (Adelaide, S.A.)

    GN345.I4 2014
    306.01—dc23

                                                                2015005752

British Library Cataloguing in Publication Data

A catalogue record for this book is available from the British Library.

Printed on acid-free paper

CONTENTS

INTRODUCTION
In the Event—toward an Anthropology
of Generic Moments

Bruce Kapferer

Against the Case as Illustration: The Event in Anthropology

The exploration of events and situations has long been at the focus of anthropological ethnographic description. In common with many other disciplines in the social sciences and humanities, this has been so in two main and frequently combined senses: (1) as exemplifications or illustrations, usually in the form of case studies, of more general ethnographic descriptive or theoretical assertions, or (2) as happenings or occasions, slices of life, that establish a conundrum or problematic that the presentation of an ethnography and its analysis will solve or otherwise explain. Most anthropological ethnographies offer examples or variations of the first. The second is relatively common, especially among historians, but perhaps the work of Clifford Geertz is the most celebrated example in anthropology. An outstanding instance is Geertz's (1980) study *Negara*, which opens with the mass suicide of the Balinese court before the Dutch invaders. This event sets the stage for his exploration of the Balinese theatre state, Geertz demonstrating the suicide as consistent with a Balinese political logic that presents power as defined and determined in the performance of status.

The concern with events and situations in this book seeks to extend beyond these more or less conventional usages and to argue for a deepening of the methodological significance of events and situations in anthropological ethnographic practice. The overall direction of the approach that I essay is one that takes the event as central to anthropological analysis rather than the concept of society, in relation to which the event or the event-as-case is commonly engaged, either to substantialize the abstract (society) or to provide a means to grasp the foundational or general organizational principles of society. The argument that I develop and toward which the chapters in this book are variously directed expresses both a continuity with conventional event-as-case approaches and, most importantly, a break with such perspectives. Ultimately, the aim is toward

Notes for this section begin on page 23.

the exploration of the event as a singularity of forces in which critical dimensions of socio-cultural existence reveal new potentials of the ongoing formation of socio-cultural realities. The approach to the event discussed here is one that goes beyond conventional perspectives of the event as representational of the social or of society and, instead, as a moment or moments of immanence and the affirmation and realization of potential. This orientation to the event is along the lines currently indicated in the work of post-structuralists, especially of a post-Nietzschean Deleuzian persuasion (see Deleuze 2004; Deleuze and Guattari 1987), who stress the idea of the social or society as a continual becoming, an open, a virtual in the differentiating process of multiple and shifting affirmations and realizations. The social or society in this perspective is not a closed totality representable in the event that if it expresses its world, it is also a force in its making, going beyond what it might be said to represent. Hitherto, such a view has largely been presented as a philosophical abstraction despite claims to the contrary, as in assertions of transcendental empiricism (Deleuze and Guattari 1994) in opposition, for example, to a Kantian transcendental idealism that underpins much Durkheimian anthropology and sociology in which the social or society is a relative closed organismic totality.

I start this discussion with the early development of an event approach in anthropology, initiated by Max Gluckman's Manchester School, which was partly motivated in the direction of more recent post-structuralist orientations. In certain respects it anticipated these later directions. The efforts of the Manchester group continue to be instructive regarding the limitations of event/situational analysis, as well as its renewed potential in the context of the current, if in critical ways distinct, methodological turn toward the event (Badiou 2006; Deleuze 2004).

Events and Situations: Gluckman's Manchester School

For the Manchester School,[1] events and/or situations (or situated practices) were not to be regarded in Gluckman's words as 'apt illustrations' of ethnographic generalizations concerning patterns or types of socio-cultural practice. The events or situated events that they analyzed were not significant as typical slices of lived reality as generally descriptively understood.[2] They were not to be seen as examples of a general pattern of action that might otherwise be indicated through interviews or social surveys. If anything, the events or situated practices attended to by the Manchester anthropologists were atypical, even unique, and their close investigation would reveal dimensions of the potentialities of the realities within which they irrupted. The atypicality of the events was of primary interest, most especially those that expressed conflict and crisis or threw into relief the social and political tensions that were conceived as being at the heart of everyday life. Events of conflict or of tension effectively constitute what the Manchester School (and before them the Rhodes-Livingstone Institute in Zambia) defined as significant events or practices that were likely to reveal the social and political forces engaged in the generation or production of social life. Rather than normative harmony or social integration—a common structural and functional orientation of the times in which cases or events were selected for their typicality—it was events that broke the apparent calm or routine of everyday life that were the focus of Gluckman's Manchester anthropology. Events of conflict or events that manifested social and political tension were not conceived of as dysfunctional or pathological, as in so much functional analysis; rather, they were seen positively as being vital in the definition and reproduction of social and political relations.[3] In Gluckman's analyses, irresolute contradictions in the social principles underpinning social life gave rise to recurring conflicts that could also drive radical social and political transformations of a kind that broke with patterns of the past and produced original institutional orders. For example, contrary to colonialist European imaginaries, some forms of chieftainship and kingship in southern African situations were relatively egalitarian and were centers of redistribution rather than accumulation, as in Europe. Gluckman was interested, especially with regard to his Zulu research, in how such institutions of rule could transform into dictatorial tyrannies.[4] This interest was connected to Gluckman's distinction between, on the one hand, change that involved a series of adjustments to dynamics of conflict (often expressed in patterns of social and political rebellion that appeared to repeat or reproduce the same institutional structures and customary values) and, on the other hand, repetitive change that involved a series of system-sustaining adjustments in response to dynamics of conflict (often expressed in patterns of social and political rebellion that appeared to repeat or reproduce the same institutional structures and customary values) and, on the other hand, change that took a more radical transformational and revolutionary form, involving the creation of new institutional and customary orders, as in the political-military system established by Shaka Zulu. However, despite the recognition of these two kinds of change, Gluckman and his colleagues stressed change as integral to all socio-political systems: it underpinned their key concept of process, which they introduced into the anthropological lexicon.

The Manchester approach to the analysis of apparently atypical non-normative events was that such events express incommensurabilities or incontrovertibilities that are integral to social relations. In terms of the Deleuzian perspective, which will be addressed later, the events of conflict upon which Gluckman and his colleagues concentrated were 'plateaus of intensity' (Deleuze and Guattari 1987). That is, they were moments in which the intransigencies and irresolvable tensions ingrained in social and personal life (the two being inseparable) boiled to the surface and became, if only momentarily, part of public awareness for the participants as well as for the anthropologist.

The methodological value that the Manchester group placed on events—specifically, events of conflict and contestation and not just any event or act or practice—was that they revealed what ordinary and routine social practices of a repeated, ongoing kind tend to obscure. Gluckman argued that events of conflict or eventful irruptions of social and personal crisis should be neither sidelined in ethnographic description in favor of the typically routine nor treated as exceptions, as in much anthropological accounts of the period. The innovation of Gluckman and the Manchester School was to make the event of crisis, the event of vital conflictual intensity, a primary focus of anthropological attention. Moreover, the critical event—atypical and often unique but not necessarily exceptional—was switched from being of secondary importance in anthropological ethnography (of 'the exception proves the rule' kind) to being of primary methodological worth (a site of potential), calling for more thorough investigation of its ethnographic realities.

Accordingly, Gluckman made the methodological recommendation that events be recorded in their fullest detail and in excess of the analytical requirements of those that struck the fieldworker as appropriate at the time. Thus, events were no more to be regarded as mere examples that necessarily supported the general ethnographic accounts within which they were nested. Effectively, they were to be treated as singularities and critical ethnographic moments in themselves to be addressed in the fullness of ethnographic detail. Furthermore, he advocated the description of events, as much as possible, from multiple perspectives or positions in the process of the forming of the event (see also Fibiger, this volume). Gluckman insisted that the ethnographers should make thoroughly evident their own positioning, including the sociological and personal factors involved in their own access and situating in the action of the event.

Here it should be added that Gluckman's insistence on detail was connected to his belief in anthropology as an empirical science whose arguments should be testable in terms of the evidence provided.[5] Although he accepted the importance of mathematics and statistics as methods for the validation of anthropological assertions, Gluckman understood anthropology to be thoroughly grounded in fieldwork observation. This, in his view, did not permit the abandonment of scientific rigor. The common representation of anthropology as a qualitative, interpretive discipline is often used to excuse anthropologists from certain criteria of scientific validation. The measures employed in anthropology might be different from many of the physical or biological sciences, but in Gluckman's opinion they should be no less exacting. Thus, a major objective of the emphasis on apparently excessive detail over and above the analytic or interpretive needs of the ethnographer was to enable reanalysis by other anthropologists in order to test the veracity of both the argument and the observation. For Gluckman and others to become associated with his group, no ethnographic fact or interpretation was independent of the individual bias of the ethnographer or observer. Interpretive assumptions were seen as likely to skew the way that ethnographic information was selected for presentation, perhaps resulting in the exclusion of crucial details. Therefore, Gluckman demanded that as much of the evidence as possible upon which argument was based should be presented, the aim being to open analysis to independent falsification. Moreover, such details had to be presented, along with the interpretations that were being made of them, to assist with reanalysis. This expands on some of Gluckman's methodological thinking, and that of his colleagues, behind the advocacy of 'situational analysis' to describe a method that did not separate data or information from the interpretational architecture leading to the establishment of analytical significance. The stress was not merely on the presentation of the facts of practice but also on the process of the analytical unfolding that laid claim to an understanding of the practice in the course of ethnographic presentation. Gluckman stressed the importance of the empirical while avoiding empiricism. Situational analysis demanded a setting out of the steps that are involved in abstract understanding while descriptively laying out the dynamics and process of action encompassed in events.

The focus on events in situational analysis, in other words, addressed the teleology implicated in general ethnographic description (what C. Wright Mills described as 'abstract empiricism') and in the conventional presentation of case material. The point is underlined if it is compared with Geertz's notion of 'thick description', which he exemplified in ethnographies such as *The Religion of Java* (1960) and especially *The Social History of an Indonesian Town* (1965). Geertz advocates a density of description, but it is not oriented to an internal destabilization of interpretation, which is an important objective behind the Manchester situational analysis approach.[6] Quite the reverse, in fact. Geertz's thick description appears to be a concern with the demonstration of complexity, a perspective developed further in North American postmodernist anthropology (see, e.g., Clifford and Marcus 1985), consistent with an atheoretical and anti-generalist relativism that would become a kind of fetishism of detail, diversity, and individual subjective variation in itself. Veena Das's (1995) approach to events in *Critical Events* should also be distinguished. Although superficially it might be seen as affiliated with the Gluckman orientation (due to the focus on conflict and crisis), the argument that she presents is another instance of the case as exemplary, as demonstrating general patterns—the case as illustration.

The Manchester stress on the steps in anthropological argument through the presentation of the event-ful practice upon which an anthropological analysis is built, along with an attention to the positioning of the anthropologist in the course of witnessed processes, bears some comparison with Husserl's recommendation for a scientific approach to human action. Husserl (1970) stressed that the distinction between a science of human being and other sciences was that the key instrument of the former is human being itself. This has major importance for the general anthropological recommendation of participant observation, and Gluckman's situational analysis was intended to carry it forward. I comment here that Gluckman was avowedly Durkheimian, particularly in the sense that he was convinced of a science of society,[7] but in an anti-sociological positivist way. Gluckman did not consider that the facts spoke for themselves, and the result was the situational analysis that he and his colleagues advocated. What Gluckman took from Durkheim was the emphasis on the social principles and institutional order of human social existence and the need for a methodology that was founded in this fact. Situational analysis and the event approach that Gluckman pioneered were to constitute just such an approach.

Much of the foregoing is made relatively clear in Gluckman's ([1940] 1958) now classic account of the bridge-opening ceremony in Zululand, Natal, South Africa. The bridge opening is significant as a critical event in the sense that it related vitally to the South African racial divide, the dominant socio-political cleavage as Gluckman wrote about it, and the complexities in its bridging (both literally and metaphorically). In many ways, the analysis that Gluckman was to build out of the event anticipated later discussions on the nature of hegemonic forces, the structures of discipline in colonial orders, and the dynamics of the invention of tradition, among other topics. The order of his essays connected to this event, with the last pursuing a problematic abstract discussion about social reproduction and the relation between equilibrium and change (Gluckman 1968), is partly intended to demonstrate that his argument arises out of the kind of detailed evidence he provides and the questions that it raises. Whether this is achieved is a matter of debate. Much of the argument he presents might have been made regardless of the details that he sets forth, although they do demonstrate a depth of penetration into the minutiae of social practices of the larger socio-economic and political forces that were at work globally and in South Africa at the time—details that a colonialist and traditionalist anthropology of the time ignored. However, these merits should not obscure the methodological point in Gluckman's concern with detail as a way to facilitate the necessity for the anthropologist to lay out the grounds and the kinds of observational evidence or sources from which the anthropologist's explanations and general descriptive assessments emerged.

Gluckman (1949) made this explicit in a trenchant attack on Bronislaw Malinowski's (1945) attempt to use anthropology in a consultant role to the white South African government, in which Malinowski appeared to abandon his anthropological and methodological prescriptions for sound understanding—among them, long-term immersion in the ethnographic context. Gluckman presented Malinowski's statements regarding change in Africa as being based on a superficial understanding fueled by theoretical opinions that had no basis in fact. Malinowski's demonstration of the worth of anthropological ethnography was subverted by the master himself. Gluckman regarded his recommendation of the methodology of situational analysis as an extension of the importance of Malinowski's own discoveries of the importance of participant-based ethnography and the attention to detail.

Gluckman's situational analysis was developed further by his Manchester colleagues. J. Clyde Mitchell[8] extended the method in his important essay *The Kalela Dance* (1956a), which explored practices of urban ethnicity in the Zambian Copperbelt. The *kalela* dance satisfied the notion of the event as crisis and as the playing through of conflict. It was a competitive contest, and in the dances and songs a conflict of interpretations was played out regarding the forming of customary life from the point of view of the diverse multi-ethnic African population of the Copperbelt.[9] Through the *kalela* event, Mitchell examined the processes underpinning the social construction of ethnicity and the role of identity in the constitution of social relations (what he described as 'categorical relations') that were situationally relative. The analysis is sometimes presented as an example of established sociological understandings concerning social and cultural stereotyping, but in keeping with the anti-normative orientation of the Manchester School, Mitchell was concerned with the situated limitations (i.e., the occasions governing the appropriate use of identity categories) of such stereotyping and the social circumstances of its engagement. In anthropology, the work was well in advance of its time. Anticipating Fredrik Barth's *Ethnic Groups and Boundaries* (1969) by more than 10 years, it stressed a similarly labile constructivist dynamic but without the individualist rationalist assumptions, whereby Barth conceived the use or not of ethnic categories being a matter of individual choice and having little connection to the structuring of situated relations.[10] One of Mitchell's critical concerns was the degree to which the practices that he recorded indicated the emergence of new directions in socio-cultural conceptions and practices, which he attempted to test through statistical analysis.

Here I underline Mitchell's use of statistical (and later mathematical) concepts in anthropological work and, in Mitchell's opinion, its conditionality upon situational analysis. Statistical work—the construction of interviews and the statistical search for significant patterns—was seen by Mitchell to be dependent on the insights gained through the observation of situated practices. Nothing could be discovered regarding the complexities of interpersonal relations and the social processes implicated in the relatively gross patterns that statistical analysis might pick up without the intensive analysis of situated action. Theory was to be derived from such action and to some degree tested through statistical work, which was to define its testable criteria on the basis of grounded observational experience that also facilitated the interpretation of statistics. Undertaking a statistical and mathematical analysis of human social phenomena without the kind of research that situational analysis afforded was to risk reification, that is, to constitute social realities out of essentially non-socially constituted arrangements and categories of data. This kind of statistical work, along with the development of general statements using statistically derived information, was for Mitchell thoroughly secondary to the anthropological method of situational analysis. The atypicalities of the event provided the basis for the establishment of the patterns and typicalities of statistics—the effectively normative direction of the descriptive statistics of much sociology. The study of statistical analysis was, in Mitchell's view, thoroughly dependent on ethnographic work that was alive to social variation and its situated production.

Gluckman's orientation was built around the idea that human realities are in constant flux: change rather than stasis is their circumstance. A protagonist of historical interpretations that aligned with this viewpoint, he maintained it steadfastly with regard to the southern African context. This was at the root of his critique of the anthropology that Malinowski appeared to advocate—the notion of so-called traditional societies as static, totalized entities in themselves for whom change was deeply problematic. Gluckman insisted that the focus of anthropology should be on change, as this was the normal condition of all societies. Further, his implication was that the idea of society as it had been sociologically developed, especially by Durkheim, was a conceptual abstraction, a fiction that was designed to enable the theoretical understanding of the innumerable and differentiated complexities of everyday life and that, in some sense, must always be speculative. Gluckman's concept of equilibrium, which was much misunderstood at the time,[11] was a theoretical construct that would be directed to the understanding of process rather than stasis and would be continually open to reformulation on the grounds of situated evidence. His notion of equilibrium was effectively a model in the scientific sense—a way of conceiving the totality that was continually subject to reformulation as a consequence of situated analyses (see Gluckman 1968).

Mitchell stressed the situationally relative nature of social action. Not only are there multiple kinds of social orders through which human beings pass in contemporary societies, but also these are variable in terms of the way that they determine or influence the particular definition of the person and the structuring of social relations. In modern Zambia, people could be part of kinship-based tribal social worlds, at one moment, and participants in social and political action that had everything to do with the class processes of urban society, at another moment. The concepts of 'modern' and of 'tradition' made little sense. In the Zambian context, tribalism—that is, the attachment to tribal or, rather, ethnic identities—was thoroughly a dimension of urban modernity (in Mitchell's analysis, most evident in situations outside the highly controlled contexts of industrial mine labor) and was most observable in everyday, casual contexts of social interaction that were not dominated by overarching institutional orders. Tribalism, as used by Mitchell, was a contemporary form of the invention of tradition (in effect, a break with the traditional and its reinvention), rather than the continuity of customary practices that is most apparent in rural areas, where tribal identity was assumed and not involved in the everyday construction of social intercourse as it is among erstwhile strangers in town.[12]

Mitchell's urban work focused on the heterogeneity of municipal life. He did not envisage life in the towns of Zambia as part of coherently ordered, functionally interrelated systems; rather, he viewed city life as a multiplicity—as sets of different practices emergent under a variety of different and continually differentiating situated circumstances. He was moving away from Gluckman's more totalizing system constituted around fundamental social contradictions that were manifested in a diversity of conflicts at the surface of everyday life.[13]

Gluckman's notion of situational analysis had been highly influenced by Evans-Pritchard's ([1937] 1976) concept of situational selection, whereby different social logics come into operation relative to the social issue or the particular social problematic arising and the kinds of social relations involved. The idea had been developed in the context of a discussion about Zande witchcraft practices to show how apparently contradictory practices and understanding could co-exist without threatening the socio-cultural order of the overall system as such. The point being made was that human beings do not live their worlds as coherent wholes but always in a situated and fractionalized way. This was the real (or actuality) in Gluckman's sense and why situational analysis was an appropriate method. However, this did not rule out the analytical value of the concept of system and the determination of underlying system-related contradictions. In Gluckman's Marxist-influenced understanding, the always situated nature of lived existence was the primary factor that inhibited the emergence to consciousness (or withheld from participants an awareness) of contradictions running through the diversities of lived practice. (In other terms, a consciousness of the system as a whole.) Mitchell was less convinced of such an orientation than was Gluckman, and in his urban work and later his research into social networks (see Mitchell 1969), he was moving away from the idea of system altogether.

Germinal to both Gluckman's and especially Mitchell's situational orientation is a shift away from a totalizing concept of society (or community) as a bounded, integrated whole. Furthermore, the critical focus of analysis was not society but rather the event or situation as entities of practice. These were not necessarily microcosms of the macrocosm or particular expressions of the social whole as some kind of static social order but aspects (or moments) of its continual historical formation along a multitude of dimensions. In other words, the social whole is itself relative and dependent on the kind of issue being addressed. Thus, certain problems might see the social whole as related to global processes that are very distant from the particular events or situations of ethnographic description and involve processes that affect, but are not integral within, the social institutions or relations that are characteristic of a particular social order. With reference to some of Gluckman's own examples, the Zulu wars against the Boers and the British were driven by political developments in Europe that were not immediately apparent to the Zulu themselves, an argument that, much later, Eric Wolf (1982) would independently develop more strongly. Similarly, tribal relations, as well as African and white colonial political conflict in the Copperbelt, had to consider the structure of capitalist socio-economic orders in Northern Europe and the Americas. A focus on event and situation in relation to the problematics that they addressed made it difficult to write about society as some kind of integrated, coherent whole. Thus, those in Gluckman's Manchester School began to prefer more fluid and open concepts, such as social field and social arena (see Bailey 1969; Kapferer 1972; Turner 1957, 1974). Both John Barnes (1954) and Mitchell (1969) were to push beyond conventional social-institutional analysis and to pioneer social network approaches that stressed different patterns of relationality.

Events Over the Long Term: Extended Case Analysis

The directions pioneered by Gluckman and Mitchell were further developed by Jaap van Velsen and especially Victor Turner. Broadly, they were concerned not with events as one-time occurrences but with the effects of events over the long term and their realization of original structures of action and meaning.

In his now classic monograph on the Ndembu of Zambia, *Schism and Continuity in an African Society,* Turner (1957) explored a series of interlinked events of crisis (or social dramas, as he termed them) that were driven by political ambition and influenced by contradictory principles involving marriage and the relationships of powerful males vis-à-vis their matri-kin, women especially. In Turner's analysis, Sandombu (the key protagonist whose career Turner followed) is in many respects an outsider whose actions throw into relief underlying systemic tensions and who brings into play new possibilities as a result of changes in the political economic environment, such as cash farming, and new modes of settlement unconstrained by village orders. Van Velsen (1964) followed a similar course of analysis as that of Turner, breaking away even more strongly from the structural functionalism of the time and its tendency to stress system integration without paying due attention to the innovations that actors applied toward the apparent rules of practice. Through a series of events, van Velsen explored how individuals worked customary conventions in novel social directions, thus effecting new arrangements and rules of social practice. But it was Turner who realized most of all a key implication of Gluckman's situational analysis—that it is through a focus on events that anthropologists can come to grips with social processes in their creative and generative moments.

Here I underline the significance of the move of both Turner and van Velsen to the consideration of the event as such. This involved a stronger shift away from the idea of society as a bounded and institutionally interrelated whole, although the emphasis was sustained concerning the nature of the principles involved in the constant creation of the system as a whole. A distinction in van Velsen's approach is related to his interest with how the principles and rules integral to social action themselves change and, therefore, the constitutive logics of the relevant social whole. Implicit in van Velsen is a notion of the social whole as a continually open whole rather than a closed totality—an orientation that is the vital dimension of a Deleuzian perspective to be discussed later (see Deleuze and Guattari 1994).

Gluckman stressed the idea of system overarching or fundamental principles ever-present in society or the realities of lived existence; thus, the diverse local social orders and situated social practices in South Africa were thoroughly overarched and underpinned by the racist principles of the color bar of apartheid, which constituted what he regarded as an overdetermining dominant principle (or cleavage) that shaped conflicts at all levels (Gluckman 1955b, 1965). These in Gluckman's understanding were historical and cultural expressions that had critical force as such but were no less produced or given intense effect through the energies of capitalism present in globalizing industrial and political economic processes. Turner and van Velsen maintained much of this systemic vision but shifted more strongly toward an event-focused interactional perspective and, in Turner's case, a more phenomenological one.

Turner is chiefly responsible for the development of the event as a locus of creativity and change. This was already explicit in his early *Schism and Continuity in an African Society* (1957) and in *The Drums of Affliction* (1968), although it was constrained by his effectively Hegelian processual formula of the social drama (breach, crisis, resolution, reintegration). It is in his later ritual work that Turner realizes the fully generative potential of the event. He saw particular events in ritual to be critical in the reconfiguration of existential realities (cognitive and social structural), overturning the conventional anthropological orientation to rite as the reproduction of an unchanging tradition, the repetition of the same. This is evident in Turner's stress on the liminal events of ritual (see Turner 1969) in which counteracting forces or principles are at play—an idea that owes as much to Nietzsche's (1993) Apollonian/Dionysian contest as it does to van Gennep (1960). But Turner does not remain bound to the problematic of ritual. He quickly expands the notion of the critical and generative event to an array of historical and contemporary world-changing occurrences, from Thomas à Beckett's murder to Hidalgo's *Grito* that sparked the Mexican War of Independence to the events of Paris in 1968 (Turner 1974). In his analyses, he concentrates on the accidental, the fortuitous, the way in which the contingent eschews the overdetermination of events in structure, and the forces that they may unintentionally unchain. With Turner, the event is a relatively open phenomenon that manifests a multiplicity of potential, a diversity of possible outcomes (perhaps best exemplified in his discussion of Hidalgo).

The development of the event and situational analysis concepts continued at Manchester. Kapferer's (1972) study of African factory workers in Zambia applies a Turner-style analysis of interconnected events of crisis to an urban-industrial context, showing how the emergence of various forms of social association within the larger circumstances of political transition out of colonial rule influenced efforts for better work conditions. However, the argument was framed through an attention to exchange theory approaches (see Blau [1964] 1986; Gouldner 1965), effectively maintaining the idea of the event as an illustration or representation of external theory and, in so doing, reducing the intention of situational analysis to develop theory from the ethnographic grounds of lived practices. The capacity of the event to be in itself the source of new conceptual understanding and theoretical comprehension—as indicated in Mitchell's *The Kalela Dance* and in van Velsen's and especially Turner's work—was diminished. This was much less so with Handelman's (1977) study of a sheltered workshop in Israel. In it, Handelman addressed Erving Goffman's interactionist perspective, which had quite independently treated events or routine interactive encounters as the source of novel conceptualization and theorization. Handelman challenged many of Goffman's abstract formulations with similar kinds of ethnographically grounded evidence.

In a later work, Handelman (1998) extended further in his event-centered direction, attempting a classification of types of events involving reanalyses of a range of different ethnographic materials. There are important methodological questions at the root of Handelman's development on event and situational analysis, among the more crucial being a major concern with the generalized classification and definition of events. The event is no longer essentially defined in terms of the dynamics of conflict or contradiction but in terms of its degree of institutionalization and routinization. Handelman effectively establishes a continuum from open, unstructured events, at one end, to highly formalized and institutionalized events, at the other end. Overall, his work is designed to explore the ways in which events either dominantly represent (and can therefore be studied in terms of how they express structuring principles and the key processes by which human beings systematically assemble their realities) or else exhibit a high degree of openness, perhaps leading to new kinds of structural arrangements or systematizations of practice. The approach deserves attention, not only because it offers a means for classifying events, but also, and perhaps more significantly, because it presents a way to discriminate between events independently of how they relate to larger structural/cultural forces within which they are embedded. Handelman develops a sociology of events as such.

One difficulty in the powerfully interactionist perspective of Handelman (and also Kapferer) is the implication that the circumstances of face-to-face interaction are also those of large-scale processes. To put it another way, all processes, in some way or another, are small group processes, despite any major global effects that may be rooted in them. The suggestion is that although such encounters may appear to be on the order of a different register or scale, similar interactional principles may be observed in them: what is transpiring in the Oval Office is essentially little different from the kind of negotiation that may be taking place in the classroom. There is a potentially immanent reductionism in this perspective (which Gluckman's systemic emphasis was intended to combat), and it is exacerbated by a tendency to overlook the likely possibility that the dynamic quality of particular events may vary according to the forces at which they are the locus and which may affect the internal processes of events but are not reducible to them. The relation between apparently larger, encompassing molar processes and local or small everyday interactive events is of major issue in any analysis based in events,[14] as Charles Tilly (1989) indicated and as Marshall Sahlins (2005) has pursued more recently in the context of a somewhat different approach to the event. Sahlins's work is significant, as I shall discuss, due to his introduction of cultural value into event analysis. This adds another dimension to the dynamics of event that counteracts certain aspects of the reductionism to which event analysis may be prone.

Elaborations and Innovations

What counts as an event for analysis is highly problematic, and there is always a risk that the event merely becomes 'Society' writ small—a micro representation of society or systems that, furthermore, is often treated as representing the dynamic processes of the whole. This was a clear dimension of the approach to the examination of situated events by the Manchester anthropologists and is a factor underlying their expressed frustration at the incapacity of much situational analysis to escape the critique of the use of events as mere illustrative cases or representations of normative processes.[15] Mitchell would complain that even though the Manchester concern with events demanded a greater attention to ethnographic complexity and detail, the approach was nonetheless saddled with the event as a gimmick, a device for introducing a problem for analysis, rather than being vital in itself to the creative and productive work of analytical ethnographic conceptualization and understanding. The event as a descriptive device still dominates in most anthropology. However, the stress in the Manchester orientation to focus on events of crisis—in which the participants are effectively engaging with the taken-for-granted assumptions of reality and redefining the nature of their orientations to reality—is still a fruitful course.

The Manchester situational analysis approach to events was methodologically innovative in anthropology. Obviously, as Gluckman and his colleagues recognized, similar perspectives had been adopted elsewhere in the humanities and social sciences. The study of jural practices (Gluckman 1955a), psychoanalysis, and Kurt Lewin's psychodrama perspective were influential, as was Marx's (1852) analysis of the events of the 18th Brumaire of Louis Napoleon.[16] Turner's discussion of major events that constituted turning points in history (referred to above) parallels Max Weber's attention to historical switch points whereby political and social processes took a new direction. In these senses, the Manchester situational perspective demonstrated an anthropology that not only was addressing critically normative paradigms but also was opening the discipline up to other orientations. Despite its potential, situational and event analysis saw little expansion outside the domain of the Manchester School and largely faded as an anthropological methodological experiment. The event was maintained as exemplary or illustrative rather than as in itself a dynamic process (the Manchester innovation) that potentially constitutes an original structuring of relations or plane of emergence that is irreducible as a representation of the order of surrounding realities.

However, more recently there has been a growth of interest in event analysis, partly in response to a collapse in the totalizing paradigms of society and system. Some have consciously expanded on the Manchester initiative. Michael Burawoy (2000), a student of van Velsen, has adapted it to the exploration of contemporary transnational contexts of globalization. Others such as Das (1995), who makes no reference to Manchester, and Alexander, Giesen, and Mast (2006), who make use of Turner's dramatic and performance perspective, have given events a critical place in their analyses. However, none of these extend beyond the event as illustrative or as encapsulating a density of detailed practice whereby larger forces can be intensively explored. Indeed, there has been a widespread tendency to reduce the study of events, including the Manchester approach, to a concern with the dynamics of practice or to look at it in terms of micro-history, which in the view expressed here tends to miss the central points of situational analysis.

The Event in a Structuralist Register

Marshall Sahlins's (1980, 1985, 2004) studies of Hawaii and Fiji, which offer a relatively novel orientation to the event, are motivated out of a concern to overcome the ahistorical aspects of Lévi-Straussian structuralism. This and the fact of his Boasian cultural emphasis might explain why Sahlins makes no reference to Manchester. It should be added that Gluckman and his colleagues were developing from within Radcliffe-Brown's Durkheimian structuralism—despite their criticism of it, especially that of van Velsen (1967)—from which Sahlins is distanced. They were also critical of Malinowski, with whom Sahlins is altogether more sympathetic. I add that major proponents of the situational and event perspective, including Victor Turner, were openly hostile to structuralism and championed event analysis as a radical alternative. Nonetheless, Sahlins's approach to events extends a course of analysis that parallels Manchester, overcoming some of its limitations but itself perhaps being vulnerable to difficulties that situational analysis avoided.[17]

Sahlins begins his attention to the event in his now classic discussion of the crisis confronting the Hawaiian king, Kalani'ōpu'u, when Captain James Cook, by unexpectedly returning to Hawaii, placed himself outside the cultural categories that had been adapted by the Hawaiians to make sense of his appearance (see Sahlins 1980). In the accident of his return, Cook effectively changed in practical value from being a beneficent fruitful god into the figure of a usurping king. He revealed an intense ambiguity that was a potential threat in the Hawaiian mytho-political scheme of things and its appropriate practice. The critical occurrences that Sahlins explores are those focused on the making of Cook into the figure of the god Lono, which leads to his killing. In the Hawaiian construction of things, Cook is 'sacrificed' (an after-the-fact invention) and positively *made into* the god (a construal that persists as such in cultural cum historical memory). The possibility of Cook being a realization of the stranger king who usurps the kingship (which is part of the mythopoetic potential of Hawaiian kingship) was thereby thwarted. This is hardly a resolution of the crisis of the situation that Cook's arrival effected, but it becomes integral to a whole series of further critical events that are vital to the creation of new potentials in the construction of Hawaiian social and political arrangements. There are shades of Gluckman's notion of the event as part of a repetitive structure in that the changes that events manifest are part of the reproduction of the system as a whole (which does not obviate its constant, internal changing system of differentiation and diversification). There is no transformational revolution in the process (that Gluckman might have detected)—merely a dissolution of the past into the present via different meaningful arrangements of the cultural categories. There is a Malinowskian ring to Sahlins's approach, but rather than the disorganization and pathological entropy that Malinowski stresses in his functionalism, with Sahlins (as in Geertz's culturalism) culture or value operates positively in the creation and generation of the new or a particular adaptation to modernity.

Both Sahlins and Manchester concentrate on the dynamics of events as driven in conflict and contradiction. For the former, this is a critical dimension of what he terms the structure of the conjuncture, which in his Hawaiian example represents a close affiliation with notions of culture contact to which the Mancunians were staunchly opposed. They argued that cultures—as interrelated systems of value, for instance—never come into contact as wholes and only ever in a partial way through the action of particular agents. This is in practice how Sahlins's analysis operates, but the idea of conflict and contradiction as being integral to systems (the Manchester position) is nonetheless underplayed, the contradictions and tensions within the system being effectively produced and opened up through the action of the structure of the conjuncture. However, the importance of Sahlins's approach is the very idea of the event *as a structure of the conjuncture*. That is, it is a structural dynamic in itself that is irreducible to any one cultural or social order and simultaneously is in effect a site of emergence out of which novel articulations of practiced reality arise. Sahlins ties this to a linear notion of historical change (how the Hawaiians became part of the globalized modern but in their own cultural way), as also does the different Manchester approach. But Sahlins's emphasis on the original and originating structure of the event effectively gives it a relatively external independent force, rendering it unencompassed, as it were. More than a representation of systemic socio-cultural processes, the event is the site for innovative practice and (importantly in Sahlins's work) for the practical construction of cultural memory.[18] For example, the murder of Cook, born out of the emotional and chaotic tensions of the moment, becomes creatively reconstructed as an intended act of sacrifice, now a part of historical memory—the event as myth—that influences subsequent action, such as the Hawaiian insistence on being British. The Manchester concern to avoid the idea of the event as mere illustration is overcome by Sahlins's attention to the structure of the event as a dynamic in itself that is also thoroughly situationally specific. It is the very specificity of the situated event (as also a dramatic site of revaluation) that gives it the potency to switch the path of change in a certain direction rather than another through both its particular actualization of a mythic consciousness and its validation via a historicized constructed memory.

New Articulations of the Event in Post-structuralist Thought: Becoming as Always Not Yet

In retrospect, Sahlins's 1980 work and later analyses anticipate for anthropology certain post-structural developments in the philosophy of the social sciences and humanities. Here I comment on the significance attached to the event in the social philosophical orientation of Gilles Deleuze and Félix Guattari (1987, 1994) and also that of Alain Badiou (2001, 2006). The last claims a distinction from Deleuze, but in the framework of anthropological and ethnographic concerns, it constitutes a Freudian 'narcissism of minor difference'. This is not to reduce the importance of Badiou in relation to Deleuze in the context of philosophical argument (Badiou expresses a closer link with Platonic traditions than Deleuze avowedly does), but to state that for anthropology, or the kind of anthropology that I pursue, which is ethnographically driven (see Kapferer 2007), such philosophical distinction is of little import. Both Deleuze and Badiou argue a philosophical direction that is of ontological rather than epistemological proportions. The Deleuzian turn to the event is part of a general approach that strives to break away from various oppositions and exclusivist positions that, for example, overprivilege the individual subject or the idea of society as a coherent totalized order.

In many respects, Deleuze aims for an ontological shift away from the assumptions that lie at the heart of Western modernist social and psychological theories. The emphasis is on the multiplicity of sensory and cognitive processes, which permits all kinds of agency or effect (human, non-human, structural, etc.) and patterning of relations. Rather than the notion of society *sui generis* in the Durkheimian sense, Deleuze and Guattari stress the concept of assemblage whereby particular concatenations of relation and process are actualized or brought into existence or lived practice. This orientation excludes neither systemic processes (which are characterized as different potentials of centered hierarchical dynamics) nor others that Deleuze and Guattari characterize as rhizomic and relationally a-centered but which may be intertwined (entangled) with systemic dynamics. The interconnection is not, in their conception, dialectic but rather thoroughly tensional, involving entirely distinct structural logics in a dynamic that may be mutually annihilatory and irresolute in any dialectic or Hegelian sense.[19] The event in the Deleuzian orientation becomes the critical site of emergence, manifesting the singularity of a particular multiplicity within tensional space and opening toward new horizons of potential. In Deleuze's sense, the event is present-future oriented and not to be reduced to terms of orders, structures, and relations that can be understood only through a connection to a past or a reality that can be completely grasped in its own terms. In this, Deleuze and Guattari break out of any essentialism or determinism of a historicist, structuralist, or psychological kind without excluding such considerations altogether. These aspects are part of a continuing tensional mix, and the event may be conceived as a particular plateau of intensity that has immanent within it a potential that effectively becomes knowable through the actualizations or realizations in the event itself. The event, in their analysis, is a wellspring of emergence that is not merely a reflection (or illustration) of the world around it, as this may be described independently of the occurrence of the event, but is itself a creative crucible of new, hitherto unrealized potential.

Deleuze and Guattari, I think, articulate more explicitly the direction that the Manchester School and, more recently, Sahlins had already set. With regard to Manchester, Deleuze and Guattari clear away some of the analytical and theoretical baggage—the Durkheimian, Radcliffe-Brownian structural legacy—that may have burdened the Manchester anthropologists and prevented them from escaping the case as example or as mere microcosm. The Hegelianism implicit in the development of the extended case—as in Turner's Ndembu ethnography—is committed to a teleological, linear dialectical course, as to some extent is Sahlins's Hawaiian work, which he, perhaps self-critically, recognizes as 'afterology'. Husserl, I note, suggested that social understanding could be condemned to such a position, but the course indicated by Deleuze and Guattari offers one way out. Their approach conceives of the event not only as being delinked in critical ways from the past but also as opening up numerous pathways into various potential futures. It does not determine the future so much as it is determined by the event in the future in the sense that Deleuze develops in *Difference and Repetition* (2004). The future event, therefore, is not the inevitable and necessary outcome of a preceding event (as certain structural perspectives of a Hegelian or Marxist persuasion might insist), nor is it part of a determined and linked series. The connection, as it were, is made by events in the future that do not flow as a necessity from specific preceding events. In such an orientation, the importance of the detailed consideration of the practices of the event is not to demonstrate the logic of a relatively closed (and therefore repetitive) system, which I think dogs the Manchester approach and also, if less so, that of Sahlins (which he self-consciously quips as being 'afterology')—rather, it is to explore the novel potentiality of a becoming that is always not yet.

The importance of the event as a creative and generative nexus in the philosophy of Deleuze and Guattari opens up new space for the importance of event analysis in anthropology. Notwithstanding the potential of their philosophical arguments (and those of others such as Badiou), their orientation demands the kind of grounding that anthropology always offered. But the point of the discussion here is that anthropologists have been grappling with the potential of event analysis for some time and have already demonstrated the value of such an approach, well beyond the treatment of the event as a mere exemplification or illustration of what is already known. The major anthropological positions I have explored here were already engaging the event in a way that was breaking away from what Deleuze would describe as 'royal' and 'ruling' theory and were demonstrating the potency of anthropological methodological thinking in the face of ethnographic commitment and a recognition of ethnography as being at the root of theoretical and philosophical discovery.

The Chapters

The impetus and inspiration for the chapters that are presented in this book arose from two research seminars on event analysis organized by Lotte Meinert and myself on behalf of the Danish Research School of Anthropology and Ethnography in 2008 and in 2009. The discussions initially focused on the work of the Manchester School and similar perspectives that had some influence on the Manchester approach, such as the American symbolic interactionists (see Evens and Handelman 2006; Kapferer 2005b). The discussions then turned to the relatively new orientation pioneered by Sahlins and, more recently, the line of thought of the social philosophers Deleuze, Guattari, and Badiou. The chapters here express various lines of inquiry involving what can be broadly termed event analysis within the spectrum that has been presented in the foregoing discussion. They can be regarded as part of an ongoing discourse and in various ways represent differing positions. This introductory essay has outlined the structure of my thought, but many of the positions taken in the essays demonstrate some of the limitations of certain of my directions, often a dimension of the very ethnographic contexts and the problematic chosen, and stress other possibilities. Thus, the chapters in this book might be considered events in themselves—particular points in the development of specific ethnographic understandings and, most importantly, approaches that may offer a variety of analytical directions via a focus on events. The book as a whole should be considered as a kind of becoming, offering varying and still developing approaches to ethnographic methodology that are framed by a concern with the event as the grounds as well as the plane of emergence for analytical and theoretical knowledge. In this regard, I stress the distinction of anthropology as, above all, an ethnographic discipline that conceives the source of theory and knowledge concerning human being to be in and through the creative and generative action of human beings participating in the situated circumstances of the changing and perduring problematic character of realities as always being in the process of becoming (see Kapferer 2007, 2013).

A critical issue that underpins many of the essays concerns the status of the event. What exactly is an event, and what are the reasons behind its selection? My suggestion is that an event should not be selected on the basis of its illustrative dimensions or because it is in some way or another a micro example of macro dynamics. These are difficult to avoid, for the event, I contend, is always likely to have these dimensions. It is because the event, at least in some intuitive way, seems to point up problematics and questions in the contexts of anthropological work that it is selected. Thus, all the events addressed in this volume are in some way or another illustrative. But they are also more than this, for by and large they contain in themselves the evidence or the evidential grounds for the analysis that builds upon them and which further may be the grounds for the establishment of new theoretical directions that are thoroughly founded in existential practice.

Events are not natural phenomena. They are always constructions and do not exist as events apart from this fact. As Sahlins expressly points out in his Hawaiian work, events achieve their import and effects through the meaning or the significance that human beings attach to them, and it is this which yields their generative impact. Initially, they might be conceived of as happenings or occurrences without any necessary meaning or significance. When they become significant, it is in their becoming an event in this sense that they achieve their import. So the events that Sahlins considers, or the happenings made into events—for example, the unforeseen and in all likelihood accidental happening of Cook's killing, which becomes an event of defined significance as the sacrifice of a god—achieve their force in a process of conjunctive cultural construction that is both a specific arrangement and an invention of meaning. As I have already intimated, there is a similarity here with the Manchester approach (although less set within a culturistic concern with meaning that exists above and independent of the dynamics of the event), whose orientation to events is as moments of social definition that facilitate as they may alter the terms for ongoing intercourse. The discussion of events in all the chapters in this book are thoroughly concerned with the event as a construction that in various ways concentrates on the manner in which participants constituted the event as an event (and the potential of such a construction). Furthermore, the analyses presented are in different ways concerned with laying out the kinds of evidence that form the basis for the specific and more general anthropological assessments of the processes described. Event and situational analyses effectively set out the terms internal to their analytical program as regarding the selection and intense considerations of the lived practices *in situ* that they address.

I underline here the constructionist approach to the event. I do so in response to the development of an anti-constructionist direction in some of the more recent discussions concerning the event, especially those influenced by the poststructuralist turn. This has been brought about by the interest of some (e.g., DeLanda 2006; Latour 2007) to break away from the anti-science directions that have received emphasis in many subjectivist postmodern orientations that seek to avoid what they see as the positivist objectivism of science.[20] Deleuze, Guattari, and certainly Badiou are not anti-science (with the last often appearing to take a neo-Platonist stance), and I do not conceive of them as anti-constructionist (see Hacking 2000), although they must be seen as decentering the position of human being. For some social scientists, we are in an era of the post-human (Haraway 2007; Latour 2007; see Hayles 1999 for a critique) and must therefore take into account forms of agency, effect, or constructional impetus other than those created by human beings. In other words, constructions of reality are embedded in processes that are not entirely of human invention; they are able to exert an effect on human being because they are insensible to human action. There is a reinsistence on a certain materialism, which is already powerfully apparent in Marxist perspectives and, I consider, in some phenomenology, in what may be glossed as post-structural directions. The significance of events as constructed and defined (usually in multiple ways) by human beings is emergent upon processes—for example, ecological/environmental or biological systems, interspecies relations, socio-political forces not within the direct or immediate awareness of participants—that, in their relative intransigence, force a diversity of human reactive constructions. The kinds of events upon which the authors of this volume concentrate are specifically moments of emergent consciousness that in themselves give expression to novel realizations of ongoing existence.

The chapters of the collection begin with Thomas Fibiger's analysis of the 'Ashura Shi'i ritual celebrations in Bahrain. His analysis provides an immediate connection to the birth of event analysis in the Manchester group, especially Turner's development through the analysis of ritual drama. This brief introduction to the essays ends with Morten Nielsen's contribution, which deals with the crisis of a natural disaster (an initiating point for two other chapters in this book, those by Jonas Østergaard Nielsen and Mikkel Rytter) and its socially generative effects. Morten Nielsen explicitly places the Manchester orientation in critical conjunction with a Deleuzian perspective.

The major significance of the event that Fibiger addresses is self-evident. As an annual calendrical rite of the Shi'i majority of Bahrain, which attracts over 100,000 participants (and involves the Sunni minority as well), it is already replete with significance and the kind of repeated occasion that should immediately attract anthropological attention. Such ceremonial and ritual events are windows into the real and imagined realities of human existence, both inside and outside ritual performances. The rite that Fibiger addresses is a manifestation of the fundamental religious and socio-political cleavage, as Gluckman would have described it, in Bahrain. As in Gluckman's analysis of the Zululand bridge opening, Fibiger presents the diverse positions and interpretations of the significance of the practices by participants. He stresses the ceremony as a complex multiplicity that, in itself, does not reduce systematically to the kind of dominant cleavage that is integral to the overarching mythos it expresses. What Fibiger's account addresses is the way that novel directions in Shi'i-Sunni relations, as well as a host of other problematics, take form during the commemoration of a mythopoetic and defining event in Shi'i-Sunni cultural and historical memory. Potentials that were hitherto only virtual can be realized. By way of contrast, in Gluckman's kind of situational analysis, the dominant cleavage in the system permeates the meaning of the event. Fibiger suggests a more Deleuzian approach. As evidenced in his conversations with participants, the ritual is a kind of Deleuzian open, a creative moment giving rise to new social and political potentials that press well beyond its historical reference. As Turner might have said, the repetition of an old history allows for a diversity of new possibilities that may transcend the past and, as Deleuze might have noted, are determined in a future and not conditioned in preceding processes.

Bjarke Oxlund's chapter describes a mock funeral held for student organizations that were aligned with the African National Congress (ANC), which had heralded in the new post-apartheid era in 1994. The essay addresses further some of the aspects raised by Fibiger. Discussing Gluckman's situational analysis, Oxlund is explicitly concerned to avoid the case as mere illustration. He observes that he was drawn intuitively to the event because it clashed with many of his expectations or normative understandings of the South African context in which he was collecting ethnographic materials. In other words, it appeared as a generative, innovative moment in which new directions away from the immediate post-apartheid era were emergent. The mock funeral explicitly buried the ANC—creative in its very playfulness—and manifested a kind of hiatus between understandings that drew their meaning from the past, as well as a new import born of the present becoming a future. The processes engaged in the construction of the event are what Deleuze may have grasped as a dynamic of delinking from a virtual past (the plethora of potentiality and multiplicities of experience that might have made the immediate post-apartheid era) and a reorientation toward a virtual future (the potentialities that the post-apartheid student population may, over the course of their lives, come to actualize).

Vital for any discussion of events is what may be termed their locus. Where they occur in time and in space (place) is integral to what they are and can become. This is of heightened significance in ritual events, whose space (often of mythological significance) feeds imaginal potential into ritual practice, as the practice may in its own way generatively realize such potential. Jesper Oestergaard's essay on a Tibetan sacred cave underlines such a point, emphasizing the symbolic emplacement of events and how reference to them excites the situated dynamic of events. The place or space of events is not inert or mere background setting (context)—it is itself active in the event. This is explicit in Oestergaard's discussion, but I suggest that it is an aspect of most events, not just those that are rituals. I add that Oestergaard's analysis has relevance for an understanding of the virtual/actual features of events. The cave expresses a virtuality as a pregnancy of potential—a phantasmagoric space (see Kapferer 2002) that excites the imagination, perhaps aligning it in certain mythopoetic directions. It is activated and actualized via various techniques of the memory, in this case aided by photographs and their interpretation, as described by Oestergaard.

Jonas Østergaard Nielsen's chapter takes up what I have stated is a post-structural interest involving the constructivist import of non-human agency in the production of socially generative effects. He is directly concerned with environmental processes that are integral to the realization of new constructions of social reality and the events of their realization. Thus, Nielsen shows how climate change and drought as non-human forces enter within the situated dynamics of social constructional events, giving them moment and facilitating a major restructuring of social relations. The essay illustrates how an ecological crisis in a small village in Burkina Faso stimulated processes of creative social emergence, giving rise, for example, to new definitions of gender relations.

A similar argument is developed in Rytter's chapter, which discusses the constructional processes activated by the Pakistan earthquake of 2005 in which some 70,000 people died. Following Das (1995), Rytter describes this as a critical event around which new definitions of the relations between local Pakistanis and those of the diaspora (with specific reference to Denmark) were defined. Here I note that a hallmark of the situational perspective that Gluckman and his Manchester colleagues developed related to the effect of global forces (largely industrial-economic) on situated practices that appeared to be well outside them. They in effect argued that there was no such thing as a pristine, traditional society, as often celebrated by anthropologists. Even those societies that are the most apparently radical and isolated are nonetheless enmeshed in processes that are implicated in what may otherwise appear to be their own independent self-generation, as Gluckman ([1940] 1958, 1949) and Wolf (1982) stressed. Burawoy (2000), in his readdressing of the Manchester methodological innovation, expands upon such a point and redraws situational analysis to deal more explicitly with contemporary global interconnections. As Rytter points out, globalization and cyberspace have rendered notions of society or territorially bounded and insulated social orders thoroughly redundant. They lead to more intense intertwinement, realizing unexpected mutual effects and resulting in redefinitions of the nature of relations. The unity that the Danish-Pakistani doctors felt when identifying with the earthquake victims was belied by the suppressed imperial-hierarchical relation that was implicated in the Danish doctors reaction to the disaster.

In the following chapter, Anja Kublitz discusses the construction of the now (in)famous matter of the 2005 Danish cartoon controversy into an event involving irruptions of angry demonstrations by Muslim immigrants, from which emerged a new value of Muslim identity in Denmark. Interestingly, as a major point of social and political emergence, the controversy could be seen as counteracting the polarization between immigrants and those locals who stayed behind, as discussed by Rytter. Through this cartoon incident, major cleavages in Danish realities (which had been hitherto obscured or repressed) achieved definition, agency, and new meaning in the course of its construction into an event. Danish Muslims realized a greater sense of global unity, which, of course, continues to have reverberations in the structuring of both global and local relations.

The phenomenon of contemporary globalization, as I have already noted, has been implicated in a reframing of many of the key problematics of anthropological practice, some of which are evident in the chapters of this volume. Corporate structures are significant drivers of global interconnections and networks, and their processes cannot necessarily be reduced to the statist kinds of discourse and dynamics that have shaped much anthropological conceptualization. A shift away from such approaches was implicit, if far from fully expressed, in Manchester situational analysis, but Jakob Krause-Jensen's essay realizes more explicitly such a potential in his discussion of a Danish electronics company. It could be argued that the Manchester emphasis on conflict and contradiction embeds a modernist-cum-statist analytical commitment. Krause-Jensen indicates that the social practices of a managerial rather than bureaucratic order refract a different style of political and social discourse (and organization of work) that might modify some of the theoretical assumptions at the root of situational analysis.

Clearly, within the corporatizing and managerial realignments of the political and of the state in globalizing contexts (see Hardt and Negri 2001; Kapferer 2010), the organization and patterning of opposition and resistance are altering. What is widely discussed as terrorism and its spread are indicating as much. The clear-cut socio-political cleavages that motivated the arguments behind Gluckman's situational analysis (especially of the bridge opening) are becoming less apparent. Stine Krøijer, whose chapter analyzes violent protests on a bridge near the French-German border during a 2009 NATO summit, takes issue directly with the case as an actualization or representation of underlying social forces. She explores the event as expressing a dynamic of emergence in itself, in which there are specters of the real or shades of potentiality in Deleuze's sense. The analysis demonstrates the multi-positionality and shifting multi-relationality of the dynamics of the event, arguing against any solid actualization in its process of orders in a past or of those necessitated in a future. Engaging the ideas of Deleuze, Strathern, Viveiros de Castro, and others, Krøijer goes well beyond the representational dimensions of Gluckman's bridge opening (in which the order of South Africa is realized), taking up the event in its vibrational, shadowy, virtual potentiality as a domain of becoming that cannot be grasped as an actualization of the world external to it. Nonetheless, perhaps the character of such events and their theoretical mode of understanding are related to dimensions of the crises and uncertainties of the current historical social and political juncture.

The final chapter, by Morten Nielsen, places Manchester situational analysis firmly within the Deleuzian post-structural frame. Rather than specific, concrete events of practice, it deals with the situational complexity and multi-directional dynamics of an urban context in which there is no clear-cut structure of control that is similar to the colonial orders addressed by Manchester situational analysis. The post-colonial and post-war realities of Maputo, Mozambique, are thoroughly in flux. Nielsen's account addresses the strategies of securing urban residences following the Mozambique floods, which contributed to a plateau of critical intensity that opened up new forces of differentiation and lines of flight. He shows how the statist, oversystemic Gluckman approach to situated events must give way to a more Deleuzian perspective in post-flood and post–civil war Maputo. The analysis that Nielsen presents of the ways in which people secured building plots and established their urban status, among other dimensions of forming an urban way of life, demonstrates the ontological (rather than epistemological) shift that surrounds post-structuralist approaches to the event. Most importantly, Nielsen sets out an approach to the event that may avoid the dilemma of the case or event as an illustration of external realities and realizes a more generative dynamic, one that both constitutes its reality and opens up to new potential.

This book as a whole traces a variety of orientations concerning the idea of event and situational analysis, exploring specific methodological problematics within a larger set of debates in anthropology. At times, the discussion involves critical reconceptualizations of the nature of anthropological work and the processes whereby it may generate analytical and theoretical understanding within the constantly changing lived circumstances of human existence.

Bruce Kapferer is a Fellow of the Australian Academy of Social Sciences and is currently Professor of Social Anthropology at the University of Bergen, Norway. He was affiliated with the Rhodes-Livingstone Institute (1963–1966) and was later appointed to the Department of Social Anthropology at the University of Manchester (1966–1973). He was subsequently Foundation Professor of Anthropology at the University of Adelaide and later at James Cook University, as well as Professor and Chair at University College London. He has held research fellowships at the Center for Behavioral Sciences, Palo Alto, the Netherlands Institute for Advanced Studies, and the National Humanities Center, North Carolina. His published books include *A Celebration of Demons* (1983), *Legends of People, Myths of State* (1988), *The Feast of the Sorcerer* (1997), and *2001 and Counting: Kubrick, Nietzsche, and Anthropology* (2014). He has edited *Beyond Rationalism* (2002) and has co-edited, with Angela Hobart, *Aesthetics in Performance* (2005) and, with Bjørn Bertelsen, *Crisis of the State* (2009). He was formerly joint editor of *Anthropological Theory* (2012–2015) and is chief editor of *Social Analysis*. He was Director of the Challenging the State project, supported by the Norwegian Research Foundation, and is currently Director of an egalitarianism project funded by the EU under the ERC Advanced Grant Scheme. This involves an international team of researchers inquiring into historical and current egalitarian/inegalitarian social and political processes.

Notes

1. For detailed analyses of the Manchester School, see Gluckman ([1940] 1958, 1961a, 1961b), Mitchell (1956a, 1956b, 1969, 1974, 1983), Turner (1957, 1968), and van Velsen (1964, 1967). For overviews and extensions, see especially Evens and Handelman (2006) and Werbner (1984).

2. In the Manchester perspective, there is some lack of clarity concerning the relation between event and situation. There was a tendency at Gluckman's time to associate the notion of the situation with context. If the idea of context refers to the background setting for the irruption of events, then this does not always fit with the usage of situation, which includes the structural processes emergent in the irruption of events. In this essay, I tend to discuss the events of focus in situational analysis as situated events and do not conflate the notion of situation with the idea of context as a kind of background setting or behind-the-scenes systemic order for events.

3. Gluckman stressed the positive role of witchcraft accusations and ritual demonstrations of rebellion against the kingship in the definition of social and political relations (see Gluckman 1955a, 1955b, 1963, 1965).

4. Gluckman noted that many chieftainship systems in Africa were of a *primus inter pares* sort. The chief, who was in many instances relatively impoverished, served as a conduit for the redistribution of benefits and resources rather than as an accumulative center. Moreover, those in centralized positions of power had their authority tempered by the encompassing social orders of which they were a part. The assumption of dictatorial and tyrannical powers by the nineteenth-century Zulu warrior king Shaka (also known as Shaka Zulu) was an innovative realization of an existing potentiality in the Zulu political order. Gluckman's argument had resonance with Edmund Leach's (1961) classic discussion of the emergence of authoritarian hierarchy out of relatively egalitarian processes—an approach that influenced Deleuze and Guattari's (1987) seminal discussions on rhizomic and statist-hierarchical dynamics. Gluckman, however, was committed to a linear orientation to change (very much influenced by a continuing Durkheimianism in his thought), which he tended to see as being impelled by external forces of a global nature.

5. Heidegger (1977: 115–128) discusses the historian's concern with the status of sources as being equivalent to the scientist's concern with the experiment. In different ways, both have the same aim to validate rigorously their descriptions and assessments. Gluckman—completely unaware of Heidegger—was arguing a similar position. For him, events were the grounds for anthropological judgment, description, and theory. In order for the assertions of anthropologists to have authority, the nature of the events upon which the analyses depended had to be as thoroughly presented as possible. In other words, a science of anthropology depended on a methodology, such as that of situational analysis.

6. Geertz's (1973) famous study of Balinese cockfighting is an example of an analysis of an event, but not along the lines developed at Manchester. It is more a detailed account of an event as an illustration of the cultural nature of Bali with regard to status (developed in his discussion of *negara*). Asserting a highly cultural, relativist view, this approach does not involve a plane of emergence, which was the direction of Gluckman's methodology as developed by Mitchell, Turner, and others.

7. As an example, Gluckman admired Durkheim's analysis of suicide in which there is a marked attempt to make the definitions and logic of analysis transparent.

8. Mitchell's (1956b) study of the Yao, which explored social life through a series of events, was important in the development of situational analysis and had a major influence on the work of both Victor Turner and Jaap van Velsen. Mitchell was involved in the supervision of these two scholars during their doctoral work.

9. See Kapferer (1995) for a critical appreciation of Mitchell's analysis of the *kalela* dance.

10. For Mitchell (1956), the capacity of individuals to exercise choice was a property of structural aspects of the situation coupled with the problematic relevant to the exercise of choice. In his analysis, ethnic categories in urban contexts were used to establish the terms of social relations, and this was most apparent in what he described as relatively open situations that lacked overriding dominant structures. Ethnic identity, in his view, tended not to be engaged, for example, in contexts where social relations tended to be highly determined by the organization of work. However, in places where there was no overdetermining organization that governed activity, and especially where participants were strangers to one another, then ethnic categories were used. This was so, he added, because the categories had implicit within them orientations to the formation of social relations and social conduct. He concentrated especially on the development of institutionalized joking relations between particular ethnic categories.

11. Gluckman entered into a celebrated debate over the concept of equilibrium with Leach (1961), who taunted him for being overcommitted to an understanding of stable systems. Gluckman was to retort, with some justification, that his approach was similar to Leach's own famous discussion of the dynamics of change among the Kachin people.

12. Magubane (1971) criticized Mitchell, but he was confused by Mitchell's concept of tribalism, which he mistakenly interpreted as traditionalist in usage, quite contrary to the intention. Magubane's error has been compounded by Ferguson (1999). The approach that Ferguson develops is based on an extraordinary misreading of the work of Godfrey Wilson in which he attributes to Wilson a perspective that Mitchell develops in criticism of Wilson. The latter—despite his important attention to global political and economic forces—cleaved to a notion of the urban process in Zambia as a means of gradual transition away from traditional, customary values. Mitchell and Gluckman were opposed to such adaptationist and gradualist perspectives, identifying them as being aligned with colonialist administrative understandings and as failing to concentrate on the multiple structural processes that underpinned a variety of reactions to the global forces of political and economic change. Ferguson's orientation has more in common with Mitchell's position than that of Wilson, although in execution it is far more subjectivist and is ethnographically superficial.

13. Gluckman (1961a) had famously asserted that modern Zambia could be understood through a contrast of two systems: (1) the urban capitalist industrial order, the domain of tribalism (or ethnicity), and (2) the rural traditional order, based in traditionally structured politico-jural tribal kinship processes in which village, lineage, and kinship were the primary bases of everyday action, not tribal identity. He overstated his case ("the African townsman is a townsman") to make a political point against patterns of colonial administration of African populations, which insisted on a traditionalism (itself invented by the colonial rulers) that saw a non-modern tribal primitivism pervading every area of interaction among Africans. Mitchell agreed with Gluckman's anti-colonialist political point but saw dangers in the contrast as forcing too hard a distinction between urban and rural. Much of Mitchell's work was to demonstrate the inadequacy of such a dualism, concentrating instead on the continuing emergent multiplicities of social life that refuted such dualistic thinking.

14. The whole matter of scale is important in the discussion of events and the relation of particular kinds of interactive event and the events involving larger social and group processes. This is an area that demands attention for which I do not have space here. In anthropology, Godfrey Wilson (1941–1942) raised the matter, and his perspective was influential on the kinds of questions that Gluckman and especially Mitchell were asking in relation to situational analysis. I note the important work of Reidar Groenhaug (1978) in this regard. Contemporary discussion on the local and global is a version of these kinds of issues concerning scale and the relation of small-scale interactional events to larger processes.

15. An egregious misrepresentation (and trivialization) of situational analysis along these lines is that of Ferguson (1999).

16. Marx's (1852) analysis is important to the argument that Deleuze (2004) develops regarding the event. He disagrees with Marx concerning the event of Louis Napoleon as a farcical repetition. Deleuze insists that it is better grasped as an original event that does not so much tragically repeat the past as open up irreducible creative and dynamic potential.

17. The British sociological orientation in anthropology was not as prone to the kinds of culturological totalism and bounding that were prevalent in American cultural anthropology. Much of the anthropological postmodernist subjectivist approach has been initiated from within North American perspectives, and the matter of culture seems to operate as a continually nagging paradox.

18. In Sahlins's analysis, memory is a type of virtual. In relation to a Deleuzian notion of the virtual (see Deleuze and Guattari 1994; Kapferer 2005a, 2005b; Thanem and Linstead 2006), it is a kind of totality of potential (past, present, and future) that is a real but not necessarily an actual and evident overtly in practice. Sahlins's independent development of a notion of the virtual that is similar to that of Deleuze may overcome the kinds of culture contact relativism that the Mancunians would have complained about in Sahlins's work and which they would have seen as extending from the Malinowskian perspective that Gluckman criticized.

19. The anti-Hegelianism of Deleuze and Guattari—indeed, a powerful commitment to the kind of break that Nietzsche pursued—distinguishes their perspective and underpins their positivity.
20. Recent debates in 2010 involving the American Anthropological Association, which was pressured to abandon an expressly anti-science position, are a case in point.

References

Alexander, Jeffrey C., Bernhard Giesen, and Jason L. Mast, eds. 2006. *Social Performance: Symbolic Action, Cultural Pragmatics and Ritual*. Cambridge: Cambridge University Press.
Badiou, Alain. 2001. *Ethics: An Essay on the Understanding of Evil*. Trans. Peter Hallward. London: Verso.
Badiou, Alain. 2006. *Being and Event*. Trans. Oliver Feltham. New York: Continuum.
Bailey, Frederick G. 1969. *Stratagems and Spoils: A Social Anthropology of Politics*. Oxford: Blackwell.
Barnes, J. A. 1954. "Class and Committees in a Norwegian Island Parish." *Human Relations* 7: 39–58.
Barth, Fredrik, ed. 1969. *Ethnic Groups and Boundaries: The Social Organization of Cultural Difference*. London: Allen and Unwin.
Blau, Peter. [1964] 1986. *Exchange and Power in Social Life*. Chicago: University of Chicago Press.
Burawoy, Michael. 2000. "Introduction: Reaching for the Global." Pp. 1–40 in Michael Burawoy, Joseph A. Blum, Sheba George, Zsuzsa Gille, Teresa Gowan, Lynne Haney, Maren Klawiter, Steven H. Lopez, Seán Ó Riain, and Millie Thayer, *Global Ethnography: Forces, Connections, and Imaginations in a Postmodern World*. Berkeley: University of California Press.
Clifford, James, and George Marcus. 1985. *Writing Culture: The Poetics and Politics of Ethnography*. Berkeley: University of California Press.
Das, Veena. 1995. *Critical Events: Anthropological Perspective on Contemporary India*. New Delhi: Oxford University Press.
DeLanda, Manuel. 2006. *A New Philosophy of Society: Assemblage Theory and Social Complexity*. New York: Continuum.
Deleuze, Gilles. 2004. *Difference and Repetition*. Trans. Paul R. Patton. New York: Continuum.
Deleuze, Gilles, and Félix Guattari. 1987. *A Thousand Plateaus: Capitalism and Schizophrenia*. Trans. Brian Massumi. Minneapolis: University of Minnesota Press.
Deleuze, Gilles, and Félix Guattari. 1994. *What Is Philosophy?* Trans. Hugh Tomlinson and Graham Burchell. New York: Columbia University Press.
Evans-Pritchard, Edward E. [1937] 1976. *Witchcraft, Oracles and Magic among the Azande*. Oxford: Oxford University Press.
Evens, T. M. S., and Don Handelman, eds. 2006. *The Manchester School: Practice and Ethnographic Praxis in Anthropology*. New York: Berghahn Books.
Ferguson, James. 1999. *Expectations of Modernity: Myths and Meanings of Urban Life on the Zambian Copperbelt*. Berkeley: University of California Press.
Geertz, Clifford. 1960. *The Religion of Java*. Glencoe, IL: Free Press.
Geertz, Clifford. 1965. *The Social History of an Indonesian Town*. Cambridge, MA: MIT Press.
Geertz, Clifford. 1973. "Deep Play: Notes on the Balinese Cockfight." Pp. 412–453 in *The Interpretation of Cultures*. New York: Basic Books.
Geertz, Clifford. 1980. *Negara: The Theatre State in Nineteenth-Century Bali*. Princeton, NJ: Princeton University Press.

Gluckman, Max. [1940] 1958. *Analysis of a Social Situation in Modern Zululand*. Rhodes-Livingstone Papers No. 28. Manchester: Manchester University Press for the Rhodes-Livingstone Institute. (Published originally in *Bantu Studies* 14: 1–30.)

Gluckman, Max. 1949. *An Analysis of the Sociological Theories of Bronislaw Malinowski*. Oxford: Oxford University Press.

Gluckman, Max. 1955a. *The Judicial Process among the Barotse of Northern Rhodesia (Zambia)*. Manchester: Manchester University Press.

Gluckman, Max. 1955b. *Custom and Conflict in Africa*. Oxford: Blackwell.

Gluckman, Max. 1961a. "Anthropological Problems Arising from the African Industrial Revolution." Pp. 67–82 in *Social Change in Modern Africa*, ed. Aidan W. Southall. Oxford: Oxford University Press.

Gluckman, Max. 1961b. "Ethnographic Data in British Social Anthropology." *Sociological Review* 9: 5–17.

Gluckman, Max. 1963. *Order and Rebellion in Tribal Africa*. London: Cohen and West.

Gluckman, Max. 1965. *Politics, Law and Ritual in Tribal Society*. Oxford: Blackwell.

Gluckman, Max. 1968. "The Utility of the Equilibrium Model in the Study of Social Change." *American Anthropologist* (n.s.) 70, no. 2: 219–237.

Gouldner, Alvin W. 1965. *Wildcat Strike*. New York: Harper & Row.

Groenhaug, Reidar. 1978. "Scale as a Variable in Analysis: Fields in Social Organization in Herat, Northwest Afghanistan." Pp. 78–121 in *Scale and Social Organization*, ed. Fredrik Barth. Bergen: Universitetsforlaget.

Hacking, Ian. 2000. *The Construction of What?* Cambridge, MA: Harvard University Press.

Handelman, Don. 1977. *Work and Play among the Aged: Interaction, Replication and Emergence in a Jerusalem Setting*. Assen: Van Gorcum.

Handelman, Don. 1998. *Models and Mirrors: Towards an Anthropology of Public Events*. New York: Berghahn Books.

Hardt, Michael, and Antonio Negri. 2001. *Empire*. Cambridge, MA: Harvard University Press.

Haraway, Donna. 2007. *When Species Meet*. Minneapolis: University of Minnesota Press.

Hayles, N. Katherine. 1999. *How We Became Posthuman: Virtual Bodies in Cybernetics, Literature, and Informatics*. Chicago: University of Chicago Press.

Heidegger, Martin. 1977. *The Question Concerning Technology and Other Essays*. Trans. William Lovitt. New York: Harper & Row.

Husserl, Edmund. 1970. *The Crisis of the European Sciences and Transcendental Phenomenology*. Trans. David Carr. Evanston, IL: Northwestern University Press.

Kapferer, Bruce. 1972. *Strategy and Transaction in an African Factory*. Manchester: Manchester University Press.

Kapferer, Bruce. 1995. "The Performance of Categories: Plays of Identity in Africa and Australia." Pp. 55–80 in *The Urban Context*, ed. Alisdair Rogers and Steven Vertovec. Oxford: Berg.

Kapferer, Bruce. 2002. "Introduction: Outside All Reason—Magic, Sorcery and Epistemology in Anthropology." Pp. 1–30 in *Beyond Rationalism: Rethinking Magic, Witchcraft and Sorcery*. New York: Berghahn Books. (Special issue of *Social Analysis* 46, no. 3.)

Kapferer, Bruce. 2005a. "Ritual Dynamics and Virtual Practice: Beyond Representation and Meaning." Pp. 35–54 in *Ritual in Its Own Right: Exploring the Dynamics of Transformation*, ed. Don Handelman and Galina Lindquist. New York: Berghahn Books. (Special issue of *Social Analysis* 48, no. 2.)

Kapferer, Bruce. 2005b. "Situations, Crisis, and the Anthropology of the Concrete." *Social Analysis* 49, no. 3: 85–122.

Kapferer, Bruce. 2007. "Anthropology and the Dialectic of the Enlightenment: A Discourse on the Definition and Ideals of a Threatened Discipline." Keynote address to the Australian Anthropological Association. *Australian Journal of Anthropology* 18, no. 1: 72–96.

Kapferer, Bruce. 2010. "Aporia of Power: Crisis and the Emergence of the Corporate State." *Social Analysis* 54, no. 1: 125–151.

Kapferer, Bruce. 2013. "How Anthropologists Think: Configurations of the Exotic." *Journal of the Royal Anthropological Institute* 19, no. 4: 813–836.

Latour, Bruno. 2007. *Reassembling the Social: An Introduction to Actor-Network-Theory.* Oxford: Oxford University Press.

Leach, Edmund. 1961. *Rethinking Anthropology.* London: Athlone Press.

Magubane, Bernard. 1971. "A Critical Look at Indices Used in the Study of Social Change in Colonial Africa." *Current Anthropology* 12, nos. 4–5: 419–445.

Malinowski, Bronislaw. 1945. *The Dynamics of Culture Change.* Ed. Phyllis M. Kaberry New Haven, CT: Yale University Press.

Marx, Karl. 1852. "Der 18te Brumaire des Louis Napoleon." *Die Revolution*: n.p.

Mitchell, J. Clyde. 1956a. *The Kalela Dance.* Rhodes-Livingstone Paper No. 27. Manchester: Manchester University Press for the Rhodes-Livingstone Institute.

Mitchell, J. Clyde. 1956b. *The Yao Village: A Study in the Social Structure of a Nyasaland Tribe.* Manchester: Manchester University Press.

Mitchell, J. Clyde, ed. 1969. *Social Networks in Urban Situations.* Manchester: Manchester University Press.

Mitchell, J. Clyde. 1974. "Social Networks." *Annual Review of Anthropology* 3, no. 4: 279–299.

Mitchell, J. Clyde. 1983. "Case and Situation Analysis." *Sociological Review* 31: 187–211.

Nietzsche, Friedrich. 1993. *The Birth of Tragedy: Out of the Spirit of Music.* Trans. Shaun Whiteside; ed. Michael Tanner. London: Penguin.

Sahlins, Marshall. 1980. *Historical Metaphors and Mythical History.* Ann Arbor: Michigan University Press.

Sahlins, Marshall. 1985. *Islands of History.* Chicago: University of Chicago Press

Sahlins, Marshall. 2004. *Apologies to Thucydides.* Chicago: University of Chicago Press.

Sahlins, Marshall. 2005. "Structural Work: How Microhistories Become Macrohistories and Vice Versa." *Anthropological Theory* 5, no. 1: 5–30.

Thanem, Torkild, and Stephen Linstead. 2006. "The Trembling Organisation: Order, Change and the Philosophy of the Virtual." Pp. 39–57 in *Deleuze and the Social*, ed. Martin Fuglsang and Bent Meier Sørensen. Edinburgh: Edinburgh University Press.

Tilly, Charles. 1989. *Big Structures, Large Processes, Huge Comparisons.* New York: Russell Sage Foundation.

Turner, Victor W. 1957. *Schism and Continuity in an African Society.* Manchester: Manchester University Press.

Turner, Victor W. 1968. *The Drums of Affliction: A Study of Religious Processes among the Ndembu of Zambia.* Oxford: Clarendon Press.

Turner, Victor W. 1969. *The Ritual Process.* London: Routledge & Kegan Paul.

Turner, Victor W. 1974. *Dramas, Fields and Metaphors: Symbolic Action in Human Society.* Ithaca, NY: Cornell University Press.

van Gennep, Arnold. 1960. *The Rites of Passage.* Trans. Monika B. Vizedom and Gabrielle L. Caffee. London: Routledge & Kegan Paul.

van Velsen, Jaap. 1964. *The Politics of Kinship: A Study in Social Manipulation among the Lakeside Tonga of Nyasaland.* Manchester: Manchester University Press.

van Velsen, Jaap. 1967. "The Extended-Case Method and Situational Analysis." Pp. 129–149 in *The Craft of Social Anthropology*, ed. A. L. Epstein. London: Tavistock.

Werbner, Richard P. 1984. "The Manchester School in South-Central Africa." *Annual Review of Anthropology* 13: 157–185.

Wilson, Godfrey. 1941–1942. "An Essay on the Economics of Detribalization in Northern Rhodesia." Rhodes-Livingstone Paper Nos. 5–6. Livingstone, Northern Rhodesia: Rhodes-Livingstone Institute.

Wolf, Eric. 1982. *Europe and the People without History.* Berkeley: University of California Press.

Chapter 1

'ASHURA IN BAHRAIN
Analyses of an Analytical Event

Thomas Fibiger

'Ashura, an annual event in the Shi'i Muslim world, is devoted to commemorating the early Shi'i leader Imam Husayn and his death in the Battle of Karbala. This crucial event in the history of Islam took place on 10 Muharram (the first month in the Islamic Hijri calendar) in the year AH 61 (AD 680 in the Gregorian calendar). 'Ashura is therefore a double event: an event in the past and an event in the present. In this chapter I will discuss its contemporary manifestation and significance in the Arab Persian Gulf state of Bahrain, where 'Ashura continues to play an important role—socially, religiously, and politically. In 2008, 'Ashura was a key event during my fieldwork in Bahrain, and I discussed it with the many people who are involved in this annual remembrance.

This chapter examines the different ways in which various parties and participants view 'Ashura and how they perceive its significance in today's society. 'Ashura is a matter of ongoing debate in modern Bahrain, much of which is

Notes for this chapter begin on page 44.

concerned with the trichotomy above: whether it is primarily a religious, political, or social event. This analysis presents various local viewpoints—especially shedding light on the discussion of religious and political issues—in order to discuss the broader significance of the event. As a contested interpretation of a crucial occurrence in Islamic history, 'Ashura brings into play established relationships between what counts as social, religious, or political participation and analysis (cf. Asad 2003). Rather than being solely a re-creation of a historical event, contemporary 'Ashura commemorations have the potential to transform and create new orders and worldviews (Deleuze 1994; Hallward 2006). This is what makes the event so important to both academic and vernacular analyses.[1]

This point of departure raises the question of where the analysis of the event takes place. I will argue that the anthropologist's analysis is shaped in collaboration with informants in the field by discussing situations and events while observing these informants and speaking with them about the observations. The development and discussion of analyses with participants in the field is an important part of anthropology and one that deserves greater recognition. A more traditional view of anthropology as a field science suggests that what we do in the field is to record what goes on and to collect material and information for use in describing an ethnography. Then, after leaving the field, we return to our desks to analyze the data in order to come up with some sort of broader, theoretical, and therefore anthropological analysis. In his Radcliffe-Brown Lecture titled "Anthropology Is Not Ethnography," Tim Ingold (2008) discusses the relationship between ethnography and anthropology, turning the traditional understanding upside down. Ingold's argument, in brief, is that we 'anthropologize' with people in the field and then go home to write our ethnographies. He implies that what we, as anthropologists, see in the field—and *how* we see and understand it—depends on the people whom we meet, on the information that they share with us, and on the events that we experience together. Likewise, Bruce Kapferer (2003) notes how his own interpretation of the Suniyama ritual in Sri Lanka is based on "discussions with the specialists and lay participants" and how "[n]o description can stand outside interpretation" (ibid.: 110). I take my cue from them in this chapter, so that rather than aiming at a neutral description or analysis from the ethnographer's desk, I shall include various analyses as they have been related to me by different field participants. The anthropologist is not alone in doing analyses; event analyses are being conducted constantly by, and with, our informants in the field.

As a contested event in a politically unstable society, the commemoration of 'Ashura in Bahrain is a case in point. Entangled in all sorts of analyses, 'Ashura itself is analytical, interpreting historically and dramatically the battle and its outcomes that occurred at Karbala over 1,300 years ago. For a period of two weeks at the beginning of each Islamic year, speeches by religious leaders, poetry recitals, flagellation rituals, weeping mourners, and many discussions about all of these activities demonstrate the importance that is attributed to 'Ashura in modern Bahrain. The descriptions and analyses in this chapter will give an account of these many voices that are heard in the field. I will argue that the task of the ethnographer is to collect these various viewpoints, to listen to them carefully, and then to 'undo' them—to resolve them in light of their social context—and to relate the multiplicity of analyses to the contested whole. This, I suggest, will provide a broader and more coherent perspective of the event and its potentiality.

Multiple Analyses in the Field

The modern event of 'Ashura reflects analyses of what happened at the Battle of Karbala, taken to be one of the decisive events in Islamic history leading up to the split between the Sunni and the Shi'i sects. After the death of the Prophet Muhammad in AH 10 (AD 632), a discussion began as to who was his rightful successor (caliph). One group supported Ali, the son-in-law of the Prophet, but the majority opted for Abu Bakr, one of the Prophet's senior companions. Ali's faction came to be known as the Shi'a. They maintained that the leadership of the Muslims should remain within the Prophet's family, and they continued to support Ali and *ahl al-bayt*, the house of the Prophet.[2] In AD 656, Ali finally became the fourth caliph and, at the same time, was regarded as the first Imam of the Shi'a. However, he was killed as early as AD 661, and after his death the Umayyad caliphate, with its capital in Damascus, took over. The second Umayyad caliph, Yazid, was a harsh ruler and widely unpopular—at least, according to the Shi'i tradition—and in AD 680 Imam Ali's son Husayn decided to travel from Mecca to the Euphrates region to rally support against Yazid. When his small group reached Karbala, they were besieged by Yazid's impressive army and denied access to water and supplies. Rising up against their much stronger opponents, all 72 warriors and Imam Husayn were killed. Ever since then, the Arab Shi'a have felt oppressed by various Sunni regimes in the Arab world, and the split between the sects has been reified (Fuller and Francke 1999; Nasr 2006). This has created a tradition of commemoration and mourning among the Shi'a, and many hold the opinion that it is only due to the advance of the Islamic Republic in Iran in the latter part of the twentieth century that the Shi'i sect has once again achieved power in a sovereign state.

During the two Islamic months of Muharram and Safar, the streets of Shi'i areas in Bahrain are adorned with black flags and banners, and most participants wear black during the event, displaying their sorrow over Imam Husayn's death. The story of Karbala is recounted with deep emotion among the Shi'a, and even outside the sect itself Husayn is revered for his sacrifice in search of a more just Islamic world. There are many ways in which importance can be attributed to this story in modern life. Some people stress the political analogies between the situation of the Shi'a in early Islam and their circumstances under current regimes, calling for resistance against the oppressors in the spirit of Imam Husayn. Others focus on the implementation of Islamic values and on the moral, but less political, struggle of Imam Husayn for a true and sound Islam. Whereas most Sunni find the 'Ashura commemorations aggressive or backward and distance themselves from the whole event, one Sunni religious *shaykh* in Bahrain was very active during 'Ashura in 2008, preaching that Imam Husayn is not solely for the Shi'a. He maintained that the story is not about the antagonism between Sunni and Shi'a but about the struggle for a true Islam, advising that Imam Husayn should be commemorated by all as a good Muslim. Yet others, both Sunni and Shi'a of less strict religious or political devotion, view the 'Ashura commemorations to be one of the few great cultural events in the country. It is a time when people have a chance to meet old friends in the lively streets or religious community halls, to express warm feelings in many different ways, and to join forces in distributing food and drink for their neighbors and for the poor in their society. Even though 'Ashura is a sad occasion in religious terms, with much mourning and grief, and even though it is a potentially aggressive event in political terms, with many slogans and calls for political action, it also gives rise to a social atmosphere of warmth and happiness.

Observing the Event—Social Analyses

Social analyses are, by common definition, what ethnographers do. Here, however, I will use the term 'social analyses' in a slightly different way. I do not refer so much to the ethnographical observation of social aspects of events, since everything is social in the eyes of the ethnographer. Rather, I focus on vernacular analyses in the field that emphasize 'Ashura as a social or cultural happening rather than a religious or political one. In this view, 'Ashura is an annual festival that creates an opportunity to get out and about, to see the processions as cultural performances, to meet people, and to feel an attachment to one's community. Other similar approaches show that people do observe the event and relate positively to it but do not see themselves as participants. In other words, people can observe 'Ashura without any religious or political motivation.

One of my informants, a schoolteacher with a Shi'i background who had studied and married abroad, has stopped practicing religion. After returning to Bahrain, he does not normally go to *matam*, the religious community hall. Even so, during 'Ashura, he visits his old village *matam* once or twice "to meet old friends," as he explained to me. Other than that, he is critical toward the role of religion in Bahraini social life. Unlike many Shi'a, he is happy that the story of Imam Husayn has not been allowed to play a major role in the school curriculum, where the only information about the original event is that Imam Husayn was beheaded. At the same time, however, 'Ashura is a good way to maintain social contacts, since it brings even infrequent visitors, such as this schoolteacher, to the *matam*.

Likewise, a Bahraini intellectual, who describes himself as "non-religious" but with a Sunni background, responds positively to 'Ashura and regards it as a unique cultural festival. The only place in the Gulf to allow public processions, Bahrain is also the only place where 'Ashura is designated as a national holiday, a practice initiated when Bahrain was under British administration during the first half of the twentieth century. Today, many Bahraini Sunni prefer to be away when the streets are taken over by mourning Shi'i processions, using the holidays to go abroad—some on pilgrimage to Mecca. Nevertheless, some Sunni also observe 'Ashura in Bahrain for its social and cultural aspects.

In the capital city Manama, at the back of an exhibition hall that displayed contemporary art reflecting the events at Karbala, I met two men during the night of the largest processions. They sat there all evening, drinking tea and talking with each other and with passers-by. They were not actively participating in the processions, nor were they going to the *matam* for religious sermons. They just liked to observe what was happening and to experience the social atmosphere. When I met these men, both of whom were well-educated and held good jobs, they were discussing the character of one of Imam Husayn's followers—Suher Ibn al-Kheyn—who plays only a minor role in the general narration of the event. He was the character in the story of Karbala whom they liked best and held up as a role model. Suher Ibn al-Kheyn had initially been against Imam Husayn, but by pure intuition he followed the Imam on his way to Karbala and ended up fighting by his side. To these men, this figure of Suher Ibn al-Kheyn showed that "no matter how far astray you go, you can still come to the absolute truth." Like the Lebanese women portrayed by Lara Deeb (2006), these Shi'i men find role models for their lives in the old story of Karbala, and they analyze their present-day social situation in relation to past events and ideals. They went on to discuss political problems in contemporary Bahrain, problems of discrimination between Sunni and Shi'a, and issues touching on human rights and political participation. These reflections were not voiced in support of a particular political movement; rather, they were based on problems that the men had encountered in their own jobs and daily lives, such as discrimination against Shi'a with regard to employment opportunities. Even for those who observe 'Ashura as a social event and do not take part in its religious and political aspects, all three spheres easily blend together.

The various vernacular approaches indicate that today Bahrain is, in many ways, a heterogeneous society. The total population has recently reached one million, of whom around half are Bahraini citizens.[3] The majority of this group are Shi'i Muslims, although there are no official figures, and the numerical relationship between Sunni and Shi'a is much debated (see also Gengler 2011). The Sunni, who control the government and administration, tend to say that it is almost 50/50, whereas Shi'a proclaim that their majority is in the range of 70–85 percent. Many Shi'a feel socially and economically marginalized and politically oppressed, and they formed the vast majority of demonstrators during the uprising for political reforms that was set off in 2011. It is, however, much debated whether this uprising should be seen as a Shi'i uprising against Sunni or as a popular uprising against an undemocratic regime, which in Bahrain is led by the Sunni Al Khalifa ruling family (Fibiger 2014; Matthiesen 2013).

Whether or not the uprising was based on sectarianism, it is clear that Bahraini politics is structured around a Sunni-Shi'a dichotomy, and religion and politics seem inseparably intertwined. This has been the case for decades, not least after the Iranian revolution in 1979 and the growing sectarian awareness that followed on both sides. This trend is especially palpable in the Gulf region, with the proponents of Sunni reformist Salafism in Saudi Arabia on one side of the coast and revolutionary Shi'ism on the other. However, political struggles in Bahrain throughout the twentieth century have often been interpreted as a Shi'i struggle against the Sunni regime, both among Bahrainis themselves and among international scholars (Fuller and Francke 1999; Nakash 2005; Nasr 2006). While such analyses do not account for important examples of non-sectarian or cross-sectarian political identifications in Bahrain, the established political system has certainly taken a sectarian turn, which has only been reinforced in the aftermath of the so-called Arab Spring of 2011. The first parliamentary assembly in Bahrain, which existed from 1973 to 1975, was remarkably non-sectarian, even though religious scholars were key members. A new parliamentary experiment since 2002, on the other hand, has seen Sunni and Shi'a uniting against each other, and there have been no parliamentary groups outside this dichotomy.[4] Secular political societies that advocate for a negation of sectarian and religious politics do in fact exist in Bahrain, but they have not won any parliamentary seats. While this may seem obvious in a religious political structure, many Bahrainis, also outside secular ranks, believe that this failure to win seats was due to government interference with the elections. The intention of the regime, according to this analysis, was to use the relative democratization to display a clear demarcation between Sunni and Shi'a, thereby strengthening national and regional Sunni alliances and consequently the position of the regime. Following from this, the opposition accused the regime of depicting the 2011 uprising as a matter of Shi'a against Sunni, and not a matter of democratic reforms, thereby securing support for the regime from regional and international powerhouses. The result is that sectarian divisions and debates over the role of religious identity in politics are as prominent as ever.

The construction of a Sunni-Shi'a dichotomy, while certainly not novel and probably not a wholly conscious effort, may place itself within the rise of a 'Good Muslim/Bad Muslim' policy, as traced by Mahmood Mamdani (2004) in global politics, especially after 9/11. In this view, the Sunni government and its allies portray themselves as 'Good Muslims' and their Shi'i opponents as 'Bad Muslims'. To the outside world, the regime seems to balance Muslim faith with a relatively modern and secular way of governing, while the 2002–2011 parliament was deadlocked in Sunni and Shi'i blocs and therefore appeared as sectarian and backward, thus justifying the limited powers given to this elected council. Moreover, the opposition to the regime is depicted as being strictly Shi'i. As the most important public display of Shi'i Islam in Bahrain, 'Ashura may serve to underline the image of backwardness and religious fanaticism among this opposition and sectarian group. In the following, I hope to challenge this notion of Good Muslim/Bad Muslim by exploring vernacular analyses of the relationship between religion and politics as it was perceived through the 'Ashura commemoration in 2008. Analyzing these important debates among Bahrainis may enhance an understanding of this contested and flexible relationship, both within and beyond Bahrain and 'Ashura itself.

Creating the Event—Religious Analyses

Despite their social and political grievances, Shi'a in Bahrain in some ways enjoy greater religious freedom than their sectarian peers in neighboring Arab countries. Bahrain is the only Arab Gulf country where 'Ashura is allowed to take place as a public event during which participants can carry out rituals in the streets. During 'Ashura, Bahrain almost seems to be an all-Shi'a community. In 2008, organizers estimated that up to 180,000 people gathered in the center of Manama on the nights when commemorations culminate, around 10 Muharram. Moreover, this number was swelled by people gathering in villages and in the country's other few urban centers. While some groups, especially from Kuwait and the eastern province of Saudi Arabia (Shi'a dominated al-Ahsa), traveled to Bahrain, the vast majority of participants were Bahraini Shi'a—old and young, women and men. 'Ashura is clearly the most important annual event in the Bahraini social calendar, and it requires large-scale organization.

The main public element of 'Ashura is the *mawkab*s, or processions, in which men from the various *matam*s walk together through the streets while rhythmically beating their chests, accompanied by the recitation of poetry about Imam Husayn and Islam.[5] These processions are organized by a committee representing the *matam*s. The committee plans the route through the city center and decides the order in which *matam*s follow each other; the largest *matam*s with the most *mawkab* participants come last. This is the main task of the organizers, who must also handle the many general aspects of controlling an event with so many participants: security, medical assistance, stalls for food and drink, stands for selling or distributing religious merchandise, special areas for the women,[6] negotiating agreements with the authorities, and so on.

After 'Ashura 2008 (or rather 1429, since the event follows the Islamic calendar), I spoke to one of the organizers, a businessman from a reputable urban Shi'i family who is well aware that people take part in the event for different reasons. When we discussed the matter of the interrelation between the religious, social, and political aspects of the commemoration, his own main concern was that 'Ashura should be seen as a religious event, devoted to Imam Husayn, and must not be appropriated for political purposes. Prior to 'Ashura, he had met with the main religious leaders of the non-parliamentary opposition group al-Haq, who, in his understanding, had agreed not to include any political agendas in the event.[7] However, activists from al-Haq did set up a stall in one of the main procession streets, which they used as a base to organize speeches and to distribute leaflets and a petition for constitutional changes (issues that I will discuss below). The organizer was clearly disappointed with this exploitation of 'Ashura for political purposes. He had had to negotiate the event with Bahraini ministries and authorities, and he was afraid that this politicization might compromise the freedom to have such public events in the future.

> I am against mixing in the political issue during this period because it will affect the religious issue. We have our opposition here, but unfortunately in Bahrain, they use this occasion to put out their political agenda during 'Ashura, which is wrong … I talk to all the opposition, [I say to them] leave the 10 days for Muharram, for Imam Husayn. You have 355 days. Maybe before I would sympathize with that, because we did not have a method of expressing our needs in political issues. Now we have freedom of speech … There is a level of communication. So why should I take advantage of this holy season, which is 10 days of the year, and inject it with a lot of political agendas? I am against it completely. I am in charge

of this, [and] my worry is that tomorrow the authorities will come to say: "Look, you misuse this occasion. This is being done to celebrate Imam Husayn and his death, and your people have been using it as a political issue and all kind of issues." This is my worry—that in the future they will not allow it.

"Religion is pure, politics is dirty," he summarized, and the two should not be mixed. The message of Imam Husayn and the Battle of Karbala are too important to be corrupted by current political issues.[8] Participants should focus instead on the story of Imam Husayn, which, according to this organizer, contains messages with a moral content that is removed from politics—issues such as family responsibility and education—and this is what he would like the commemorative event to focus on. Organizers urge religious *shaykhs* to take this approach in their *matam* speeches, in which they discuss 'Ashura each night during the two weeks of its duration.[9] This would help to "implement the true Islamic way of living with others," the businessman concluded.

The *matam*s are the primary centers of activity in relation to 'Ashura. *Matam* activities, which are separate for men and women, may be held in private homes, but larger and more public gatherings are held in specific community halls that are established either by individuals or by local residents. The *matam*s are active all year, being the center for weekly sermons, for weddings and funerals in the community, and for commemorations of the other Imams and key Islamic figures. But their main purpose is to commemorate Imam Husayn—which is why they are also known as *husayniyya*. During 'Ashura, many *matam*s invite special religious *shaykhs*, from Bahrain or abroad, as guest speakers. The speeches follow a special order in which the chronology of the Battle of Karbala is narrated day by day. After a speech on relevant contemporary issues, the last part of the sermon is devoted to mourning a special figure or issue from the battle. During this narration, both the *shaykh* and his audience weep and cry, touched by the emotions attached to the death of Imam Husayn and his companions. It is said that every tear shed for Imam Husayn opens the gates to Paradise. A young woman told me how she was moved to cry in the *matam*: "Every time I hear this story, it feels like a tragedy that has just happened, as if Husayn died only yesterday. I have heard this story more than twenty times … but the way I cry is as if I am hearing it for the first time."

In virtually all *matam*s, the first two nights in the month of Muharram are devoted to a general narration of what happened in the battle and how Imam Husayn went from his home in Mecca to Karbala near the Euphrates River to rise up against Yazid. The third night introduces the small army of 72 companions, all of whom fought for Imam Husayn in the battle and died at Karbala. After this night, the narration focuses on specific heroes in the course of events, rising in the order of importance until the tenth day, 'Ashura itself (the word 'ashara meaning 10 in Arabic). This was the day of the actual battle and the death of the Imam. Before then, on the fourth night, the *shaykh*s speak of Hurr, originally a leader in Yazid's army who switched sides and was killed next to Husayn. The fifth night is dedicated to Habib Ibn al-Madaha, known for his great knowledge of the Qur'an and for being a senior adviser to the Imam, and the sixth is for Husayn's cousin Muslim Ibn al-Akeel, who had traveled to the city of Kufa near Karbala to raise support for Imam Husayn there. When Imam Husayn reached Kufa, he learned that his cousin had been killed and that he would get no support from the Kufans. On the seventh night, the intensity rises as the losses move closer to Imam Husayn's immediate family. His brother Abbas died after both of his hands were cut off, following an attempt to fetch water for Imam Husayn's besieged camp. The next two nights are devoted to the young warriors Ghasem, son of Imam Hassan, and Ali al-Akbar, son of Imam Husayn. The speech on the night before the tenth day (an Islamic calendar date begins at sunset) is about Husayn's baby son Abdulla Radia. As the narrative goes, Husayn held his infant son in his arms and showed him to the opposing army to ask for water and relief for those besieged. In response, the baby boy was killed. This cruel act deepens the *matam* mourning prior to the day of 'Ashura, when the speech is finally about the death of Imam Husayn himself. During the following nights, the guest speakers relate stories about the women and children who were taken prisoner; the famous speech of the prisoner Zaynab, Husayn's sister, who told the world about the event;[10] and finally the funerals that took place three days after the battle.

The key individuals are also represented in a number of exhibits around the procession areas. Life-size figures of Husayn, Abdulla Radia, Abbas, Zaynab, and others are posed in crucial situations from the story. In many cases, the figures are added to the display one by one, as they appear in the *matam* narratives. Abbas is depicted with his hands cut off, the infant Abdulla Radia is impaled with arrows, and Husayn is on his knees. They are all covered in blood, which adds to the emotional atmosphere. The exhibits make visible the episodes recounted in the *matam* and in the procession poetry, and they help give the event a sense of immediacy, drawing it closer to the present, the here and now.[11] Most Shi'a know the individual characters by heart. The annual narration serves to reinforce the collective memory of the event, and the ensemble of heroes makes way for a plurality of interpretations and analytical connections.

The organizer of 'Ashura quoted above notes how the various stories of these mythological figures may be used by the preaching *shaykh*s and how this legend should be employed in the present time:

We have women, we have elderly, we have young people who believed in [Imam Husayn's] mission and followed him. We focus on this in our new life. When we talk about the elderly, the priests reinforce how we should respect the elderly today. When it comes to the day about brotherhood, when Abbas sacrificed himself for his brother, we talk about the relations between brothers—how they should be united. When talking about Abdulla Radia, we talk about the relation between mother and son. We try to take advantage, during this period, [to make] the emotional things an educational thing. It is not simply mourning and mourning and mourning. There is a time for that, but this is a time when everybody comes together. Like when you go to church, you know what I mean— you want to listen to what is being said to you. In the same way, we like to pass the message to the new generation to respect their religion. Because if a person does not have religion, [if] he does not have faith and belief in God, he does not have faith in others.

As this quote shows, while the organizer distances himself from the political uses of the event, in which Imam Husayn's suffering and battle against an unrighteous ruler is inspirational for current struggles against oppression, the events from the past may well be used in order to understand the present and the moral order of Islam. When regarded as exclusively concerned with *matam* speeches and official organization, 'Ashura may be seen as primarily religious rather than political. Nevertheless, the event takes place in the streets with a greater multitude of voices, and a more direct political agenda is involved.

After the *shaykh's* speech, the male audience gathers to do *'aza*, the chest-beating ritual in which participants inflict the pain of Imam Husayn and his followers upon themselves. During the initial nights, *'aza* takes place inside the *matam*. Each night more participants join the ritual, both young and old. Later, usually on the sixth night, the processions take to the streets. On the two nights of culmination, the processions last for hours, and the *mawkab* groups from the various *matam*s follow each other closely, forming into one long line. In the capital city, these processions sometimes do not end until dawn, at the call for morning prayer.

Debates about Flagellation among Bahraini Shi'a

Chest beating is the primary way in which procession participants flagellate themselves in order to take part in the pain suffered by Imam Husayn and his companions. Some participants strike themselves very hard, whereas others perform the act more symbolically. Some groups in specific *mawkab*s take flag-ellation somewhat further, performing either *zanjil*, using chains, or *haydar*, using a sword. The *zanjil* chains are used to beat one's back, while the sword is used to make a small cut into one's forehead and then take part in the pro-cession with raised sword and blood pouring over one's face and clothes. *Zan-jil* represents the prisoners who were put in chains when taken from Karbala to the caliph in Damascus. *Haydar* represents the people of the city of Kufa, who are said to have carried out this ritual when they learned that their failure to help had contributed to the death of Imam Husayn.

Both rituals are carried out by only a minority of participants in contem-porary Bahrain. While *zanjil* is generally accepted, *haydar* is widely disputed. The *zanjil mawkab*s take place at night, along with the general processions, while *haydar* takes place only on the morning of the tenth day.[12] In 1993, the Iranian supreme leader Ayatollah Khamenei issued a *fatwa* against *haydar*, stating that it was dangerous to one's health and would not benefit the image of Shi'i Islam around the world (see also Pinault 1999). While this *fatwa* has prompted most Bahrainis to disapprove of *haydar*, the ritual has gained impor-tance among others who do not follow Ayatollah Khamenei.[13]

The antagonism between the groups for and against *haydar* was particularly strong in the neighborhood where I lived during my fieldwork, that is, in the urban part of the island Muharraq next to the capital area. During the last few years, a minority of Shi'a in Muharraq, known to follow the religious leader

Muhammad Shirazi rather than Khamenei, have organized a *haydar* procession, an activity that has otherwise been confined to Manama. This initiative has been fiercely resisted by other Shi'a. Whereas the *haydar* supporters argue that this is acceptable due to their religious freedom as both Shi'a and Bahrainis, opponents have put banners at their *matam*s, quoting Ayatollah Khamenei's arguments against *haydar* and insisting that all Shi'a should stand together on this issue. This group also filed a petition with the municipality to call for a ban on *haydar*. Despite this attempt to ally with the authorities, accusations were also voiced against the Bahraini government for deliberately supporting the *haydar* groups— both morally and in practice (by providing ambulances, security, etc.)—in order to split the Shi'i community. Once I even heard the American embassy being accused of supporting the *haydar* processions by furnishing new swords. The *haydar* ritual may seem, to the outside observer, to be an aggressive sectarian ritual, but it is apparently more aggressive when it comes to creating divisions within the Shi'i community, rather than against other sects or regimes. I asked whether the petition submitted to the municipality would be seen as a victory for the government's hidden agenda to divide the Shi'i community, if indeed such an agenda existed. This point had already been raised within the group, I was told, but the matter was deemed too important to shy away from on such strategic grounds. As long as *haydar* was there, an alliance between the Shi'i groups was impossible.

A good friend invited me to go with him from Muharraq to Manama on 9 and 10 Muharram, the nights when the 'Ashura commemorations would culminate. Like many Shi'a, he was named after one of the legends of early Shi'i Islam, so I will refer to him as Abbas. In his early forties, Abbas was from the Persian community in Muharraq and, like many Muharraqis, worked in Bahrain's international airport, which dominates the island. He was deeply involved with his religious community, and his primary interest in 'Ashura was religious devotion. Abbas used to perform *haydar* and also had beat himself with knives on his back (a ritual rarely observed in Bahrain today), but he turned against these practices completely when Khamenei issued his *fatwa*. Abbas now took part in the chest-beating *'aza* of his *matam* in Muharraq, and while in Manama he wanted to see the large-scale processions and visit some central *matam*s. He had singled out one *matam* in particular because a certain religious *shaykh* was invited as the speaker that year. Abbas knew that this *shaykh* was very skilled in evoking emotions, and the mourning that night was indeed very intense. As the narration progressed, the *matam* audience increasingly hid their faces in their hands, and their shoulders shook with weeping. After the sermon—apparently past the phase of ritual mourning—Abbas and I went around Manama to see the processions. We passed the stand of al-Haq society as they were calling for people to sign a petition for amendments to the constitution. Abbas had already signed, but he took no great interest in the matter. "We can sign all the petitions we want," he told me in resignation, "but there is not going to be any change." Abbas's interest in 'Ashura was religious not political. Therefore, it was only later that I found out about a major gathering that had taken place that night around al-Haq's stall near the large *matam*s of Manama. The charismatic leader of al-Haq had spoken to the crowd, conveying messages about the political side of 'Ashura. While this was deeply important to some participants, others were more engaged in the social or religious activities that relate to 'Ashura: going to *matam*, seeing processions, or meeting friends.

Using the Event—Political Analyses

I will, however, now focus my attention on the political aspects of the event. Historically, 'Ashura has been the starting point for some of the most important social uprisings in the history of Bahrain, especially in the 1950s and 1990s (Khalaf 2000). The reason for this is obvious: thousands of people are gathered, they are highly charged with emotions, and, as noted above, the story of Imam Husayn is often analyzed as a righteous struggle against oppression and against an unjust regime. In Bahrain, the Al Khalifa family and their Sunni allies are seen as invaders who, by force and through regional alliances, have come to dominate an island nation that was once exclusively Shi'a.[14] In the politico-religious climate of contemporary Bahrain, drawing analogies between the Shi'a situation at present and at the time of Imam Husayn is inevitable.

Thus, in his speech, the leader of al-Haq, mentioned above, likened the present regime to the regime of Yazid at the time of Imam Husayn. He urged people not to believe the government's promises of democratic development and political participation in Bahrain, as it was exactly such unfulfilled promises that misled Muslims at the time of Husayn, causing them to turn their backs on him. In the speaker's view, the fact that Bahrain's ruler, King Hamad Al Khalifa, supported some *matams* with alms and food was simply an indication of the regime's treacherous behavior and divide-and-rule motives. Such gifts were "poisoned by Yazid," he asserted. By making an analogy between Yazid and the Al Khalifa government, the speaker aimed to spark an emotional uprising in his audience with the eventual aim of overthrowing the regime—the goal of Imam Husayn.[15]

While many other speeches and slogans during 'Ashura were outright political, they were less radical than this. The petition, which was prepared just before 'Ashura in order to take advantage of the many gatherings, called for specific changes to the constitution and especially for Prime Minister Khalifa bin Salman Al Khalifa to leave office. It was thus argued that when the crowd had shouted "Step aside Khalifa," this call was directed solely at the prime minister and not at the Al Khalifa family as a whole. This discussion and division within the opposition has been highlighted in the 2011 uprising and aftermath (Kinninmont 2012). Politicians of the parliamentary Shi'i opposition, and especially the leader of the party, Ali Salman, were invited to numerous events. Being an educated religious *shaykh* himself, Ali Salman spoke to the masses about both religious and political topics. The day after 'Ashura itself, a massive procession took place in the village of al-Deih, and Ali Salman was one of the people who recited poetry, narrated the story of Karbala, and contextualized the event for the participants, while walking along with them. He was clearly the speaker who received the most attention and gained the largest following during this procession. At the same time, political banners and slogans called for a new constitution.

The processions in al-Deih, with many thousands of participants, took place in the same streets that just a few weeks earlier had been the site of demonstrations and clashes with security forces—and even the death of one demonstrator, a rare case back then. Such violence and confrontations were remarkably absent during 'Ashura, and also after the 2011 uprising 'Ashura processions take place with fewer clashes than outside this ritual season. While the commemoration is accepted by Bahraini authorities as a religious and popular procession, demonstrations held outside the framework of 'Ashura are often countered by security forces armed with rubber bullets and tear gas. Authorities know very well that any attempt to break up the 'Ashura processions would be hazardous, even uncontrollable, and for the same reason participants avoid violence and vandalism. In 2008, more than after 2011, this implicit agreement made some groups take advantage of the event to present political messages, contrary to the wishes of the organizer quoted above.

In 2008, the violent clashes in the month before 'Ashura had a great impact on the political atmosphere of the commemorative event. The unrest began at another religious-political event, known as Martyrs' Day, in which people killed during the then last uprising of the 1990s are remembered. When the outbreak of bloodshed on Martyrs' Day added yet another martyr to the list, the mood against the regime worsened. This prompted the petition that was distributed during 'Ashura and was later forwarded to the government but received no response—in part leading to the uprising of 2011 and onward.

In Muharraq, one Sunni religious *shaykh* went against this antagonism between Sunni and Shi'a in his response to the Martyrs' Day violence and in his subsequent activities during 'Ashura. In mosque sermons and in the media, he argued in favor of commemorating martyrs, but stated that this should represent all Bahrainis, both Sunni and Shi'a. People from both sects, he pointed out, had died in the struggle for what they believed would be a better Bahrain. Opposition political societies have supported this idea, while the government ignored the matter. The *shaykh* then continued this line of reasoning during the 'Ashura events. As he had done in previous years, he went to Shi'i *matams*, Sunni mosques, and religious and political societies to argue that Imam Husayn should be remembered not only for the Shi'a but for all Muslims, since his struggle was for the implementation of true Islam for them all against the unrighteous Umayyad caliphate. Moreover, Husayn was a grandson of the Prophet Muhammad. This message was not intended to unite Shi'a and Sunni politically against the present regime; rather, it was meant to bring the sects together religiously in the spirit of one peaceful Islam.[16]

Most Sunni think differently about 'Ashura. Many fast during 9 and 10 Muharram, which have also long been national holidays in Bahrain. But to most Sunni, the fast and the holiday are not in commemoration of Husayn but of the Prophet Musa (biblical Moses), who, according to Sunni tradition, fled the pharaoh on those dates, and the Prophet Muhammad fasted in remembrance of this. The increase of sectarian awareness and religious education in recent decades has strengthened this interpretation. A Sunni informant noted how he had to convince his mother that the fast was not in sympathy with Imam Husayn and the Shiʻa, but with Musa and the Prophet Muhammad.[17] Many also use the holidays to go to Mecca for *'umra* (the 'small pilgrimage', which can be done anytime outside the season of the main pilgrimage, or *hajj*), which is promoted by travel agencies now as 'Umra al-'Ashura. This gives the name 'Ashura a meaning outside the Shiʻi ritual, creating an option to pay respect to both the Prophets Muhammad and Musa and also to leave Bahrain during the 'Ashura processions.

To the Sunni religious *shaykh*, all of these interpretations are good religious acts. One can commemorate Musa or Husayn and, in both circumstances, also the Prophet Muhammad. He uses this to stress the possibilities of peaceful co-existence, not only between Sunni and Shiʻa, but also among the faiths of Islam, Christianity, and Judaism:

> If somebody will fast for Musa, it is good, and if somebody is sad for Imam Husayn, it is also good. Between Musa and Imam Husayn is our Prophet Muhammad. Because our Prophet said about Husayn that he is my son, and he said about Musa that he is my brother—I must fast and you must fast. So you can enjoy three in one: Musa, and Muhammad, and Husayn. And so we can see that Islam and other religions can be one. Why are Muslims fighting with Christians or Jews? Our God is one. All of them are from the same family, the same tree, and all of them have Musa and Isa and Muhammad. Their father was Ibrahim. Christians believe in Ibrahim, right? And Jews also believe in Ibrahim. And Muslims also believe that Ibrahim is their father. So all of them can come in one way. It is not difficult.[18]

As these local analyses exemplify, there are various possibilities for interpreting the event—religiously, politically, and socially—in order to integrate the messages of what happened at Karbala over 1,300 years ago into contemporary Bahraini society. 'Ashura is a powerful event, one that is laden with emotions that have the potential both to gather and to split social groups, to be both political and non-political, depending on who is doing the analysis.

Conclusion: Undoing Analyses

Whether 'Ashura should be recognized as an opportunity for voicing Shiʻi political aspirations or should be seen solely as a means of religious commemoration is an important and ongoing debate among Bahrainis. As one of the organizers quoted earlier put it, the message of the event gets muddled when politics is involved—and religion should stay pure. The desire to separate religion and politics is evidently not confined to Western politicians and intellectuals. From a quite different perspective, Bahraini Muslims call for the purity of religion and the exclusion of politics from what they see as a religious event. However, this analysis of the significance of 'Ashura faces difficulties among other Bahrainis, who basically see the event in terms of Shiʻi political aspirations, in both the past and the present. In this view, the annual commemoration is an ideal occasion for expressing political viewpoints. Others see it instead as a chance to socialize. They regard it as a key event in the Bahraini social calendar and a unique cultural festival. Thus, motivations of a social, religious, and political nature all come together in 'Ashura.

This trichotomy is important to bear in mind when analyzing an event like 'Ashura. In this chapter, I have focused primarily on my informants' religious and political analyses of the event, because this is an important debate, both within and outside of Bahrain. In the broader discussion of the relationship between religion and politics, these analyses of 'Ashura suggest that the potential of religion to form political ideas and motivations should be acknowledged without being dismissed as fanatical or backward. As the Bahraini debate reflected in this chapter demonstrates, this does not mean that 'Ashura is seen only, or even primarily, as a political event. What is important is to discuss how various positions in society relate to the event. 'Ashura shows how different interpretations and potentials of the relationship between religion and politics are debated in Bahrain. This point is based on event analyses done in, and working with, the field, and it can most probably be applied to many other fields and situations.

Seen in this way, 'Ashura is not entirely political or religious. It is neither a sectarian event nor a reflection of backward traditions in an otherwise modern society. Such analyses are often seen in the field, when situated participants prefer one interpretation over others. However, this is no less the case in academic research that is aimed at achieving unambiguous clarity. When such analytical reductionism attempts to extract the essence of a given event, as if the study was done in a laboratory, it fails to listen to the various voices in the field and does not pay sufficient attention to the potential and the analyses embodied in the event.

The importance of an event analysis of 'Ashura is, therefore, to reflect the significance of the event as it is carried out in contemporary society. In this chapter I have focused on how a variety of analyses of 'Ashura are created among its participants. These analyses, as seen in the event, are not one-sided and static, but may unfold in different ways at different times and in different places. Moreover, event analysis shows that a double event like 'Ashura, as a present commemoration of a past event, is not analytically fixed to the original happening. This, of course, calls for anthropological rather than historical analyses, but also for an understanding of contemporary Muslims rather than a search for some brand of 'true' or 'original' Islam. This argument in favor of event analysis challenges essentialist interpretations, which are frequently presented by Muslims and non-Muslims alike. The statement "If you want to understand this, don't look at what Muslims do, but look at what Islam is" has often been encountered in the field, and it could easily be repeated by opponents of Islam who believe that they can find the true agenda of contemporary Muslims hidden in the original Islamic scripts. As the French scholar Olivier Roy (2004: 10) notes: "The key question is not what the Koran actually says, but what Muslims say the Koran says." Event analysis, I suggest, follows this attempt to reverse the relationship, with a focus on practices and the social situation itself rather than on a possible text or source that lies behind it. From the perspective of event analysis, Islam is what Muslims do and how contemporary Muslims analyze their own social situation.

In following this methodology, it is both possible and necessary to record multiple analyses in the field. There are various ways of using 'Ashura as an analytical event. My hope is that, by including such various analyses from the field, anthropological analysis may come to represent more fully the perspectives and potentiality of the event.

Acknowledgments

The author would like to thank Lotte Meinert, Bruce Kapferer, and Gareth Doherty for their careful comments on earlier versions of this chapter, as well as the participants in the research seminar that led to this collection for their valuable suggestions. The chapter has been revised from its original publication in the journal *Social Analysis* in order to include perspectives of the 2011 Arab Spring uprising on the event of 'Ashura and the general situation in Bahrain.

Thomas Fibiger is an Assistant Professor in Anthropology at Aarhus University. He has carried out extensive fieldwork in Bahrain in the period 2003–2010 and has co-edited (with Mads Daugbjerg) the 2011 special issue of the journal *History and Anthropology* on "Globalized Heritage." He has recently begun fieldwork in Kuwait as part of a trans-Nordic research group studying perceptions of religious authority among contemporary Shi'a Muslims.

Notes

1. Here, the word 'vernacular' means informal, non-academic, or lay, rather than the linguistic meaning of the term, which signifies colloquial, local language. Interviews quoted in this chapter were actually carried out in English.
2. *Ahl al-bayt* includes the Prophet, his daughter Fatima, and the Imams, the early leaders of the Shi'i sect. The first Imam is Ali, Fatima's husband, followed by their sons Hassan and Husayn. The title 'Imam' is given to a spiritual leader, whereas the title 'caliph' is given to a worldly leader only (Momen 1985: 11). According to the main Shi'i tradition, there are 12 Imams directly descended from the Prophet. The last of these, the Mahdi, went into occultation in AH 260 (AD 874) and is expected to return to save the world. For more on the history and beliefs of Shi'i Islam, see Momen (1985). For more on the history and theology of 'Ashura in particular, see Ayoub (1978).
3. In 2007, Bahrain's government adjusted the official figure of the total population upward from approximately 700,000 to 1,000,000 in order to account for naturalizations and new registrations of migrant workers. The updated number came as a shock to many Bahrainis, sparking a debate about the country's demography. The non-Bahraini population mainly consists of South Asian workers.
4. The Shi'a were represented by the political society al-Wifaq, the only opposition group in parliament. Following the quash of the uprising in 2011, al-Wifaq withdrew from parliament, which since then has had no acknowledged opposition. A minority of the current MPs are Shi'a. Al-Wifaq continues to play a role outside the parliament. The history and development of Shi'i political societies in the Gulf is well-documented by Laurence Louër (2008, 2012).

5. *Matam*, *mawkab*, and other Arab words in this chapter are presented in the singular. To simplify, I have added the English suffix -s when such words are used in the plural. In general, the chapter follows a simplified version of the transcriptions suggested by the *International Journal of Middle East Studies*.

6. Women and men are separated in the *matam*s and in the processions, which women do not take part in, except for one special procession on 11 Muharram that commemorates the women and children taken into captivity after the Battle of Karbala. Rather, they watch the processions from certain designated areas. As a male, I had no access to these special areas for females, neither in the *matam*s nor in the streets, and so this chapter primarily refers to male areas, activities, and viewpoints.

7. Al-Haq is a political group that represents the part of the opposition that aims for the overthrow of the regime, while the main official Shi'a political society al-Wifaq was represented in parliament up to 2011 and aims for reforms within the regime (see also note 4 above).

8. In the aftermath of the ill-fated 2011 uprising, 'Ashura organizers as well as Shi'i religious authorities have further urged ritual participants to avoid clashes with security forces during the event, stressing its religious importance. There seems to be a truce between the regime and opposition during 'Ashura, as it was noted to me by Bahraini informants shortly after the event in 2013.

9. A *shaykh*, in religious terms, is educated in religious studies, one level above the *mulla*. A Shi'i *shaykh* is distinguished by his white or black turban, while a *mulla* wears a loose head scarf (*ghitrah*).

10. Both Zaynab and Husayn's surviving son, the later fourth Imam Zain al-Abedin (who did not take part in the battle due to illness), are responsible for sharing their knowledge of what happened at Karbala. One informant referred to them as "the great myth-makers."

11. Two other rituals are performed with the same intention of bringing the past into the present: *ziyara*, the symbolic 'visiting' at the graves of key figures, done by turning in their direction during *matam* sermons, and *shabih*, theatrical performances of certain parts of the Battle of Karbala. According to Momen (1985: 244), these rituals were not performed in Bahrain at the time of his study, but they have since become an important element, especially in the large processions that gather all of Bahrain's Shi'i villages and urban neighborhoods on 10 and 11 Muharram.

12. *Haydar* may also be carried out at *arba'in*, when the whole story and ritual is repeated during one night and day, 40 days after 'Ashura, and during the similar three-night commemoration of the death of Imam Ali, Husayn's father and the first Shi'i Imam, which takes place on 19–21 Ramadan. During the year, there are smaller processions with chest beating for all dead Imams.

13. In Shi'i theory, the individual Muslim is obliged to emulate a *marja*, a religious authority for guidance in religious and moral affairs. As the supreme spiritual leader (*wilayat al-faqih*) of Iran, Ayatollah Khamenei is currently one of the most important such authorities in the Shi'i world. However, there are a number of alternate *marja*s. This is the focus of my current postdoctoral research in Kuwait, as part of a trans-Nordic research group studying alternative perceptions of religious authority in different Shi'i communities.

14. The historical perception of the Al Khalifa family itself is that its ancestors did indeed come from mainland Arabia, but that they liberated Arab Bahrain from Persia, implemented true Islam, protected its inhabitants, and, during two centuries in power, have led the country into the modern age.

15. This same al-Haq leader was arrested for his activities during 'Ashura in 2009. Other leaders from the society were later arrested and charged with conspiring to carry out terrorist attacks in Bahrain. Leaders and several hundred political activists were again arrested in 2010, in part leading up to the uprising in 2011. Since then, political activists have been in and out of custody, and as of 2014 many people, especially those related to al-Haq, remain in prison, including this particular leader.

16. After the quash of the 2011 uprising it seems that the 'sectarian gulf', aptly termed so by Toby Matthiesen (2013), has deepened, and even fewer Bahrainis stand up for a

cross-sectarian agenda. I have no knowledge of how this particular *shaykh* has reacted to the new circumstances or of his activities during 'Ashura in recent years.

17. Hylén (2007) notes how Sunni Muslims in Pakistan serve water to 'Ashura procession participants, in accordance with an Islamic tradition. While some Bahrainis recall that this tradition was observed in the past, it is apparently absent today.

18. In the biblical tradition, Isa is Jesus and Ibrahim is Abraham.

References

Asad, Talal. 2003. *Formations of the Secular: Christianity, Islam, Modernity.* Stanford, CA: Stanford University Press.

Ayoub, Mahmoud. 1978. *Redemptive Suffering in Islam: A Study of the Devotional Aspects of 'Ashura in Twelver Shi'ism.* The Hague: Mouton.

Deeb, Lara. 2006. *An Enchanted Modern: Gender and Public Piety in Shi'i Lebanon.* Princeton, NJ: Princeton University Press.

Deleuze, Gilles. 1994. *Difference and Repetition.* Trans. Paul R. Patton. New York: Continuum.

Fibiger, Thomas. 2014. "Stability or Democracy? The Failed Uprising in Bahrain and the Battle for the International Agenda." *Critical Interventions* 14: 81–94.

Fuller, Graham, and Rend R. Francke. 1999. *The Arab Shi'a: The Forgotten Muslims.* New York: St. Martin's Press.

Hallward, Peter. 2006. *Out of This World: Deleuze and the Philosophy of Creation.* London: Verso.

Hylén, Torsten. 2007. "Husayn, the Mediator." PhD diss., Uppsala University.

Ingold, Tim. 2008. "Anthropology Is Not Ethnography." Radcliffe-Brown Lecture in Social Anthropology. *Proceedings of the British Academy* 154: 69–92.

Gengler, Justin. 2011. "Ethnic Conflict and Political Mobilization in Bahrain and the Arab Gulf." PhD diss., University of Michigan.

Kapferer, Bruce. 2003. "Sorcery, Modernity and the Constitutive Imaginary: Hybridising Continuities." Pp. 105–128 in *Beyond Rationalism: Rethinking Magic, Witchcraft and Sorcery*, ed. B. Kapferer. New York: Berghahn Books.

Khalaf, Abdulhadi. 2000. *Unfinished Business: Contentious Politics and State-Building in Bahrain.* Research Reports in Sociology, 2001:1, Department of Sociology, University of Lund.

Kinninmont, Jane. 2012. *Bahrain: Beyond the Impasse.* London: Chatham House.

Louër, Laurence. 2008. *Transnational Shia Politics: Religious and Political Networks in the Gulf.* London: Hurst.

Louër, Laurence. 2012. *Shiism and Politics in the Middle East.* New York: Columbia University Press.

Mamdani, Mahmood. 2004. *Good Muslim, Bad Muslim: America, the Cold War, and the Roots of Terror.* New York: Pantheon Books.

Matthiesen, Toby. 2013. *Sectarian Gulf: Bahrain, Saudi Arabia and the Arab Spring That Wasn't.* Stanford, CA: Stanford University Press.

Momen, Moojan. 1985. *An Introduction to Shi'i Islam: The History and Doctrines of Twelver Shi'ism.* New Haven, CT: Yale University Press.

Nakash, Yitzhak. 2005. *Reaching for Power: The Shi'a in the Modern Arab World.* Princeton, NJ: Princeton University Press.

Nasr, Vali. 2006. *The Shia Revival: How Conflicts with Islam Will Shape the Future.* New York: W.W. Norton.

Pinault, David. 1999. "Shi'a Lamentation Rituals and Reinterpretations of the Doctrine of Intercession: Two Cases from Modern India." *History of Religions* 38, no. 3: 185–205.

Roy, Olivier. 2004. *Globalized Islam: The Search for a New Ummah.* New York: Columbia University Press.

Chapter 2

'Burying the ANC'
Post-apartheid Ambiguities at the University
of Limpopo, South Africa

Bjarke Oxlund

In late October 2006, two days after the elections held for the Students Representative Council (SRC) at the University of Limpopo, the youth wing and the
student arm of the ruling African National Congress (ANC)[1] were symbolically
buried in an ironic re-enactment of the funeral processions normally accorded
to fallen heroes of the struggle against apartheid. The funeral was organized
by members of the Pan-Africanist Student Movement of Azania (PASMA), the
student wing of the Pan-African Convention, to celebrate their electoral victory over the better-resourced ANC. Although the event played on a humorous
and ironic symbolism, it soon proved to reveal a number of serious tensions
and ambiguities underlying post-apartheid South African society. The students
at this former 'Bantu institution', which was reserved for the black population
only during apartheid, still struggle to carve out a path for themselves. They
question an ANC movement that is divided and has failed to deliver on its

Notes for this chapter begin on page 61.

promises, while relations with white people continue to be shaped by racial prejudices and separation.

Inspired by Gluckman's ([1940] 1958) classic piece on the opening of a bridge in Zululand and by the Manchester School in general, this chapter provides a detailed account of the outcome of the student elections at the university. Following a brief introduction to situational analysis, the essay takes its cue from specific events that unfolded in a single day and then makes connections to incidents of the immediate past and to the struggle against apartheid that took place on campus in the 1960s and 1970s. In subscribing to an understanding of a social situation as a generative moment in a series of generative moments, the analysis provides a micro-historical outlook on the ambiguities underlying post-apartheid South Africa and the ANC movement in relation to the University of Limpopo. The concluding section sums up the argument and discusses the strengths and limitations that an updated situational analysis approach brings to South African ethnography.

On Situational Analysis

When in 1940 Gluckman wrote his *Analysis of a Social Situation in Modern Zululand*, he outlined at the same time an approach to the study of social change, as well as the central analytical concepts that came to be considered the germ of later case methods by members of the Manchester School (Werbner 1984: 162). This status was underscored when the volume was republished in 1958 by the Rhodes-Livingstone Institute, since the three essays were presented in a manner delineating an analytical progression from event over history to theoretical abstraction (Kapferer 2006: 123). Through the provision of an excess of detail in the ethnographic account of the events of a single day, Gluckman took a snapshot of the complex social realities underlying South African society from which he could develop a general understanding of the inter-ethnic relations in Zululand between the dominated majority of Zulus and the white minority of Europeans (Werbner 1984: 160).

In thus shifting the ethnographic focus from the normative to actual practice, Gluckman succeeded in turning the relationship between case and statement on its head (Evens and Handelman 2006a: 1–3). This approach to case material departed from Malinowski's method of 'apt illustration', whereby cases were presented as appropriate illustrations of larger systems or structures, and asked instead for the analysis of new cases to represent new stages in ongoing processes "of social relations between specific persons and groups in a social system and culture" (Gluckman 2006: 16). In the South African context, the difference in perspective between Malinowski and Gluckman had political implications, given that Malinowski's approach to island-like, cultural wholes of specific groups could be used to legitimize policies of separate development for blacks and whites, while *Analysis of a Social Situation* demonstrated that Zulus and Europeans were in fact interlocked in one social system that was, however, characterized by a dominant cleavage (Gluckman [1940] 1958: 64).

Gluckman referred to the term 'situation' as a total context of tension and conflict qualifying as a turning point, or as "moments of social life in the very process of formation" (Kapferer 2006: 125; see also Evens and Handelman 2006a: 2). Although the concepts of case, extended case, event, and situation were only vaguely defined, they all seemed to refer to a turning point from which processes of analytical revelation could take their beginnings (Kapferer 2006: 125). Gluckman himself defined event and situation in the following manner ([1940] 1958: 9): "Where an event is studied as part of the field of sociology, it is therefore convenient to speak of it as a social situation. A social situation is thus the behaviour on some occasion of members of a community as such, analysed and compared with their behaviour on other occasions, so that the analysis reveals the underlying system of relationships between the social structure, the physical environment, and the physiological life of the community's members."

Situational analysis is often presented as a method (see Burawoy 1998) or sometimes, due to its ability to capture flux and societal change, as a method with profound theoretical implications. Kapferer (2006: 118–122) argues that it is no coincidence that situational analysis, with its focus on complexity and process, was developed at a time of crisis, when the post-colonial nation-state was in decline, or that it is resurfacing now, during a new period of crisis in the form of globalization and neo-imperialism. It is a case in point that South African sociology has recently seen a renewed interest in the extended case method (Alexander 2006: 16), as evidenced by the publication of an anthology of 12 extended cases titled *Globalisation and New Identities* (Alexander, Dawson, and Ichharam 2006). The anthology was inspired by a volume organized by the sociologist Michael Burawoy, titled *Global Ethnography* (Burawoy et al. 2000), and makes use of his elaborated and updated version of the extended case method to study issues of globalization (Burawoy 1998).

In what follows, however, it will be demonstrated that it is not just globalization that brings about crisis, tension, and conflict in contemporary South Africa. Although the divisions noted by Gluckman between black and white persist to this day, the present situational analysis shows that tensions are brewing in other corners of post-apartheid South African society where material conditions have improved only marginally after 15 years of democracy and the rule of three consecutive ANC governments. Moving from an analysis of student politics at the University of Limpopo, the chapter aims to show that situational analysis may be fruitfully used to create a 'micro-history' (see Evens and Handelman 2006b: 47) of events that connects previous generative moments with generative moments of the present. Whereas Gluckman analyzed South African society in the context of the opening of a bridge and the complexities that were laid bare by that event, this essay seeks to shed light on current political dynamics from the vantage point of student politics at a former Bantu institution, where young people strive through education to carve out a position for themselves in the new South Africa. The analysis of the ironic burial of the ANC-aligned student organizations reveals that the failure to deliver in the higher education sector has made the ANC vulnerable to severe criticism and abandonment among students. This vulnerability is evident in several other sectors, such as health and employment, where the ANC government has also failed to deliver on its promises.

Election Celebrations and the 'Burial' of the ANC

In the early hours of Wednesday, 25 October 2006, I was called on my cell phone by my field assistant Solomon, who told me that the results of the SRC elections had finally been announced. PASMA supporters were now touring the campus, singing and dancing with joy, because their opponents—the African National Congress Youth League (ANCYL) and its sister organization, the South African Student Convention (SASCO)—had won only three seats each, which left five seats for PASMA and three seats for the Student Christian Organisation (SCO). Since I was living on campus in a guest house located a few hundred meters away from the majority of the student residences, I could hear the PASMA supporters *toyi-toyiing* (a protest style of dancing and singing in South Africa during apartheid) from afar.[2] I got up and quickly ran to the central part of the campus, where between 150 and 200 students were dancing and singing resistance songs, waving the PASMA flag, and wearing PASMA T-shirts. The procession entered the fenced compound that was designated for first-year female students, and everybody made a circle around the PASMA flag that was put on the ground. Supporters now danced and cheered each other. Some of the female students had attached tiny branches of wood with green leaves to their bodies, which made for a vibrant appearance. It was, in a way, surprising to see such jubilant celebrations, considering that PASMA had not won a majority vote and thus still had to negotiate with the Christian students to ensure that its members would be able to rule.

Later in the day, PASMA's president-elect, Elvis Modikela Nkoana, called for his members to gather at one of the lecture halls in close proximity to the university administration. Nkoana informed his followers that, due to ongoing negotiations with the SCO, the funeral for the ANC 'Baby League' (as he had dubbed the ANCYL) and SASCO would be postponed until the following day. Nkoana then celebrated his group's victory in oratory, making references to Marx and renowned anti-apartheid heroes such as Onkgopotse Tiro and Steve Biko, before initiating *toyi-toyiing* in the hall. Finally, Nkoana declared: "Nothing can stop PASMA or the revolution. Even if I am killed, comrades will rise from the ground where I fell." He then left the lecture hall to resume overnight deliberations with the Christian students on the exact positions to be awarded each organization in the new student council.

By the time that the university's Turfloop campus had awakened the next morning, the announcement about the funeral had been pasted on blackboards everywhere. It stated:

> Students are hereby informed of the funeral of the ANC 'Baby League' and SASCO
> Time: 16h00PM
> Dress: Black
> Theme: "We were the future, and PASMA has stopped us."

No indication was given as to where the funeral procession would begin, but in the afternoon several hundred students gathered at Gate Two. This is the pedestrian entrance used by students to go to the Mankweng Shopping Centre, erected in 2005, which contains supermarkets, clothing stores, bank branches, and a few take-out restaurants. While Gate One is the official university entrance for vehicles, Gate Two opens into a more chaotic and commercial space, with street vendors coming up to the campus's very entrance. In the 100 meters from the campus to the shopping center, students can buy everything they need, ranging from vegetables, beer, and roasted chicken to air time for their cell phones or newspapers and sweets.

Gate Two is thus the prime spot for student life and activity. Bheki, a PASMA student leader, used to say: "Everybody loves [Gate Two] because it is so African. It looks just like something in Zimbabwe." In view of the Afrocentrist ideology proclaimed by PASMA and the pride taken in things African, it was therefore only natural that the funeral processions organized by the Pan-Africanists would start at Gate Two. In the middle of the crowd, elevated above everybody else, stood three PASMA student leaders, who were preparing their commemoration speeches that would ridicule the losing organizations on account of their election slogans. I was observing these activities with two of my friends and key interlocutors, Basala and Erad, at the outskirts of the gathering. Basala, a first-year student, was wearing an ANCYL T-shirt, since he, like his 'homeboy' Erad, had supported the losing organization that was about to be buried. In this regard, they were similar to many other students who had been members of the ANCYL in their home areas before coming to the university. Upon matriculation, however, some students developed new political or religious affiliations during their first or second year, throwing their support behind the Pan-Africanists or the Christian students because they seemed to be better attuned to the bleak socio-economic realities that students face today. Meanwhile, the leaders of the two ANC-aligned student organizations were seen to be too caught up in career politics inside the ANC movement and were therefore liable to accusations that they were becoming either 'fat cats' or 'babies'.

After brief initial speeches were made at Gate Two, the coffin finally arrived, along with carriers and 'mourners' who were dressed in black and holding flowers. Being supporters of the losing organization, Basala and Erad quietly drifted away from the scene, but I continued to be part of the procession when it began to move from Gate Two toward the official campus entry at Gate One, where the setting lent an official aura to the whole spectacle. According to an agreement with Nkoana, I had brought along my camera in order to document the event by taking photographs. The coffin was manufactured from the election posters used by the losing organizations during the campaign, and it was carried by six tall male students. In front of them walked four veiled female students who performed the role of weeping mourners, pretending to hide tears behind their sunglasses. The procession, which now consisted of more than 300 students, slowly moved past the university pond and Sovenga Hill toward Gate One. Finally, the procession moved outside of the campus and arrived at a dumping ground in Sovenga Township. The coffin carriers and the mourners took center stage, while the rest of the procession formed a giant circle around them.

Speeches inspired by the slogans of the losing organizations were held at length, although the content amounted to mere ridicule, while the designated mourners howled loudly, to the great amusement of the crowd. I noticed that another friend and key interlocutor named Jack, a PASMA supporter, was also part of the gathering. On this occasion, however, he seemed to avoid me, and the more the speeches developed the point that PASMA (unlike ANCYL) promotes a racialized policy of Africanism, the more white I felt. All of a sudden, the humorous touch to the event had evaporated, and I was rather perplexed to find that I was the only white person in the middle of a political event and that I might be perceived as taking photographs inappropriately. The situation seemed to resonate with Collier and Collier's (1986: 25) observation that interlocutors may become doubtful of the researcher's motivation if he or she acts in an evasive or hurried manner while taking photographs. Although I had cleared the snapping of photos with the PASMA president, this was unknown to the huge crowd that made up the procession, and it made them more than suspicious of my presence. Once the coffin was set alight, a shout sounded from the back of the circle: "Burn the *legkowa* [white man] as well." The call was in many ways reminiscent of the anti-apartheid slogan 'Kill the Boer, kill the farmer', which was coined by Limpopo's hero Peter Mokaba and became widely used during pre-election rallies in 1993 and 1994. What is more, the slogan was chanted by crowds at Mokaba's funeral and by students at the memorial service held for him at the University of Limpopo in 2002 (BBC News 2002).

I knew, of course, that the call for my burning was a further elaboration of the joking metaphor of the funeral, but it was still an awkwardly lonely walk back to the campus amid this huge crowd of jubilant PASMA supporters. With regard to my own position in the field, I acted swiftly to have the photos developed and printed the very same day and put on display at the Student Center. Avoiding anger and embitterment, the public display of the photos turned the methodological blunder into a positive event, since students now gathered enthusiastically in large groups to look for their own photo. Leaving that aside, the proposal to 'burn the white man' conveyed the ongoing tensions that underpin racial relations in South Africa in spite of attempts to found the post-apartheid nation on the value of non-racialism (MacDonald 2006: 92–93), or what the former chairman of the Truth and Reconciliation Committee, Archbishop Desmond Tutu (1999: 77), coined the "rainbow people of God." A striking example of how difficult it has been to change the social landscape of race in South Africa is the fact that the University of Limpopo, a former black university (sometimes termed a 'historically disadvantaged institution'), still does not have any white students. This is partly explained by the historical foundations of the university and the fact that its trademark became that of activism and anti-apartheid activities rather than academic endeavors. At the same time, the higher education policies adopted by the ANC government since 1994 have produced an environment in which historically disadvantaged institutions are destined to fail, since they are expected to compete overnight in a free and open market economy despite decades of oppression and systematic underfunding.

The ironic and ambiguous content of the funeral for the ANC can thus be understood both as a celebration of the fight against historical oppression based on race and color and as a revolt against the present market orientation in higher education. This last phenomenon has been furthered by the ANC government through its macro-economic framework,[3] which has been severely criticized by commentators on the Left who have accused the government of pursuing neo-liberal policies (Seekings and Nattrass 2006: 380). Inspired by Marxism and their own experiences, students are equally critical of these policies; hence, the need to bury the ANC and its policies in the realm of student politics. Being white and using a camera, I came to represent the other half of the equation; hence, the call to burn me as well. In trying to situate these events in a historical context, the next section touches on the foundation of the university and how its trademark became that of anti-apartheid activism. The section ends with a brief consideration of how the university and student activism have been influenced by recent policy changes.

Historical Anti-apartheid Events at the University of Limpopo

The current University of Limpopo was set up in 1959 as the University College of the North under the trusteeship of the University of South Africa with the specific aim of serving only the black population (Maja, Gwabeni, and Mokwele 2006: 24). The then minister of Bantu education, Hendrik Verwoerd, underscored that separate universities were established precisely because the apartheid government did not want white students to study side by side with black students and let them "feel that there was no difference between them and the natives" (quoted in White 1997: 3). The ideology of separation was also a determining factor for locating the institution in a rural township 30 kilometers east of the provincial capital, Polokwane (formerly known as Pietersburg). The naming of the township as Sovenga was drawn from the three main ethnic groups of the area—Sotho, Venda, and Tsonga—and served to emphasize the ethnic basis of the institution (ibid.: 75). In 1970, the university college started operating independently as the University of the North, which remained its name until its merger with the Medical University of South Africa in 2005. The institution then became the University of Limpopo, with the Turfloop campus designated for the former University of the North and the Medunsa campus for the former Medical University of South Africa.

As the second-largest black university in South Africa, the then University of the North had a proud history of student activism. It was here that in 1969 the legendary Black Consciousness Movement leader Steve Biko, among others, launched the South African Students' Organisation (SASO), which aimed to promote a strong sense of identity among black students (Dawson 2006: 278). The Turfloop campus therefore came to have a history of tension, riots, demonstrations, and unrest. Students were expelled for their political activism, and the phenomenon of informers sowed distrust in the student community (White 1997: 100). With the black African freedom movements lingering in the neighboring countries in the 1970s, black South African students had plenty of inspiration to draw from in their struggle. An article titled "Turfloop Tension," which appeared in the *Sunday Express* on 20 October 1974 (quoted in ibid.: 109), gives an indication of how the university campus was viewed by the white minority rulers: "Turfloop has been the scene of Black student militancy almost since the day it opened ... It has been the stronghold of SASO, the Black students' movement and has provided it with three presidents. Strife reached a peak two years ago when a student leader, Abram Tiro, was summarily expelled for criticizing the Bantu Education system in a speech at a graduation ceremony. This sparked off Black and White student demonstrations—and a corresponding police crackdown—around the country. Now the militancy at Turfloop has been given a fresh spurt by the triumph of the Frelimo terrorist movement in Mozambique."

Tiro was the president of the SRC in the early 1970s, and his critique of the Bantu education system was launched at a graduation ceremony held in April 1972. He described the paradoxical nature of the fact that family members of black graduates were not allowed to attend the ceremony, while the families of white academic staff were present in numbers. The university administration was humiliated by the speech and decided to expel Tiro, who refused to make an official apology (Mawasha 2006: 72f.; White 1997: 104–107). Tiro's expulsion was followed by mass protests across the country as an expression of black solidarity. So heated were the fights that police were called to the campus and the entire student body was expelled, while SASO activities were suspended.

Beyond Turfloop, SASO organized sympathy protests at all black universities, which led to SASO leaders being periodically banned across the country. Tiro's speech not only resulted in his expulsion from the university but also set the course for his continued anti-apartheid activities, which saw him murdered by a letter bomb in Botswana in 1974. The white authorities partly bowed to some of the pressures a few years later, and in 1977 they appointed the university's first black vice-chancellor (White 1997: 24). Turfloop, however, continued to be a virtual battleground for intense clashes between students and the armed forces during the height of the apartheid crisis in the 1980s. Student activism is still the order of the day, but obviously for reasons that are not directly related to the struggle against apartheid.

In brief, the post-apartheid sector has seen a difficult transition from the racially segregated system under the former regime to an open and competitive free market system since 1994. The new system brought with it different and less favorable funding regimes, as well as increased competition for students (Nkomo and Swartz 2006: 2–3). In this set-up, the former black universities have been particularly prone to funding shortages and decreasing enrollments, since black students (and the best-qualified black academics) have now been allowed entry into the well-funded, former white universities in the urban centers of Johannesburg, Cape Town, and Pretoria. Since the turn of the millennium, the ANC government has pushed through merger reforms in an attempt to improve the higher education sector and make universities more responsive to public service needs (ibid.: 3).

The government's policy frameworks are very ambitious, but judging from the University of Limpopo, they seem to be somehow out of tune with the reality on the ground. Given its funding shortages, the University of Limpopo keeps increasing the tuition fees and costs related to on-campus accommodations. This means that the majority of students, who come from poor backgrounds, find themselves in jeopardy during the annual registration, while students of the black upper or middle class will often have drifted to former white institutions. In this environment—with the University of Limpopo facing funding shortages every year, accompanied by media reports of bankruptcy,[4] ministerial investigations (Nhlapo 2000), and forced turn-around plans—students still feel that there is a struggle to be fought and that the realm of student politics is a pertinent arena in which to mobilize and fight for their rights.

When student activism continues to seem relevant and worthwhile, it is probably because the policies of higher education have become a primary example of what is wrong with post-apartheid South Africa—namely, the inability of the state to deliver key services, such as health and education, in accordance with promises made to black sectors of society at the advent of democracy. Given that the ANC had at that point in time led three consecutive governments since 1994, this failure to deliver had obviously become an obstacle to the ANC-aligned student organizations. When on top of that the image of these organizations was tainted by divisions over leadership issues at the national level, as was the case at Turfloop in 2006, the scene had been set for an electoral defeat, as documented in the next section.

The 2006 Election Campaigns at the Turfloop Campus

Recent history at the Turfloop campus has seen two blocs of student politicians competing for majority rule of the SRC: PASMA (with support from the SCO) and a coalition called the Progressive Youth Alliance (PYA).[5] The PYA has consisted of three alliance partners: ANCYL, SASCO, and the Young Communist League (YCL). The constitution of the alliance has stipulated that it be led by SASCO. Up until 2003, the Christian students had supported this alliance, but then they withdrew and threw their support behind the Pan-Africanist students instead. See figure 1 for a graphic representation of the tendencies in coalitions and alliances from 2003 to 2006.

Despite the fact that SASCO is generally understood to be the student wing of the ruling ANC party (Dawson 2006: 282), the situation at Turfloop in October 2006 was slightly confusing, given that ANCYL suddenly entered the arena of student politics as an independent player two weeks prior to election day, leading to serious divisions and infighting between ANCYL and SASCO. For the remainder of the election campaign, the former coalition partners spent most of their time arguing over who had actually split up the alliance and on what grounds. One of the main points of division was that ANCYL and YCL

FIGURE 1 Student Coalitions and Alliances at Turfloop, 2003–2006

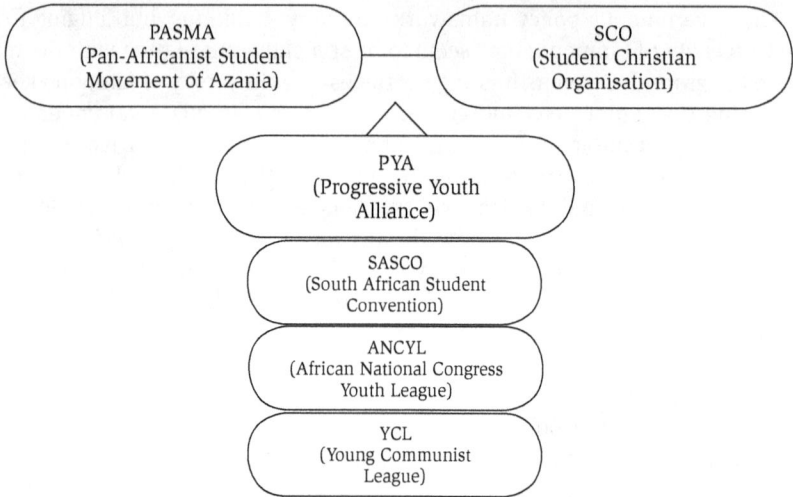

PASMA
(Pan-Africanist Student
Movement of Azania)

SCO
(Student Christian
Organisation)

PYA
(Progressive Youth
Alliance)

SASCO
(South African Student
Convention)

ANCYL
(African National Congress
Youth League)

YCL
(Young Communist
League)

threw their support behind South Africa's former deputy president (and current president), Jacob Zuma, in his campaign to wrest the ANC presidency from the then president, Thabo Mbeki, who had dismissed Zuma from office in 2005 due to charges of rape and corruption. Meanwhile, SASCO sided with Mbeki, which meant that the SRC politics of the Turfloop campus became the first battleground for the clashes of a divided ANC movement. This was probably no coincidence, given that the ANC's national conference, at which an electoral confrontation would be staged between Zuma and Mbeki, was scheduled to take place at Turfloop in December 2007.

PASMA took advantage of the divisions and differences suffered by PYA by making reference to odd statements about HIV/AIDS that a discredited Zuma voiced at his rape trial in 2006. In so doing, they succeeded in propelling into prominence the lines of division within PYA. At the same time, PASMA leaders did all they could to claim anti-apartheid credentials for their own organization: "Our history is written in blood and no amount of lies can change that" was the message that appeared on the back of T-shirts distributed among PASMA supporters. As the heirs to Biko's Black Consciousness Movement, the Pan-Africanists promote a radicalized policy of Africanization, which differs from the non-racialism of the ANC.[6] During the presentation of manifestos at Turfloop's Tiro Hall, Nkoana, PASMA's presidential candidate, vowed: "We are going to fight to the last drop of our blood to ensure that we achieve an increase in student subsidies." Through a sustained emphasis on their willingness to 'bleed' for their fellow students, the Pan-Africanist leaders established a clear connection with the struggle that their organization has been part of in the past. It also implied that PASMA was not part and parcel of the governing party and therefore had the ability to pursue freely the cause of the students' best interests.

However, PASMA was not alone in making claims to anti-apartheid history during the course of the SRC elections at Turfloop in October 2006. In a widely distributed poster, SASCO made reference to the 1976 uprising in which children of Soweto marched in protest against being taught in Afrikaans. The poster used as a background the world-famous photograph of 13-year-old Hector Peterson, who had just been struck by a bullet to his head. In the photo, he is being carried by his friend, while his sister is running alongside in her school uniform. Through its nation- and worldwide distribution, this photograph came to symbolize the brutality of the apartheid regime and the discrimination of the Bantu education system.[7] Using this iconographic image in conjunction with the messages "Realize the 1976 dream" and "Fight for quality student services," SASCO could hardly have been more explicit in its references to the anti-apartheid history of the organization.

Among the competing organizations, ANCYL probably made the least reference to its anti-apartheid history, although in its election leaflet the tenth point read: "Vote ANCYL, which was formed by comrade Nelson Mandela and later led by the forever roaring young lion, comrade Peter Mokaba [of the Youth League of the ruling party, the ANC]." The Youth League was very confident when it entered the Turfloop campus. The ANCYL presidential candidate, Justin Mafa, kept saying that the ANC was sure of winning the elections and "did not even consider the option of losing." Through its direct political connections to the ANC, the Youth League had access to resources in the form of vehicles, T-shirts, money for pre-election parties, and other social events. So confident were ANCYL leaders of eventual victory that they were already planning their celebration party—ordering food and DJs—when I conducted participant observation at one of their pre-election parties. Overall, both ANCYL and SASCO suffered the problem of looking too caught up in "old-style politics, careerism and the administration of student councils to relate well to the majority of students" (Alexander 2006: 36).

This goes a long way toward explaining how PASMA succeeded in framing the Youth League as the ANC 'Baby League' in their written materials and public speeches. Through this nickname, the Youth League was ridiculed as a bunch of immature children with little or no credibility in terms of holding student political office. The jokes about ANCYL were emasculating in the sense that its members were seen to be lacking not only adulthood but also manhood (see Oxlund 2008). The 'baby' accusation left the Youth League struggling to assert its self-image of being 'young lions' or 'comrades' of the north. After the elections, ANCYL's presidential candidate disappeared, confirming to some that he was indeed an ANC 'baby'—not man enough to survive an electoral defeat.

Irrespective of whichever organization students belonged to, during the weeks of heavy campaigning they addressed each other almost solely in military jargon, using titles such as general, commander, colonel, and lieutenant. Many even dressed up in camouflage clothing or wore T-shirts with Che Guevara emblems or green army caps. In terms of language, many turned to the use of violent metaphors and allegories when speaking of wars, bombs, bullets, fights, revolutions, killings, oppression, and liberation. After PASMA emerged as the victor in the elections, it therefore seemed only natural to extend the metaphors of struggle and death to encompass the highly symbolic and humorous burial of ANCYL and SASCO.

An Analysis of Ambiguities at the Turfloop Campus

Even though the symbolic burial of the ANC-aligned organizations must first and foremost be understood as a ritual form of ridiculing political opponents, it also involved an important element of recognition, since funerals are crucial events at which past achievements of individuals are acknowledged. It is when a man is buried that one can ultimately tell whether he has succeeded in achieving the status of full personhood (*motho*), which in a Northern Sotho understanding is indicated by the ability to cast a shadow (Mönnig 1967: 50). The number of people present and the nature of the funeral rites indicate whether the social status entitles him to become one of the ancestral spirits (*badimo*). Judging by this measure, ANCYL and its sister organization SASCO were accorded a very honorable, although symbolic, funeral in which they would have been sure of joining the ancestral spirits.

The funeral held for ANCYL and SASCO was thus an ambiguous undertaking. On the one hand, it ridiculed them for having lost the elections, while, on the other, it accorded them a status equal to that of fallen anti-apartheid heroes. The theme listed in the announcement of the funeral pointed to the dilemma of past versus future achievements. "We were the future, but PASMA has stopped us," it stated. The implicit understanding would have to be that the ANC-aligned organizations were the past and that the future belongs to PASMA. At least, this was the case at Turfloop, although at the national level, support for the mother party of PASMA, the Pan-African Congress, was crumbling to as little as two seats in the Parliament of South Africa. Still, the message sent by PASMA clearly highlighted the notion that ANC-aligned organizations should no longer take victory for granted.

An analysis of events at Turfloop reveals that anti-apartheid history continues to play a vital part in how contemporary student politicians understand their roles and responsibilities. Whereas in the 1970s Turfloop witnessed black student protests against white supremacy, the last 15 years have seen protests against a system that has not delivered what it promised at the advent of democracy in 1994. Students politicians continue to fashion and mold their campaigns and political strategies according to metaphors of war and revolution, and they understand the present situation through the prism of the past. Even though they are urged to "recognise that the context of activist action has fundamentally changed," as Njabulo Ndebele (2007: 57), the novelist and former vice chancellor of the University of the North (Limpopo), has stated, they continue to employ activist strategies in the pursuit of the fulfillment of rights.

Beneath the ANC rhetoric of non-racialism and the 'rainbow nation', relations between blacks and whites in South Africa still make up a prominent cleavage in social and economic terms. This is evidenced by the lack of white students at Turfloop as well as by the suggestion to 'burn the white man' during the symbolic funeral. At the same time, however, it is a black ANC government and a black university management that the student politicians are now confronting in the political arena. Given their status as organizations belonging to the ANC movement, this is one of the reasons why it is difficult for leaders of ANCYL and SASCO to agitate against government policies, since it would be interpreted as a lack of loyalty toward the movement. As shown in the analysis, this makes them vulnerable to claims made by competing organizations that they are the 'babies' of the ANC.

The infighting between ANCYL and SASCO over national leadership issues during the weeks of campaigning brought about a generative moment whereby students at the University of Limpopo developed a new understanding of the ANC as a divided political movement that was capable of losing elections. This became more apparent when the national media started reporting from Turfloop that the "turf war between the ANCYL and the SA Student's Congress demonstrates how the succession battle has created divisions among the various youth organizations aligned with the ANC."[8] These divisions were revealed to the national media when members of ANCYL and SASCO started attacking each other physically at the funeral in Phalaborwa, Limpopo, of Norman Mashabane, the former ambassador to Indonesia.[9]

ANC leaders at the national level took note of this embarrassment and tried to force ANCYL and SASCO into line, since the party's national conference was about to be held at the Turfloop campus. In spite of these efforts to iron out differences before the meeting, ANCYL and SASCO failed to realign with one another and suffered the embarrassment of losing the SRC elections once again in October 2007. At the party's conference that followed in December 2007, and after a long and divisive battle with Mbeki, Zuma was elected president of the ANC. Allegations that included racketeering and corruption had been brought against him, but in April 2009 the National Prosecuting Authority dismissed the charges, citing political interference as the basis for the decision. Zuma was elected president by South Africa's Parliament in May 2009. However, since divisions are still rumbling in the ANC movement, it seems likely that generative events will continue to unfold in the future.

Conclusion

This examination of the student elections at the University of Limpopo has highlighted the continued relevance of Gluckman's situational analysis and how it can be used when researching and analyzing complex situations in post-apartheid South Africa. In understanding generative moments of the present (the defeat of the ANC-aligned student organizations) as connected to and premised by generative moments of the past (anti-apartheid events at Turfloop), the chapter has favored a micro-historical approach to situational analysis in which the complexities of politics have been captured through a detailed account of the activities of student politicians in a single setting. In terms of presentation, the text has followed Gluckman's chronology of moving from event over history to generalization, which allows the ethnographic material to be presented in an appealing *in medias res* fashion.

In making this observation, I agree with David Mills (2006: 172) that situational analysis is as much a writing style as it is a method or a theoretical frame. By this I mean that the chief case or event (such as the bridge opening in Zululand) is usually evoked so as to create a feeling of presence in a situation where the ethnographer is actively seeking new knowledge through surprising and eye-opening events. It is therefore relevant to ask whether the ceremonial opening of the bridge was truly the first time that Gluckman had observed and noted the dominant cleavage in South African society and the ways in which it was handled. This amounts to a rhetorical question, since this was obviously not the case. What makes it even more obvious is Gluckman's own recognition, as stated in *Analysis of a Social Situation*, of the importance of his prior knowledge and publications on the history and culture of the Zulu ([1940] 1958: 53): "With the background of all these other works, and my own essays, I feel that I may use my material in more piecemeal fashion, for my use of facts and arguments can be checked against these earlier publications."

There is thus reason to be cautious about claiming that new insights have derived above all from an in-depth analysis of a single event, which implies that Gluckman's situational analysis may share more with Malinowski's apt illustration than he would have liked us to believe. According to Kapferer (2006: 134), the point that situational analysis cannot fully escape the idea of illustration was often underscored by J. Clyde Mitchell (1956), whose famous study, *The Kalela Dance*, is itself a prime example of the strengths of the situational analysis approach. The crux of the matter seems to be that where apt illustration is designed to illuminate states of homogeneity and overall coherence (whether imagined or real), situational analysis aims at capturing a generative moment amid flux and change (Kapferer 2006: 136).

While acknowledging the importance and potential stylistic advantages of working through complex social situations toward larger understandings, I continue to grapple with the vague definitions of the key concepts of event, situation, case, and extended case. Considering the enormity of events that ethnographers witness and experience during long-term fieldwork, it is relevant to ask how we keep track of all these events. How do we select the truly generative cases? Where do we find space to unfold these complex situations? Finally, how do we ensure that these cases do not merely become apt illustrations of the complexity that we intended to study in the first place?

I think part of the answer lies in the open mind of the ethnographer, who gets enmeshed in the field during extended periods of fieldwork and therefore takes an interest in the real-life issues of the people under study. In my own case, I never intended to study student politics—it forced itself upon me when hundreds of students began to campaign outside my front door. Although my research primarily focused on gender studies and HIV/AIDS, it would have been ludicrous and against the spirit of good ethnography if I had not taken an interest in the issues that the students found so important. The compelling experience of the *toyi-toyiing* in the early morning hours and the efforts that PASMA followers expended when organizing the mock funeral were in themselves indications that something was brewing.

The fact that the ANC-aligned student organizations suffered an embarrassing defeat in 2006 amid serious infighting gave me the clear impression that this was a generative moment at the Turfloop campus—a time when something was about to change and new ways of viewing the situation of students was in formation. If things had developed more in the way of business as usual, the social situation would not have drawn me away from the central focus of my research. In a way, that insight puts another vague definition on offer: a social situation is an event that is so generative of new perspectives that it naturally draws the ethnographer away from his or her previously established path.

Bjarke Oxlund is an Associate Professor in the Department of Anthropology, Faculty of Social Sciences, at the University of Copenhagen. His 2009 PhD thesis focused on the social becoming of South African student youths in a context of HIV and AIDS. He lived and worked as a development practitioner with the United Nations in South Africa from 2001 to 2003 and conducted fieldwork in Limpopo in 2006 and 2007. His most recent articles include pieces on masculinity and sexuality, university reform, student politics in South Africa, and the masculine identities of uniformed personnel in Rwanda. Currently, he is involved in two new research projects on medicated aging in a rural municipality in Denmark.

Notes

1. The South African Student Convention (SASCO) is not an outright structure of the ANC, but it has aligned itself with the ruling party and forms part of the democratic movement. It also has its offices at ANC headquarters in Johannesburg.
2. In an article titled "Coloureds Don't Toyi-Toyi," Shannon Jackson (2005: 210) shows how *toyi-toyiing* operates as a signifier of ethnic differentiation among blacks and coloreds at the University of the Western Cape.
3. Arguably, through the macro-economic policy framework referred to as the Growth, Employment, and Redistribution (GEAR) strategy, the ANC government committed to orthodox fiscal policies while sidelining the more pro-poor policy framework, the Reconstruction and Development Program (Seekings and Nattrass 2006: 349–350).
4. "University of Limpopo Finances a Shambles," *City Press*, 14 October 2007.
5. There is yet another organization competing for SRC seats called the Azanian Student Convention (AZASCO), which is the student wing of the Azanian People's Organisation (AZAPO). Due to its insignificant share of votes and followers at Turfloop, it will be disregarded in this discussion.
6. Biko drew on the work of Frantz Fanon in arguing along psychological lines that black subordination was possible because blacks accepted inferiority to whites in their hearts and minds. In promoting black consciousness, he therefore rejected non-racialism to be the highest political goal, as it was perceived by the ANC (MacDonald 2006: 116–118).

7. "How One Photograph Changed the World," *Mail and Guardian*, 15 June 2006.
8. "A Fight for Young Minds," *City Press*, 28 October 2007.
9. Ibid. See also "When a Funeral Is Desecrated by Fisticuffs, You Know It's War Out There," *Sunday Times*, 28 October 2007; "Plan to Embarrass Moloto at Funeral," *Mail and Guardian*, 26 October 2007.

References

Alexander, Peter. 2006. "Globalisation and New Social Identities: A Jigsaw Puzzle from Johannesburg." Pp. 13–65 in Alexander, Dawson, and Ichharam 2006.

Alexander, Peter, Marcelle C. Dawson, and Meera Ichharam, eds. 2006. *Globalisation and New Identities: A View from the Middle*. Johannesburg: Jacana Media.

BBC News. 2002. "Row over South African Funeral." 17 June. http://news.bbc.co.uk/1/hi/world/africa/2050188.stm (accessed 30 May 2009).

Burawoy, Michael. 1998. "The Extended Case Method." *Sociological Theory* 16, no. 1: 4–33.

Burawoy, Michael, Joseph A. Blum, Sheba George, Zsuzsa Gille, Lynne Haney, Teressa Gowan, Maren Klawiter, Steven H. Lopes, Seán Ó Riain, and Millie Thayer. 2000. *Global Ethnography: Forces, Connections, and Imaginations in a Postmodern World*. Berkeley: University of California Press.

Collier, John, and Malcolm Collier. 1986. *Visual Anthropology: Photography as a Research Method*. Rev. ed. Albuquerque: University of New Mexico Press.

Dawson, Marcelle C. 2006. "Students, Activism and Identity." Pp. 275–294 in Alexander, Dawson, and Ichharam 2006.

Evens, T. M. S., and Don Handelman. 2006a. "Introduction: The Ethnographic Praxis of the Theory of Practice." Pp. 1–12 in Evens and Handelman 2006c.

Evens, T. M. S., and Don Handelman. 2006b. "Preface: Theorizing the Extended-Case Study Method." Pp. 45–48 in Evens and Handelman 2006c.

Evens, T. M. S., and Don Handelman, eds. 2006c. *The Manchester School: Practice and Ethnographic Praxis in Anthropology*. New York: Berghahn Books.

Gluckman, Max. [1940] 1958. *Analysis of a Social Situation in Modern Zululand*. Manchester: Manchester University Press, on behalf of the Rhodes-Livingstone Institute.

Gluckman, Max. 2006. "Ethnographic Data in British Social Anthropology." Pp. 13–22 in Evens and Handelman 2006c. (Paper originally presented in 1959 at the Fourth World Congress of Sociology in Stresa.)

Jackson, Shannon. 2005. "Coloureds Don't Toyi-Toyi: Gesture, Constraint and Identity in Cape Town." Pp. 206–224 in *Limits to Liberation after Apartheid: Citizenship, Governance and Culture*, ed. Steven L. Robins. Oxford: James Currey.

Kapferer, Bruce. 2006. "Situations, Crisis, and the Anthropology of the Concrete: The Contribution of Max Gluckman." Pp. 118–155 in Evens and Handelman 2006c.

MacDonald, Michael. 2006. *Why Race Matters in South Africa*. Cambridge, MA: Harvard University Press.

Maja, Botshabelo, Andile Gwabeni, and Phuti A Mokwele. 2006. "The Repositioning of Two South African Universities." Pp. 15–46 in Nkomo, Swartz, and Maja 2006.

Mawasha, Abram L. 2006. "Turfloop: Where an Idea Was Expressed, Hijacked and Redeemed." Pp. 65–84 in Nkomo, Swartz, and Maja 2006.

Mills, David. 2006. "Made in Manchester? Methods and Myths in Disciplinary History." Pp. 165–179 in Evens and Handelman 2006c.

Mitchell, J. Clyde. 1956. *The Kalela Dance: Aspects of Social Relationships among Urban Africans in Northern Rhodesia*. Rhodes-Livingstone Papers No. 27. Manchester: Manchester University Press, on behalf of the Rhodes-Livingstone Institute.

Mönnig, Hermann Otto. 1967. *The Pedi*. Pretoria: J. L. van Schaik.

Ndebele, Njabulo S. 2007. *Fine Lines from the Box: Further Thoughts about Our Country.* Houghton, South Africa: Umuzi.

Nhlapo, Thandabantu. 2000. "Investigation into the Affairs of the University of the North by the Independent Assessor Appointed by the Minister of Education in Terms of Chapter 6 of the Higher Education Act, No. 101 of 1997." *Government Gazette*, no. 21654, 16 October.

Nkomo, Mokubung, and Derrick Swartz. 2006. "Introduction." Pp. 1–14 in Nkomo, Swartz, and Maja 2006.

Nkomo, Mokubung, Derrick Swartz, and Botshabelo Maja, eds. 2006. *Within the Realm of Possibility: From Disadvantage to Development at the University of Fort Hare and the University of the North.* Cape Town: Human Sciences Research Council Press.

Oxlund, Bjarke. 2008. "Masculinities in Student Politics: Gendered Discourses of Struggle and Liberation at the University of Limpopo." *Psychology in Society* 36, no. 2: 60–76.

Seekings, Jeremy, and Nicoli Nattrass. 2005. *Class, Race, and Inequality in South Africa.* New Haven, CT: Yale University Press.

Tutu, Desmond. 1999. *No Future without Forgiveness.* London: Rider Books.

Werbner, Richard. 1984. "The Manchester School in South-Central Africa." *Annual Review of Anthropology* 13: 157–185.

White, Christopher. 1997. *From Despair to Hope: The Turfloop Experience.* Sovenga, South Africa: UNIN Press.

Chapter 3

A TOPOGRAPHIC EVENT
A Buddhist Lama's Perception of a Pilgrimage Cave

Jesper Oestergaard

Patterns in the rocks of a wall in a cave in Maratika, a pilgrimage site in eastern Nepal, and their interpretation as the physical traces of a mythological figure are at the center of this chapter. So far, it is unknown to most Buddhist pilgrims that a significant mythological figure is believed to be manifested in these dripstone formations. This analysis concerns a Buddhist lama's perception of these patterns as being part of Tibetan Buddhist mythology and how perception can be approached anthropologically.

The lama's comprehension of landscape is placed in its religious context as part of the continual retelling of the mythological narratives of Maratika. Landscape is an indispensable part of Tibetan Buddhist pilgrimage. When alleged mythological episodes are supposed to have taken place in landscape, mythological time intersects with geographical space, creating a sacred site, a location that is separated from other geographical locations. A Tibetan pilgrimage site is therefore not only spatial but also temporal, integrating geographical space and

Notes for this chapter begin on page 74.

narrative time in a particular place. This influences the understanding of the landscape around a pilgrimage site. It will be argued that the perception of the landscape at the pilgrimage site contributes to and is situated within and constrained by a larger religious context that is highly influenced by religious narratives about the pilgrimage site, as well as by the sacred landscape of the site.

This chapter will furthermore illustrate how perception may be organized in events in such a way that the perceptual process becomes available for anthropological study. In my fieldwork, the landscape became a shared third object in an asymmetrical 'joint attention' situation between the lama, as the competent perceiver of religious landscape, and myself, as an inexpert, interested observer. Situations are "moments of social life in the very process of formation" (Kapferer 2006: 125), and in the study of social processes, the temporal aspects of a situation are often emphasized. This raises the question about the role of place and the relation between time and place in situations and events. Situations may take place, but place is not merely an inactive scene for situations. Instead, places may constitute or frame the situation and may link to other situations.

In the ethnographic material presented here, the spatial aspect of situations is moved to the center of analysis. The landscape around a pilgrimage site relates different events. The related events all concern the perception of the landscape, and the topological features of the landscape are the objects of joint attention around which the events unfold. The events are all about the landscape, but they do not take place at the landscape.

Topographic Events

My fieldwork was carried out in the eastern part of Nepal[1] at Maratika, a low-altitude pilgrimage site for Hindus and Buddhists, and in Boudha, a suburb to Kathmandu, where the lama of Maratika, Karma Wangchuk, lives most of the year with his family. Maratika consists of three small hills with caves in them, but often Maratika refers simply to one specific dripstone cave, the Long Life Cave.[2] As a Buddhist pilgrimage site, it is mainly visited by Sherpa pilgrims during the Tibetan New Year, usually around February.[3] Maratika is, according to myth, the place where the Indian guru Padmasambhava[4] practiced the Buddha of Immortality's teaching and achieved immortality. According to Tibetan Buddhist history, Padmasambhava was asked to subdue demons that were disturbing the construction of Samye, the first Buddhist monastery built in Tibet. On his journey, he visited many places in the Himalayas, where he practiced religious teachings and often left behind physical marks or traces in the landscape, such as footprints, handprints, or stones in special shapes. Many of these locations throughout the Himalayan region are now pilgrimage sites, and Maratika is such a place. The site is imbued with mythology, which is manifested in the landscape through footprints or body prints in rocks; stones resembling a subdued demoness's head, heart, and intestines, or the head cap of Padmasambhava; mantra-reciting bats; stalactites resembling religious banners, flags, or protective deities; and a series of other topological features that refer to the mythology of Maratika. The physical landscape, the soil, of Maratika possesses the blessings or empowerments (Tibetan: *byin rlabs*) of Padmasambhava in material form, and pilgrims collect dust, herbs, and especially water from the site to use for religious and medical purposes.[5]

The word 'Maratika' is known, from religious texts, not as referring to any specific location but only as a geographical location in Nepal, dating back less than 200 years. What is the relation between a mythological Maratika and a geographical Maratika? Do they continually shape and reinforce each other? And what role does Maratika's double position play with regard to perception and meaning making? This dialectic between myth and landscape is predominant at a pilgrimage site where mythology is inscribed on the land through the pilgrims' re-enactment of the mythology. Over time, the topology and appearance of the landscape is slowly being modified into a replica of the mythology, thereby reinforcing that very same mythology. This mutual 'anchoring'[6] between mythology and landscape in the perception of Maratika is played out in pilgrims' practices, as explained in "Introduction to Maratika,"[7] written by Ngawang Choepel Gyatso (2000), the founder of the Buddhist monastery at Maratika.[8] Mythological events relating to Padmasambhava are situated in the landscape in and around Maratika: the landscape itself is the scene, consequence, and continuation[9] of Padmasambhava's activities. Landscape and mythology are mutually reinforced in this perception in similar ways, since it situates mythology in the landscape and mythologizes landscape.

During fieldwork, I made visits to Maratika, but since my anthropological object involved both aspects of Maratika, the study carried out was not so much *at* Maratika as it was *about* Maratika. Thus, the empirical data used in this analysis are from events that dealt with Maratika but most often did not take place there. In this sense, Maratika became objectified as an item of joint attention between my main informant, the present head and lama of the monastery at Maratika, named Karma Wangchuk, and myself. Joint attention has an asymmetrical structure. Two or more people share the direction of attention onto a third object, often for the sake of social interaction between the two or more subjects. However, the relation between the subjects is never equal, and often the culturally and socially relevant matter is going on between them. Usually, this relation is one of teaching or communicating a certain view concerning the third object, as in much teacher-student or children-adult interaction in general. Working with joint attention as a prerequisite for language acquisition, Michael Tomasello (1999: 97) defines joint attention scenes as "social interactions in which the child and the adult are jointly attending to some third thing, and to one another's attention to that third thing, for some reasonably extended length of time." Certainly, I was the novice (student), whereas Karma Wangchuk, given his religious status, was the competent perceiver of landscape (teacher). The third object, the landscape at Maratika, was important because it would frame the event. Landscape became the 'aboutness' of the situation, and I would carefully watch how Karma Wangchuk dealt with this object. His perception of the landscape, framed within joint attention situations, became my empirical data.

The First Event: Little Britain Coffee Shop

On 29 August 2008, the morning after a return from Maratika, Karma Wang-chuk asked to look at my photographs. We met at the Little Britain Coffee Shop, one of the popular cafés in Boudha where I had met Karma Wangchuk for the first time. The atmosphere was relaxed, and the three of us—Karma Wangchuk, an American nun named Anila Choying, and I—had coffee while we looked through all the photos from Maratika. It was Karma Wangchuk's hope that a new religious landscape would be exposed in the form of patterns and manifestations in the dripstone formations that could be interpreted and reflected upon. When the pictures came up on the computer screen, there was an atmosphere of excitement. The number of photos was considerable, and it took about two hours to look through them all. The conditions were not opti-mal, as the images were viewed on a computer in outdoor lighting. Nonethe-less, the photographs exposed new views of the cavescape. On the one hand, the mediation through the computer was a disadvantage, since it became an exclusively visual experience, lacking the tactile, auditory, and olfactory ele-ments that are present in the cave itself. On the other hand, it proved to be an advantage, because the visual input was easy to manipulate by regulating contrasts in the pictures.

It is important to note that the context for the initial identifications of the cavescape in Maratika was not a ritual one. As such, it was not a religious and ritual framing of the situation that altered the perception of the photos. Still, as will become clear, mythological narratives were to a large degree imposed and had great influence on how the cavescape was perceived, modifying 'ordinary' perception into a more mythological or semantic perception.

Among the many photographs, one in particular attracted Karma Wangchuk's attention (see fig. 1). The photo had been taken inside the Long Life Cave, and for most people it shows a wall of the cave where dripstones have formed irreg-ularities. However, for Karma Wangchuk it revealed a trace of Padmasambhava that was 'self-produced' (Tibetan: *rang 'byung*) from the cave. My interest was to understand the process of identifying a wall inside a cave as displaying a Guru Rinpoche[10] body trace (Tibetan: *gu ru'i sku rjes rang 'byung*), a physical manifestation of Padmasambhava. Since Karma Wangchuk believed that he had already seen the outline of the body trace in the cave in 2006 following a religious ceremony, it was his goal to find more of that trace and to elaborate on its religious significance.

During the process of finding the Guru Rinpoche body trace, other traces appeared and were discussed, but for the most part they were discarded, maybe to be taken up at a later date. Among the new traces, Karma Wangchuk saw (or might have seen, since he was only suggestive and never conclusive) a handprint, some letters such as 'Hung' (possibly written by Dakinis, female mythological figures), and a horse, which he seemed rather certain about. He was constantly looking for new traces in other places of the cave or in connec-tion with the Guru Rinpoche body trace. Among the different photographs, an impression of horses on the head of Padmasambhava caught his interest and

FIGURE 1 Dripstone patterns on the wall of Long Life Cave © Jesper Oestergaard

had to be checked against the mythology. The handprint and the letters were seen more as a sign that Padmasambhava might have been there and nothing more, whereas the impression of horses on Padmasambhava's head was an expansion of the mythological background for the cave and therefore much more interesting. In a way, it was like retelling the myth by describing the landscape but with further attributes or twists that would expand its meaning, as a result of taking more cavescape details into the narrative. The mythology itself was used as an argument for the possibility of such an image being there. "It makes sense," Karma Wangchuk later declared about the possibility of a topological trace of a horse on the wall of the cave.

The interpretation of the photographs consisted of the interplay between the perception of the cavescape and memories of the background mythology. Two processes were therefore used in identifying the traces. First, the general process of ordinary perception was important. Patterns in the walls could become clear or less clear—that is, regular visual features counted in the observation of the traces, which is hardly surprising. Furthermore, humans—like many non-human animals—tend to apply patterns to perceptual input in order to make it more predictable. For humans, this pattern is often a humanlike pattern; in short, humans tend to anthropomorphize the world through their perception (Guthrie 1993). This point may seem trivial, but visual perception was a factor in the identification process. One could not just see anything there, simply because it was mentioned in the mythological narratives. Even though mythology may override vision, it never completely overrules it. Vision is anchored by mythology, but not in a very strict sense. By anchoring, I refer to a stabilizing aspect, a constraining and scaffolding perception of the landscape. I shall argue that in this instance the narrative seemed to alter the perception from one of topological features to one of meaning.

Second, the knowledge about the place, as written in the mythological narratives connected to it, was also important. From an insider's perspective, Karma Wangchuk saw more—and saw more clearly—than did Anila and I. The identification of the cavescape is an ongoing process that combines perceptions of the landscape with the study and knowledge of the narratives. At the same time, the landscape is considered to be a living, ever-changing entity. It is therefore believed that the landscape around Maratika will in the future expose even more sacred traces. The evolution of landscape, including abrupt changes due to landslides or the discovery of new caves, is therefore considered a continuation and unfolding of the mythology of Maratika. This is in accordance with the mythological narrative concerning Maratika in which it is said that Padmasambhava concealed a great number of texts, to be discovered later when the time is ripe. This is also known in the Tibetan tradition as 'terma' (Tibetan: *gter ma*).[11] Landscape is, in this way, imbued with latent meaning, and changes in the landscape are seen as elaborations on the religious significance of Maratika.

The underlying assumption of this first event—viewing the photographs on the computer—was that the semantic and dynamic landscape is believed by Karma Wangchuk to expose religious meaning and teaching. The question to be answered, and the reason for the excitement, was whether the photos would show anything new about the unfolding religious meaning. It was decided to print out some of the most important images and then sit together with pens and mark them, in order to make more clear the patterns that could be seen in the photographs. Whereas we had been relatively passive during the first event, our active involvement now increased in order to identify more of the cavescape.

The Following Events: Drawing the Trace

The later events took place in a hotel room, a quiet undisturbed place in Boudha, over the days and weeks that followed. Instead of a leisurely look through scores of photographs, we got down to work, choosing to concentrate on only a few images, all of which had possible self-produced traces on them. These events of joint attention directed toward the landscape of Maratika in a focused and undisturbed setting allowed me to observe the lama's work on the identification of Padmasambhava and other traces. It also gave me the opportunity to ask about the process of identification, both while it was happening and later in follow-up interviews on the subject. The atmosphere was serious but also playful, with an air of creativity and imagination. Some of the same processes that were evident in the first meeting could be observed. Again, it was the body trace of Padmasambhava that attracted the most attention, and, again, this trace appeared to be "very clear" to Karma Wangchuk.

At these events in the hotel room, other possible traces were also discovered. All of the patterns that were spotted had to be checked with the mythology, which served as an interpretive scheme whereby perceptual patterns—the traces—were given meaning and connected to the Tibetan Buddhist cosmology. This emphasis on mythological narrative was reinforced by Karma Wangchuk when he expressed uncertainty about the identification of figures resembling characters that are not present at all in the Maratika mythology.

Karma Wangchuk described the difference between viewing the photographs and seeing the traces in the cave itself. The power of Maratika was not in the photos, he explained, whereas in the cave, he felt that he was inside a place where the Buddhist dharma is present. Having hardly any religious capacity and seeing the trace without even recognizing it as such, as most pilgrims would do, is also beneficial, since Maratika is said to be blessed by Padmasambhava. The identification and the benefit from the landscape are along a continuum that ranges from no recognition, at one end, to the landscape as a perceptual scaffolding for the identification of an internal, intentional conceptualization of Padmasambhava, at the other end. In Maratika, one need not visualize, since the liberating power is already present. Practices that take place there are considered more efficacious, which makes the pilgrimage all the more beneficial.

The utility of landscape varies according to the viewer's religious capacity. Different abilities to see depend on a Buddhist perspective about wisdom that is accumulated through practice and the purification of negative actions, after which one will have a clear vision. Karma Wangchuk could see the trace, but he did not consider himself able to discover the actual teaching of the trace. When the time comes, explanations will be uncovered by an accomplished religious specialist. Identifying the landscape as religiously significant is an ongoing process of building up expertise in the mythology and then going to the cave to compare perception with mythology. Karma Wangchuk continues to relate the actual cave and objects that exist naturally in Maratika with written and oral descriptions of the site. This process is open-ended, as there are many more traces waiting to be discovered. Karma Wangchuk described it thus: "It is like somebody already there waiting for us, giving us information."

In the end, after several attempts, a conclusion was reached about the Guru Rinpoche body trace when Karma Wangchuk was able to see and draw Padmasambhava in a meditation position on photo paper (see fig. 2). He had drawn not just the outline of Padmasambhava's body but also facial features, arms and legs, vase and hat. When the trace was completely unfolded, Karma Wangchuk

FIGURE 2 The Guru Rinpoche body trace, according to Karma Wangchuk
© Jesper Oestergaard

was pleased and satisfied. "I'm so happy! We really found Guru Rinpoche," he exclaimed. It seemed that he had reached the goal that he had set out for from the beginning and had longed for during the events.

The Temporality of Landscape, the Spatiality of Myth

According to Bruce Kapferer (2006: 122, emphasis added), "For Gluckman, the term 'situation' refers to a total context of crisis, not just contradictory and conflicting processes but a particular tension or turning, *a point of potentiality and multiple possibility.*" The potentiality and possibilities in the events described in this chapter are connected to the topological features of the landscape. Because mythological time is believed to be embedded in geographical space, perceiving the landscape is (also) perceptually interacting with myth and, in the case of religious specialists, elaborating on myth. As such, landscape is an integral part of generative events, although the events in this instance were not events of crisis but rather generative moments of religious development. This is what is referred to as topographic events—events that conceptualize landscape.

These topographic events were all different. The first event had the joyful atmosphere of new discoveries, whereas the following events were more like working sessions, with creativity being restricted and perception being focused on the identification of traces. But they can all be positioned along a continuum of related events. The events in themselves are not independent from the other, their relation having been established through landscape. The event at the Little Britain Coffee Shop and the following drawing events are connected because they share the reference to the sacred landscape of Maratika. The crucial aspect in these events is how the landscape of the cave was an object for joint attention and how the religious significance of the landscape was articulated through the perception of it.

So why place emphasis on Karma Wangchuk's identification of the cavescape as a Guru Rinpoche body trace? It is on exactly that level, I propose, that the most interesting processes of culturally constrained and informed perception are taking place. Not only is Karma Wangchuk's perception imbued with mythology, it is likewise contributing to the continuity of myth. The process of placing myth in landscape is, among other processes, mediated by perception. If, as Tim Ingold (1993: 152–153) argues, "[t]o perceive the landscape is … to carry out an act of remembrance, and remembering is not so much a matter of calling up an internal image, stored in the mind, as of engaging perceptually with an environment that is itself pregnant with the past," then Karma Wangchuk's perception of the cavescape is a perception of the temporality of landscape. This, however, is not the full story, and meaning is not "there to be *discovered* in the landscape, if only we know how to attend to it" as Ingold would argue (ibid.: 172; emphasis in original). Karma Wangchuk is calling up an image, not purely internal, but a religious image derived from the mythology of Maratika and Tibetan Buddhism more generally—the image of Padmasambhava in a seated position. More than giving temporality to landscape, the discovery and identification of new traces give spatiality to myth. Meaning is therefore not to be *discovered* through perception of the landscape; it is instead to be *constructed* through perception of the landscape. Meaning is naturalized by giving it perceptual support in landscape.[12]

Mythology and landscape mutually reinforce each other in religious action and perception. Mythological narratives about Padmasambhava and Maratika suggest that possible perceptual stimuli are available from the landscape at Maratika. Without any mythological content, a visual perception was disqualified by Karma Wangchuk as being 'wrong'. Unless it was very clear, it could be that the mythological connection was not yet to be found.[13] Through this perceptual process, Maratika as landscape and Maratika as mythology become continually reintegrated into each other: landscape becomes imbued with a mythological time, whereas the mythological time becomes situated. Space is temporalized, and time is spatialized and is combined in the religious perceiver's experience of Maratika.

Whether religious believers view Maratika as a sacred landscape or as a materialized mythology depends on their religious knowledge and status. Most pilgrims approach Maratika as a sacred landscape and are ready to receive its blessing, whereas religious persons with status, authority, and knowledge see it as a mythological place, interpreting the topological features in light of mythology and thereby ensuring a constant flow of meaning from the mythology into the landscape. Through an analysis of related events about the landscape at Maratika, not only was a complex system of the production and consumption of religious meaning spelled out, but the actual landscape at Maratika was imbued with new meaning, and the narratives connected to Maratika were sustained. In short, religious believers approach Maratika along a continuum from a perception of the landscape as sacred to a conception of the landscape as mythological.

Conclusion

To sum up, the asymmetrical structure of joint attention, similar to a teacher and student relationship, facilitated a situation wherein Karma Wangchuk's perception of coincidental patterns of the cavescape in Maratika as a Guru Rinpoche body trace became available for analysis from the perspective of anthropology and the study of religion. The initial observation that Karma Wangchuk noticed a trace of Padmasambhava after a ceremony in the Long Life Cave set in motion a series of events in which landscape was framed as the third shared object in a joint attention situation. These events were generative moments of potential for new religious developments. The possibility that the Guru Rinpoche body trace will become a trace revered by pilgrims is likely. The mythologically informed perception of the cave by Karma Wangchuk is part of this new religious development.

Jesper Oestergaard holds a PhD in the study of religion. His research fields include the cognitive science of religion, externalism, the anthropology of religion, Tibetan religion, pilgrimage in different traditions, internalization, conceptual integration with material anchor, and theories on space, place, and the topographic turn in the humanities. His current research focuses on the relationship between landscape and religion, connecting theories from cognitive science and geography with a focus on the concrete landscape to analyze the role of landscape in pilgrimage. Recent publications include "Walking toward Oneself: On the Mythologization of Geography and Ritualized Authenticity on the Route to Santiago" (2010) and "Pilgrimage Landscape as Material Anchor of Time" (2013).

Notes

1. For political reasons connected to the Olympic Games, the torch relay that preceded the official opening of the event, and the unrest in Tibet, during most of 2008, when I carried out the majority of my fieldwork, Tibet was off-limits.
2. The area as a geographical location is generally referred to as Halase, whereas Maratika denotes the region synecdochically from the name of a pilgrimage site. I use Maratika throughout this chapter.
3. Losar, an event in a more traditional sense, is the Tibetan celebration of the New Year. Predating Buddhism, it is the most important holiday in Tibet. For an ethnographic description of Buddhist and Hindu New Year celebrations at Maratika, see Eberhard Berg (1994).
4. A very important figure in Tibetan Buddhism, Padmasambhava is believed to have brought the pacifying Buddhism to (in Tibetan self-understanding) the fierce pre-Buddhist people of Tibet in a special ritualistic form.
5. 'Long life pills' are even produced by the monastery. Believed to be empowered by Padmasambhava, these pills are said to 'liberate through tasting' (Tibetan: *myong grol*) and to cure illnesses. For an analysis of liberation through the senses as a Tibetan soteriological concept, see Holly Gayley (2007).
6. For 'material anchoring' as a part of conceptual blending and cognition, see Edwin Hutchins (2005), Per Aage Brandt (2005) and David Kirsh (1995).
7. Guidebooks, written or oral (Tibetan: *gnas yig*, *gnas 'bshad*), are common at most Tibetan pilgrimage sites. However, pilgrims are not necessarily familiar with the content of the guidebooks in detail.
8. Maratika is a Hindu area, but in 1980 Ngawang Choepel Gyatso established a small Buddhist community of monks there. Today, the monastery, Maratika Chimey Takten Choling, houses around 25 monks. *The Guide to Maratika* (Sherpa 2000) was written because of a dispute over land between the Hindu and the Buddhist communities (see Buffetrille 1994).
9. This threefold scheme is inspired by John S. Strong's (2004) *Relics of the Buddha*. The Buddha's previous incarnations, his life as Sakyamuni Buddha, and his relics are seen as three parts of an extended biography of the Buddha.
10. Tibetans refer to Padmasambhava as Guru Rinpoche, that is, 'precious teacher'.
11. For more on terma as a Tibetan tradition, see Janet B. Gyatso (1996).
12. Although on a more general level, Kirsten Hastrup (2005: 145) has argued for a topographic turn in anthropology, a turn that includes the geographic grounding of social life where it is "not possible to 'think away' the actual geographical location of social life; lives are always grounded. Movements in space inscribe social life on the land, and with

time particular paths are cleared and certain directions presented as more natural than others." Terminological, as well as theoretical, inspiration is taken from Hastrup.

13. Karma Wangchuk believed that the number of new discoveries regarding landscape features was sufficient to write a new guidebook.

References

Berg, Eberhard. 1994. "Sherpa Buddhists on a Regional Pilgrimage: The Case of Maratika Cave at Halase." *Occasional Papers in Sociology and Anthropology* 4: 124–145.

Brandt, Per Aage. 2005. "Mental Spaces and Cognitive Semantics: A Critical Comment." *Journal of Pragmatics* 37, no. 10: 1578–1594.

Buffetrille, Katia. 1994. *The Halase-Maratika Caves (Eastern Nepal): A Sacred Place Claimed by Both Hindus and Buddhists*. Pondicherry: French Institute of Pondicherry.

Gayley, Holly. 2007. "Soteriology of the Senses in Tibetan Buddhism." *Numen* 54, no. 4: 459–499.

Guthrie, Stewart. 1993. *Faces in the Clouds*. Oxford: Oxford University Press.

Gyatso, Janet B. 1996. "Drawn from the Tibetan Treasury: The *gTer ma* Literature." Pp. 147–169 in *Tibetan Literature: Studies in Genre*, ed. José Ignacio Cabezón and Roger R. Jackson. Ithaca, NY: Snow Lion.

Gyatso, Ngawang Choepel. 2000. "Introduction to Maratika." Pp. 25–39 in Sherpa 2000.

Hastrup, Kirsten. 2005. "Social Anthropology: Toward a Pragmatic Enlightenment?" *Social Anthropology* 13, no. 2: 133–149.

Hutchins, Edwin. 2005. "Material Anchors for Conceptual Blends." *Journal of Pragmatics* 37, no. 10: 1555–1577.

Ingold, Tim. 1993. "The Temporality of the Landscape." *World Archaeology* 25, no. 2: 152–174.

Kapferer, Bruce. 2006. "Situations, Crisis, and the Anthropology of the Concrete." Pp. 118–155 in *The Manchester School: Practice and Ethnographic Praxis in Anthropology*, ed. T. M. S. Evens and Don Handelman. New York: Berghahn Books.

Kirsh, David. 1995. "The Intelligent Use of Space." *Artificial Intelligence* 73, no. 1–2: 31–68.

Sherpa, Karma Wangchuk, ed. 2000. *The Guide to Maratika*. Kathmandu: New Nepal Press.

Strong, John S. 2004. *Relics of the Buddha*. Princeton, NJ: Princeton University Press.

Tomasello, Michael. 1999. *The Cultural Origins of Human Cognition*. Cambridge, MA: Harvard University.

Chapter 4

THE OUTBURST
Climate Change, Gender Relations, and Situational Analysis

Jonas Østergaard Nielsen

Concern about the climate and its impact on rural populations in the Sahel zone of West Africa was an immediate response to the most recent of recurrent drought periods, which began in the early 1970s (Brooks 1993; Nicholson 1978; Rain 1999; Watts 1983; Webb 1995). Averaged over 30-year intervals, annual rainfall in this area fell by 20–30 percent between the 1930s and the 1950s and the three decades following the 1960s, prompting Hulme (2001: 20) to state that "[t]he African Sahel therefore provides the most dramatic example worldwide of climatic variability that has been directly and quantitatively measured." It is repeatedly argued that this change in rainfall had major economic and social consequences for the rural populations of the Sahel zone, who were already under stress from deteriorating political and economic conditions (Warren 1995).

Rural communities in the Sahel have always faced climate variability and, to a large extent, have been able to develop their livelihood strategies in a way that enables them to cope with and adapt to an unpredictable climate (Mortimore and Adams 2001). These strategies have traditionally included crop diversification,

Notes for this chapter are located on page 87.

migration, and small-scale commerce. But in the aftermath of the drought of the 1970s and 1980s, a new possibility presented itself: the arrival of international development projects (Nielsen et al. 2012). This chapter explores one of the social consequences of this new livelihood strategy by focusing on a particular event that took place in Biidi 2, a small village in northern Burkina Faso.

Following Max Gluckman's ([1940] 1958) understanding of a social situation, the visit by a development 'expert' and in particular its immediate and surprisingly antagonistic aftermath—caused by an unexpected outburst—will be analyzed as an occasion of social potentiality for the women of the village (Kapferer 2005). Social relationships are often most clearly demonstrated and negotiated in precisely such circumstances wherein the "concatenation of events is so idiosyncratic as to throw into sharp relief the principles underlying them" (Mitchell 1983: 204). This is so because conflicts are relatively 'open spaces' or 'unstructured contexts' in which normal social control is revealed, suspended, and/or negotiated, leaving actors involved in the event, such as the women of Biidi 2, relatively free to construct alternative definitions of their identity and social positions (Kapferer 1995; Mitchell 1956). As such, conflicts reveal how social life is not merely a function of normative rules and ideal principles duplicating themselves endlessly, but rather an ongoing dialectical process (Evens and Handelman 2006). In conflicts, social relations are thus both revealed and altered as actions are quickly adjusted, thereby generating new social relations. This is exactly what happened in the aftermath of the outburst: the women of Biidi 2 seized this opportunity in an attempt to change their position within the village vis-à-vis the men (Kapferer 1995; Mitchell 1956).

The chapter is organized as follow. A brief introduction to the village is followed by a presentation of the recent climate change experienced there. Two of the livelihood strategies employed in the village to negate the effects of this climatic change—working for development projects and women's economic activities—are examined. The social situation is then described, and, lastly, the situation is analyzed.

The Village of Biidi 2

Founded some 125 years ago, Biidi 2 is located approximately 14 kilometers southwest of Gorom-Gorom, which is the capital of Oudalan, the northernmost province of Burkina Faso (see fig. 1). The landscape in the region is dominated by vast, ancient pediplains cut by temporal rivers and longitudinal-oriented dune systems that are superimposed on the pediplain (Reenberg and Fog 1995). Biidi 2 is, like many other villages in this region, situated on top of one of these dunes, surrounded by more or less continuous fields. Mainly located on the pediplain, the fields are cultivated with millet, sorghum, and cowpeas (Rasmussen and Reenberg 1992; Reenberg and Paarup-Laursen 1997). The dune is rimmed on its southern side by gardens. Agriculture, pastoralism, gardening, migration, development projects, and small-scale commerce constitute the economic mainstays of the village.

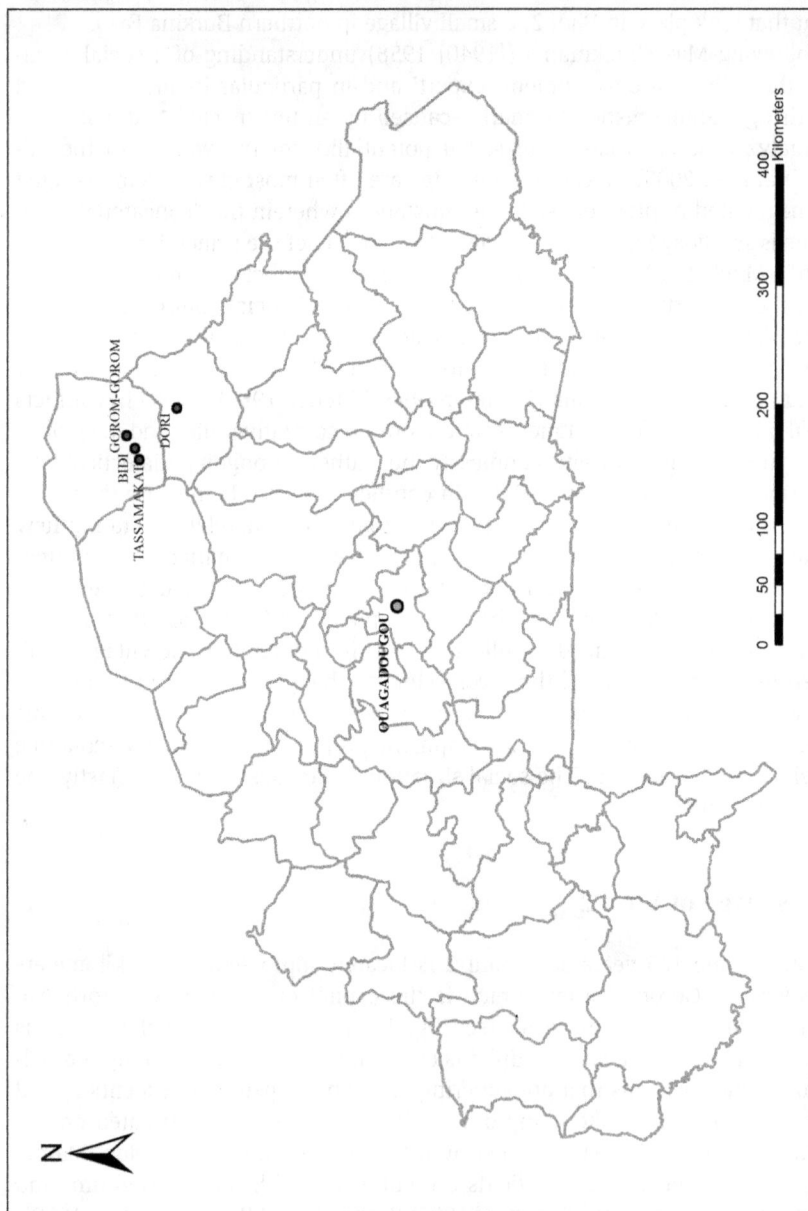

FIGURE 1 Map of Burkina Faso

The ethnic composition in Oudalan is complex, with several different ethnic groups present (Claude, Grouzis, and Milleville 1991). In Biidi 2, three ethnic groups reside: Rimaiibe, numbering 302 individuals, Fulbe, numbering 167, and Wahilbe, numbering 116 (at the time of fieldwork). Of these, 246 are under the age of 15, constituting 42 percent of the total population. Wahilbe, in their role as blacksmiths, constitute a kind of professional 'caste', which separates them from the other two groups (see also Riesman 1977). Comparisons with population figures from 1995 indicate that the village has had an annual population growth rate of 3.8 percent since then (Reenberg and Paarup-Laursen 1997). Many of the people 'belonging' to the village territory actually live in the surrounding bush, and the village center itself is populated almost exclusively by Rimaiibe and Wahilbe. Only one Fulbe household, consisting of seven individuals, is located within the village center.

A major reason behind this spatial differentiation is the historical master-slave relationship between Fulbe and Rimaiibe. Permanent villages like Biidi 2 are made up of separate slave hamlets (*debeere*) in which Rimaiibe, the former slaves of Fulbe, live in large patrilineal compounds. For Fulbe, it is considered shameful (*semteende*) to live next to their former slaves, and consequently they prefer to live in the bush (Nielsen and Reenberg 2010a). Slavery had been abandoned during the colonial period, but it was not until the late 1970s and early 1980s that this actually came into effect in the village (Nielsen and Reenberg 2010b). The slave-master relationship determines much of the interactions between Fulbe and Rimaiibe. Despite relatively good relations and significant cultural similarities between the two groups, such as a shared language, they generally do not work or live together. They do not intermarry, nor are they buried next to each other.

Climate Variability in Biidi 2

Between June and late September, Biidi 2 typically receives between 200 and 600 millimeters of rain a year. No meteorological records are available for Biidi 2, but in nearby Gorom-Gorom, rainfall data have been collected monthly since 1955. This data set indicates that the region has gone through much the same climate development as the rest of the West African Sahel, with the wet 1950s and 1960s followed, starting in the early 1970s, by a prolonged dry spell that lasted until the 1990s. The general trend seen elsewhere in this region toward more rain and greater inter-annual rainfall variability in the 1990s and early 2000s is also evident in the data set from Gorom-Gorom (Nicholson 2005).

Generally, the villagers perceive the rainfall to be less predictable today than it was 40 years ago, to have a number of 'false starts' (making it extremely difficult to know when to sow seeds), and to fall in either greater or smaller quantities than previously. The villagers attribute this last-mentioned feature to an annual rainy season that they believe to be shorter now with more dense periods of rain, often resulting in either flooding or drought. Temperatures during both the cold and the hot season are also perceived to have risen, and both seasons to have become longer. The wind is likewise believed to have increased, causing a more pronounced movement of sand that results in river beds filling up and crops being destroyed. Besides drought, flooding, and the movement of sand, the villagers mention the degradation of the soil; the disappearance of plants, trees, wild fauna, and watering holes; and growing problems with pests as consequences of the changed climate. All of these factors make rain-fed agriculture difficult and, in turn, livelihood diversification increasingly important.

Development Projects and Women's Work

Since the drought of the early 1970s, Rimaiibe, on whom this chapter largely focuses, have experimented with different types of agro-pastoral practices and, as a result, have diversified their sources of income dramatically (Nielsen 2009; Nielsen and Reenberg 2010a, 2010b).[1] Among these diversification strategies, working for development projects and women's small-scale commerce (often initiated on the basis of micro-credit loans from the projects) are two of the most important in terms of cash earnings.

Development Projects

In the aftermath of the droughts and famines of the 1970s and early 1980s, a plethora of non-governmental organizations (NGOs), the majority of which owed their existence to international aid, entered Burkina Faso, in particular the northern part, as this was perceived to be the most vulnerable to food shortage (Atampugre 1997). The impetus for these organizations and for governmental aid was the desire to alleviate the problems of poor socio-economic infrastructure and food and livelihood security (Batterbury and Warren 2001). The early development efforts focused on 'modern' technical interventions that were designed to boost and transform agricultural and rangeland productivity. When these initiatives, for various reasons, began to fail, the emphasis shifted to reforms in which issues of gender, cultural pluralism, better targeting of aid, and support to local institutions became important (Carney 1998; Vivian 1994).

In Biidi 2, the involvement of NGOs began around 1992–1993, and since then there have been about 20 projects in the village. These undertakings vary in size, duration, and efficiency, but Rimaiibe attribute enormous importance to them. A major reason for this is that many of the projects provide Rimaiibe with salaried work or with a source of cash income through the sale of goods produced with the help of the NGOs. Over the course of a year, many Rimaiibe households earn as much as $150 working for development projects. Only circular labor migration rates higher as a source of cash revenue in the village. The money is mainly used for food and to reinvest in other economic activities.

Because development projects are a main source of salaried work in Biidi 2, the villagers have become very adept at attracting new and desired projects.

While many opportunities may seem to arrive out of the blue, this does not mean that the villagers are unprepared. Common topics of conversation among both men and women revolve around projects—how to get them to come to the village, what they should aim to accomplish, and, if they arrive unexpectedly, how to get them to stay. Once they are there, the villagers are very good at working with project staff members to fulfill the goals that the staff have set up: they clearly understand that target deliverables have a high priority. The villagers are also acutely aware that fulfilling these targets and working well for projects seem to attract other projects. This is echoed by development project staff, who emphasize that Biidi 2 is a good village to work with and a suitable location in which to try out new projects. Another major incentive for the villagers to spend time on projects is that they are convinced that projects will continue to come only if the village works well and achieves results with the ones that are already there.

Women's Work

Rimaiibe women have become very economically active since the 1980s. In only 6 of the 60 Rimaiibe households in Biidi 2 did the women not participate to some extent in the cash economy during the study period—and this was due to old age. Asked about the reason behind this development, the villagers unanimously mentioned the increased resilience of the household to food shortages due to the cash income generated by women. In some Rimaiibe households, women now contribute up to half or more of the total income. Generated by working for projects and/or by engaging in small-scale commerce, the cash is used to buy food, medicine, clothes, and jewelry and to invest in animals, education, seeds, or other materials for gardens, looms, or houses.

The Social Situation

The expected arrival of the development 'expert' from the regional capital Dori was making everyone slightly edgy that morning. As is often the case with visitors, we had no idea about the exact time of his arrival. A couple of the younger boys had been sent down to the small junction to spot the dust being kicked up by the jeeps, and soon the boys' yells could be heard: the jeeps were on their way. A group of younger and elder men, with the president of the Comité Villageois de Développement (CVD, Village Development Committee) in front, quickly left for the newly established garden that had been paid for by a large international donor and was now to have its first evaluation. Haste was important. The men wanted to get there before the project expert and his staff, which was important for a number of reasons. Chief among these was making sure that the entourage parked their jeeps in a particular place.

The garden project had started a year earlier. A piece of land had been selected next to the river, in which there is always a bit of water. The garden is large and square and surrounded by a metal mesh fence. It is split into two halves: one for the women and one for the men. These two sections have been divided among the villagers who wanted a little garden plot in which to sow the potato seeds provided by the project. At the time of the visit, the two halves of the garden were very different. The men had been largely inactive, and their land had, with the exception of a few plots, not been planted and maintained. In contrast, the women's half was completely cultivated, with beautiful potato beds and small trees providing shade. The trick was to get the development expert to park as far away from the men's garden as possible and to keep him from noticing its condition. This was to be achieved by guiding him through the women's garden along a predetermined route, during which he would have his back to the men's garden most of the time. Where this was not possible, large groups of villagers would be strategically placed, blocking his view.

Things were running smoothly. The jeeps had been intercepted exactly where planned, and the villagers and I had taken up our positions. The expert and his entourage, the president of the CVD, the traditional chief, and the administrative head of the village, along with a few others, had entered the garden at the gate farthest away from the men's section, and they were now walking along the predetermined route, expertly guided by the head of the CVD. However, when the group arrived at the most precarious place closest to the men's garden—where a group of the tallest men, among whom I rank, stood to hide the view—the plan crashed to the ground.

Asoman, the older brother of the CVD's president, stepped out of our group, walked the few steps over to the expert, and, while pointing to the men's garden, told him that it had never taken off. The reason for this, he continued, was to a large extent due to his little brother, whom he thought was incompetent and a thief and who, he asserted, had stolen all the seeds destined for the men's garden. He then proclaimed that for the project to become a success, it needed a new president, an older one, and he thought that he was the ideal choice. The expert, who obviously did not want to get involved, looked at the men's garden, noted its sorry state, and proclaimed that he would return in four weeks to have another look. If the garden had not improved, he was not so sure about continued funding. The local men, sensing this opening, quickly assured him that the next time it would resemble the women's garden. The expert seemed content with this and walked on, staying for another 10 minutes before driving off.

As soon as he was gone, a huge and very animated and hostile argument broke out. During my previous five months in the village, I had never witnessed an acrimonious discussion, and I was surprised by its intensity. The argument initially centered on how Asoman's outburst had jeopardized Biidi 2's image as a good development village and how this could be disastrous for attempts to attract new projects, thus aptly illustrating the importance of development projects. But as the discussion about the garden evolved, it became clear that other things were at stake, and chief among these were gender relations.

Analysis

Gender Separation

In Biidi 2, and among Fulbe and Rimaiibe in general (de Bruijn and van Dijk 1995; Riesman 1977), men and women live quite separate lives. The men spend most of their time outside the village, working in the fields and gardens or visiting relatives and friends. In contrast, women spend most of their time in and around the village, mostly in the vicinity of their huts. There they prepare food, make mats or other handicrafts, look after the children and the small domestic animals, and socialize with other women belonging to the same lineage. Interaction between the sexes often occurs around midday and at night, when the men return to the village to eat and rest. The two groups do not sit together on these occasions, and communication between them takes place across a spatial divide. This spatial and social separation is mirrored in ceremonial life, such as name givings, marriages, and funerals, but also in political life and within the household. It is the men who hold all political offices and make the decisions regarding almost all issues of importance for the village and the household.

The Desire to Stay Married

Fulbe and Rimaiibe have virilocal residence, and the women are incorporated into their husband's lineage at marriage. All children from these unions belong to the husband's family, and if a woman is unhappy about her marriage, which is not uncommon, she is free to leave—but without her children. For the woman, this is a very strong incentive to stay in the marriage and to remain on good terms with her husband. As younger women are the most attractive marriage partners in the eyes of the men, being divorced and older makes it hard for a woman to get married again.

The separation between the sexes and women's desire to stay married thus make public critique by women of their husbands very rare. Prior to the development expert's visit, I had therefore never experienced it. But the fissure in normality created by the outburst and the ensuing discussion seemed to provide the women with an 'unstructured context' and hence a chance to suspend normal gender relations by speaking out (Mitchell 1956). With the exception of the two brothers, who had to be physically separated, it was the women who entered the discussion with most passion.

Negotiating Gender

"Look at the garden we are standing in!" Fatimata exclaimed in a high voice. "We [the women] made this," she continued. "You [the men] have made nothing, and today you have depended on us." The other women nodded and contributed to the dialogue with similar statements that grew in boldness, culminating in a series of speeches by different women that pivoted around the importance, the hardship, and the inventiveness of women's work—with the garden project standing as a perfect example. The men responded by highlighting that they already had their own gardens to look after and that they had not been given the potato seeds, which had mysteriously disappeared (or perhaps been stolen). They gave a number of other excuses, none of which made much of an impression on the women.

The debate then moved on from being a common one, in which the two groups took turns emphasizing general points pertinent to them, to one between male and female family members of individual households. The discussion now revolved around the relative importance of the women's income for the household. Many of the women pointed out how they have sold things and animals at the market for the past several years and that the income generated through such activities had made life in the household better. The women were therefore "tired of being told what to do all the time by men, because we also have money and also know things," as Awa expressed it. This coupling of increased economic importance with the expansion of gender roles taken on by the women brings us back to Asoman's outburst.

Asoman is married to Haawa, who, like many other women in Biidi 2, is involved in the micro-credit schemes set up by aid organizations. Haawa has been very successful at buying and selling chickens and goats. She also grows vegetables in garden plots and goes to the market in Tassmakat on Mondays and in Gorom-Gorom on Thursdays to sell her produce. In addition, she works for wages for development projects, and over the past four years, she has made around $150 a year through these activities. Haawa is quite aware of the importance of this money for the household, and in a subsequent interview she told me, "We can't count on the fields. The rain is never good, but we need to eat—to buy food. I buy most of it, and Asoman knows this."

Asoman has had no luck with work obtained through migration, returning home with only $50 a year before giving it up three years ago. He works in his garden, which provides him with some, but not much, income, and he is also involved in working for the development project, planting hedges in the sand dune. His lack of success in gardening bothers him, and he explains it as a result of bad luck and wrong decisions. This does not, however, change the fact that his economic activities do not add up to as much as Haawa earns, and he has been seeking employment in order to change that. The major reason is that Haawa's earnings make him feel uncomfortable about his position as head of the household. As he explained, "It is not easy to decide how the money is to be spent when I am not the one making it."

Like his control over the money, Asoman's control over Haawa is slipping. "When she has money, she is not that dependent upon me. What can I give her that she cannot buy herself?" he asked rhetorically in an interview. A few days later, he was even more pessimistic. "She could just leave me. She would be able to take care of herself. She does not need me." In a meek attempt at consolation, I suggested that this would probably not happen, as she would have to leave the children. But Asoman was not so certain, even about this: "I can't buy them food. She can."

Asoman's attack on his younger brother must be seen in this light. It was a reaction to the fact that he was losing his position as the family's major breadwinner and to the challenge that this presents to his position as head of the household. By discrediting his brother and laying claim to his paid job as president of the CVD, Asoman was trying to gain work and income in order to reassert himself as the undisputed head of his household. Indeed, he was willing to sacrifice the image of Biidi 2 as a good development village to this cause. "Development projects come and go," he later explained. And while he was aware that his outburst had been potentially damaging, he did not regret it. Why should he? he asked. "It was good to expose my little brother's incompetence." He hoped that it would result in a re-election and that he would then get elected, because "I will do a better job, and I need the money more than he does."

The Potential of Unstructured Context

Ironically, however, Asoman's outburst had provided the women with an unstructured context in which gender roles could be publicly negotiated, potentially leading to a further deterioration of his already weakened position as head of the household. Asoman sensed that "all we talked about [in the discussion] was women, their work, their money, and how well the women worked for development projects. And that did not really help me." As Asoman had rightly predicted, shortly thereafter the presidency of the CVD came up for election, due to 'bad management', but it was not he who got elected. It was instead Digga, the wife of a former administrative head of the village.

The election of Digga suited the development project staff, who, according to the local representative, prefer to work with women because "they are more committed to making the projects work." The project's satisfaction with the new president and with the "increased involvement of women in developing their village," as it was put, was quickly manifested, and the garden was substantially enlarged and better fenced. This, in turn, enhanced the position of Digga and the argument increasingly made by some of the women that they are as suited for public positions as the men.

After Digga's untimely death a couple of months later, Asoman and two other men ran for election along with Haawa. The men argued that the election of Digga had been spurred by the unprecedented situation caused by the outburst and that a return to normality in which all public offices are held by men would once and for all put the event in the garden behind them. In response, Haawa used the track record of Digga, the discourse of empowerment of women among the development projects, and the ability of women to make money for the household as arguments for continuing with a woman president.

The development project staff were present throughout the period leading up to the election and strongly emphasized that the election was to be democratic, meaning that all adults, not just the men in the village, would be allowed to vote. The women liked this, and on the day of the election they turned up in great numbers to vote for Haawa. Asked why, they emphasized two things. First, they thought that Digga had done a great job and that Haawa could be expected to do the same. Second, many of them were afraid that if Haawa was not elected, things would "become like before, when it was just men who were presidents." They felt that voting for Haawa could cement the change initiated with the election of Digga and thereby manifest the emergence of a new social reality. Haawa won.

Conclusion

This study of a social situation that took place in the aftermath of drought and climate variability demonstrates how situational analysis provides insights into ongoing social processes and their relations to wider contexts, such as climate and development projects. While the visit of the development expert and its aftermath stands as an 'apt illustration' of the importance of these two contexts for life in the village, it also revealed how gender relations were being challenged within the event and how this challenge in turn seems to indicate new directions in these relations in the village. The election of Digga and then Haawa to a public 'office' in this way illustrates how fissures in normality—in this case, created by Asoman's outburst—provide an initial context in which current social relations are both revealed and transformed as actions are quickly adjusted, thereby generating new social relations (Kapferer 1995; Mitchell 1956).

It is difficult to make definitive claims about future gender relations in Biidi 2 on the basis of Asoman's outburst and the two elections. However, increasing evidence that future climate change will strongly affect the African continent, particularly the drier regions (Adger et al. 2007; Usman and Reason 2004), implies that an emphasis on non-agricultural livelihood diversification and the continued presence of international donors remain crucial for Sahelian households. In Biidi 2, women are increasingly engaging in activities such as gardening, development projects, and small-scale commerce, and their economic importance within the household is thus unlikely to diminish in the years to come. Combined with their frequent encounters with development discourses of gender equality and the project staff's positive treatment of women villagers, it is highly likely that the event of the outburst and the subsequent elections will result in further changes in gender relations in the village. The aftermath of the outburst is, in other words, loaded with social potentiality for the women of Biidi 2. If they seize it, as Digga and Haawa did, traditional gender relations that designate men as the undisputed heads of households and public offices seem untenable.

Acknowledgments

The field research for this chapter was funded by a grant from the Danish Ministry of Foreign Affairs (grant no. 104.Dan.8-914). The final editing and writing were funded by a grant from the European Research Council (grant no. 229459 Waterworlds). This study was also part of the African Monsoon Multidisciplinary

Analysis (AMMA) project. It has been the beneficiary of a major financial contribution from the European Community's Sixth Framework Programme for Research and Technological Development. I would like to extend my thanks to the villagers of Biidi 2. The fieldwork was carried out with the permission of, and in accordance with, the Ministère des Enseignements Secondaire, Supérieur et de la Recherche Scientifique (research permission no. 2007 0089), and the Université de Ouagadougou, Département de Géographie, Burkina Faso.

Jonas Østergaard Nielsen is a Junior Professor and Research Group Leader in the Department of Geography at Humboldt University of Berlin. He studied social anthropology at Auckland University, New Zealand, and the University of Copenhagen, Denmark, and obtained his doctorate in human geography in 2010 at the University of Copenhagen. From 2010 to 2013, he worked as a Postdoctoral Fellow in the European Research Council-funded project Waterworlds, Department of Anthropology, University of Copenhagen. His research is concerned with the human dimensions of global climate change, human-environmental relations, issues of global-local interactions, and urbanization in sub-Saharan Africa. Since 2007, he has conducted extensive ethnographic fieldwork in Burkina Faso. Currently working in the capital Ouagadougou, he explores contemporary rural-urban relations and issues related to urbanization. A central theme throughout his work has been causality and how to understand the impact of different drivers of change on local lives.

Notes

1. Rimaiibe follow in this regard the trends seen elsewhere in the Sahel (Batterbury and Warren 2001; Bolwig 1999; de Bruijn and van Dijk 1995, 2001; Elmqvist and Olsson 2006; Mertz et al. 2009; Mortimore 1998; Mortimore and Adams 2001; Mortimore and Turner 2005; Rain 1999; Raynaut 1997, 2001; Reenberg, Nielsen, and Rasmussen 1998; Reenberg and Paarup-Larsen 1997; Roncoli, Ingram, and Kirshen 2001).

References

Adger, W. Neil, Shardul Agrawala, M. Monirul Qader Mirza, Cecilia Conde, Karen O'Brien, Juan Pulhin, Roger Pulwarty, Barry Smit, and Kiyoshi Takahashi. 2007. "Assessment of Adaptation Practices, Options, Constraints and Capacity." Pp. 717–743 in *Climate Change 2007: Impacts, Adaptation and Vulnerability. Contribution of Working Group II to the Fourth Assessment Report of the Intergovernmental Panel on Climate Change*, ed. M. L. Parry, O. F. Canziani, J. P. Palutikof, P. J. van der Linden, and C. E. Hanson. Cambridge: Cambridge University Press.
Atampugre, Nicholas. 1997. "Aid, NGOs and Grassroots Development: Northern Burkina Faso." *Review of African Political Economy* 24, no. 71: 57–73.
Batterbury, Simon, and Andrew Warren. 2001. "Viewpoint. The African Sahel 25 Years after the Great Drought: Assessing Progress and Moving towards New Agendas and Approaches." *Global Environmental Change* 11, no. 1: 1–8.

Bolwig, Simon. 1999. "Livelihood Practices and Land Use in the Sahel: Labour allocation and Adaptive Capability among the Fulani Rimaybe in Northern Burkina Faso." PhD diss., Department of Geography, University of Copenhagen.

Brooks, George E. 1993. *Landlords and Strangers: Ecology, Society, and Trade in Western Africa, 1000–1630.* Boulder, CO: Westview Press.

Carney, Diane, ed. 1998. *Sustainable Rural Livelihoods: What Contribution Can We Make?* London: Department for International Development.

Claude, Jacques, Michel Grouzis, and Pierre Milleville. 1991. *Un espace sahélian: La mare d'Oursi, Burkina Faso.* Paris: Orstom.

de Bruijn, Mirjam, and Han van Dijk. 1995. *Arid Ways: Cultural Understandings of Insecurity in the Sahel.* Amsterdam: Thela Publishers.

de Bruijn, Mirjam, and Han van Dijk. 2001. "Ecology and Power in the Periphery of Maasina: The Case of the Hayre in the Nineteenth Century." *Journal of African History* 42: 217–238.

Elmqvist, Bodil, and Lennart Olsson. 2006. "Livelihood Diversification: Continuity and Change in the Sahel." *GeoJournal* 67, no. 3: 167–180.

Evens, T. M. S., and Don Handelman. 2006. "Introduction: The Ethnographic Praxis of the Theory of Practice." Pp. 1–11 in *The Manchester School: Practice and Ethnographic Praxis in Anthropology*, ed. T. M. S. Evens and D. Handelman. New York: Berghahn Books.

Gluckman, Max. [1940] 1958. *Analysis of a Social Situation in Modern Zululand.* Manchester: Manchester University Press for the Rhodes-Livingstone Institute.

Hulme, Mike. 2001. "Climatic Perspectives on Sahelian Desiccation: 1973–1998." *Global Environmental Change* 11, no. 1: 19–29.

Kapferer, Bruce. 1995. "The Performance of Categories: Plays of Identity in Africa and Australia." Pp. 55–80 in *The Urban Context*, ed. A. Rogers and S. Vertovec. Oxford: Berg Publishers.

Kapferer, Bruce. 2005. "Situations, Crisis, and the Anthropology of the Concrete: The Contribution of Max Gluckman." *Social Analysis* 49, no. 3: 85–122.

Mertz, Ole, Cheikh Mbow, Anette Reenberg, and Awa Diouf. 2009. "Farmers' Perceptions of Climate Change and Agricultural Adaptation Strategies in Rural Sahel." *Environmental Management* 43, no. 5: 804–816.

Mitchell, J. Clyde. 1956. *The Yao Village.* Manchester: Manchester University Press for the Rhodes-Livingstone Institute.

Mitchell, J. Clyde. 1983. "Case and Situation Analysis." *Sociological Review* 31, no. 2: 187–211.

Mortimore, Michael. 1998. *Roots in the African Dust: Sustaining the Drylands.* Cambridge: Cambridge University Press.

Mortimore, Michael, and William M. Adams. 2001. "Farmer Adaptation, Change and 'Crisis' in the Sahel." *Global Environmental Change* 11, no. 1: 49–57.

Mortimore, Michael, and Bill Turner. 2005. "Does the Sahelian Smallholder's Management of Woodlands, Farm Trees, and Rangeland Support the Hypothesis of Human-Induced Desertification?" *Journal of Arid Environments* 63, no. 3: 567–595.

Nicholson, Sharon E. 1978. "Climatic Variations in the Sahel and Other African Regions During the Past Five Centuries." *Journal of Arid Environments* 1: 3–24.

Nicholson, Sharon E. 2005. "On the Question of the 'Recovery' of the Rain in the West African Sahel." *Journal of Arid Environment* 63, no. 3: 615–641.

Nielsen, Jonas Ø. 2009. "Drought and Marriage: Exploring the Interconnection between Climate Variability and Social Change through a Livelihood Perspective." Pp. 159–177 in *The Question of Resilience: Social Responses to Climate Change*, ed. K. Hastrup. Copenhagen: Royal Danish Academy of Sciences and Letters.

Nielsen, Jonas Ø., Sarah D'haen, and Anette Reenberg. 2012. "Adaptation to Climate Change as a Development Project: A Case Study from Northern Burkina Faso." *Climate and Development* 4, no. 1: 16–25.

Nielsen, Jonas Ø., and Anette Reenberg. 2010a. "Cultural Barriers to Climate Change Adaptation: A Case Study from Northern Burkina Faso." *Global Environmental Change* 20, no. 1: 142–152.

Nielsen, Jonas Ø., and Anette Reenberg. 2010b. "Temporality and the Problem with Singling Out Climate as a Current Driver of Change in a Small West African village." *Journal of Arid Environments*, 74, no. 4: 464–474.

Rain, David. 1999. *Eaters of the Dry Season: Circular Labor Migration in the West African Sahel.* Boulder, CO: Westview Press.

Rasmussen, Kjeld, and Anette Reenberg. 1992. "Satellite Remote Sensing of Land Use in Northern Burkina Faso: The Case of Kolel Village." *Danish Journal of Geography* 92, no. 1: 86–93.

Raynaut, Claude. 1997. *Societies and Nature in the Sahel.* London: Routledge.

Raynaut, Claude. 2001. "Societies and Nature in the Sahel: Ecological Diversity and Social Dynamics." *Global Environmental Change* 11, no. 1: 9–18.

Reenberg, Anette, and Bjarne Fog. 1995. "The Spatial Pattern and Dynamics of a Sahelian Agro-ecosystem." *GeoJournal* 37, no. 4: 489–499.

Reenberg, Anette, Trine L. Nielsen, and Kjeld Rasmussen. 1998. "Field Expansion and Reallocation in the Sahel: Land Use Pattern Dynamics in a Fluctuating Biophysical and Socioeconomic Environment." *Global Environmental Change* 8, no. 4: 309–327.

Reenberg, Anette, and Bjarke Paarup-Laursen. 1997. "Determinants for Land Use Strategies in a Sahelian Agro-ecosystem: Anthropological and Ecological Geographical Aspects of Natural Resource Management." *Agricultural Systems* 53, nos. 2–3: 209–229.

Riesman, Paul. 1977. *Freedom in Fulani Social Life: An Introspective Ethnography.* Chicago: University of Chicago Press.

Roncoli, Carla, Keith Ingram, and Paul Kirshen. 2001. "The Costs and Risks of Coping with Drought: Livelihood Impacts and Farmers' Responses in Burkina Faso." *Climate Research* 19: 119–132.

Usman, Muhammad T., and C. J. C. Reason. 2004. "Dry Spell Frequencies and Their Variability over Southern Africa." *Climate Research* 26, no. 3: 199–211.

Vivian, Jessica. 1994. "NGOs and Sustainable Development in Zimbabwe: No Magic Bullets." Pp. 167–193 in *Development and Environment: Sustaining People and Nature*, ed. Dharam Ghai. Oxford: Blackwell Publishers.

Warren, Andrew. 1995. "Changing Understandings of African Pastoralism and Environmental Paradigms." *Transactions of the Institute of British Geographers* (n.s.) 20, no. 2: 193–203.

Watts, Michael J. 1983. *Silent Violence: Food, Famine and Peasantry in Northern Nigeria.* Berkeley: University of California Press.

Webb, James L. A., Jr. 1995. *Desert Frontier: Ecological and Economic Change Along the Western Sahel, 1600–1850.* Madison: University of Wisconsin Press.

Chapter 5

EVENTS AND EFFECTS
Intensive Transnationalism among Pakistanis in Denmark

Mikkel Rytter

In October 2005, an earthquake hit the region of Jammu and Kashmir in the northern part of Pakistan, killing 75,000 people. Even more were injured, and almost 3,000,000 lost their homes. From an analytical perspective, the natural disaster was a 'critical event' (Das 1995) that, in a single moment, turned life upside down for thousands of families in the affected mountain region. But the event also had consequences, or effects, in different Pakistani communities around the world, such as the migrants who have been living in Denmark since the late 1960s. The period following the earthquake was one of immediate activity, which saw people in this migrant community striving to provide emergency treatment for the many victims in Pakistan. Such liminal periods, which suspend regular, everyday life and mobilize people to help victims of disasters in other parts of the world, have been called 'intensive transnationalism' (Holm and Fabricius 2008: 87). One significant development in the aftermath of the disaster was the ad hoc establishment of an association of Danish-Pakistani medical professionals, Medical Doctors in Assistance to the Earthquake Victims in Pakistan (Læger til hjælp for jordskælvsofrene i Pakistan), which, in the following months, sent trained medical staff to the disaster area. In this chapter I discuss the origins, developments, and impacts of the doctors' initiative, both within and beyond the Pakistani community in Denmark. In a more general respect, the dynamic period of intensive transnationalism that emerged after the earthquake will be used to explore the relationship between events and effects on a global scale.

An overall argument of this chapter is that events today can be radically different in character and scope from those that anthropologists studied in the middle of the previous century because contemporary modes of telecommunication and mass media set up new premises for human relations and sociality. I do not contest the fact that Max Gluckman and other scholars of the Manchester School developed an innovative methodology and analytical framework. Nor do I dispute the fact that, very early in the history of modern anthropology, these scholars, who may have been among the first to do so, emphasized the importance of connecting their local ethnographic data from Africa to broader historical processes, economic conjunctures, and global regimes, such as imperialism and colonialism. Their awareness of local-global interconnectedness stimulated a shift away from the conventional focus on 'society' to develop the much more flexible notion of 'social fields' (Gluckman 2006: 20).

In this respect, the study of local social situations was never analytically restricted to what was immediately observable. J. Clyde Mitchell ([1983] 2006: 27) emphasizes this point when he defines social situation analysis as "a detailed examination of an event (or series of related events) which the analyst believes exhibits (or exhibit) the operation of some identified general theoretical principle." Nevertheless, I suggest that the analytical approach of social situational analysis needs to be updated so that it can cope sufficiently with the challenges of contemporary ethnography in the twenty-first century.

One of the most obvious changes since the heyday of the Manchester School has been the appearance and expansion of advanced communication technology—an imprint of late modernity itself. Different media have not only conquered our local worlds and intimate spheres of life but also enabled the creation of bonds between people, places, and spaces around the globe in ways never before seen or imagined. Currently, we are subjected to the experience of 'time-space compression' (Harvey 1990) and 'simultaneity' (Levitt and Glick Schiller 2004), as shown, for instance, by the fact that an event in one local site can (and often will) become a topic of discussion and motivate people into action in different settings around the world. Critical local events are often communicated worldwide by international television news or radio broadcasts, or through more idiosyncratic and less controllable channels, such as Internet sites, Facebook, blogging, or chains of SMS (short messaging service) communications. The Rushdie affair, 9/11, the 2005–2006 cartoon controversy, and the 2011 democracy movement in the Middle East are all examples of how purely local events can spread worldwide via chaotic networks within networks and bring about unpredicted outcomes as the events generate new configurations of identity and imaginaries, creating spaces for political action that were not accessible, or even thinkable, earlier.

The Kashmir earthquake became just such a global, media-borne event. This chapter analyzes some of the effects of the earthquake among Pakistanis in Denmark and especially how it motivated the rise and fall of an organization, Medical Doctors in Assistance to the Earthquake Victims in Pakistan. Almost as an inevitable consequence of the earthquake turning into a media event, this initiative became a kind of reflexive performance through which the Danish-Pakistani doctors enacted, fulfilled, or disappointed the expectations and promises of their profession. The significance and impact of this organization will be explored in three interconnected contexts: the migrant family, the Pakistani community, and the arena of national identity politics.

The Disaster

On the morning of 8 October 2005, the city of Muzaffarabad, situated in Azad Kashmir, was hit without warning by a huge earthquake estimated to measure 7.6 on the open Richter scale. In the beginning, there was no exact information about the damage. Initial reports from Islamabad, the capital of Pakistan situated a couple hundred kilometers south of the earthquake's epicenter, stated that the Mangla Towers, a high-rise block of apartments, had collapsed, killing nearly 100 people. It was not until national and international media entered the mountain regions that people in Pakistan and around the world realized the full extent of the damage and human casualties that this natural disaster had caused.

Many Pakistanis in Denmark followed the course of events on Pakistani television channels, the BBC, CNN, or the Internet. Migrants with relatives or friends in Islamabad, in the neighboring city of Rawalpindi, or in the northern areas telephoned Pakistan to make sure that their loved ones were safe. As most Pakistanis in Denmark had emigrated from the lowlands of the Gujrat district of Punjab, only a few families actually lost relatives as a result of the earthquake. Pakistanis who had settled in the United Kingdom were much more affected by the disaster, as more than 80 percent are Kashmiri and originate from Azad Kashmir (Rehman and Kalra 2006: 311).

When Pakistani and international teams of relief workers finally entered the mountain region, the reported number of casualties shot up dramatically. Every hour of every day brought new and higher figures. During this critical period, Pakistanis in Denmark suffered and identified with the many victims whom they were confronted with in the media. Three circumstances intensified the immediate identification and emotional connection with the victims. First, the earthquake hit ordinary people and families, who, for the most part, had lived lives very similar to those of the first generation of migrants before they moved to Denmark about 40 years earlier. Secondly, the disaster happened in the month of Ramadan, a time where everyone is focused on helping those in need by giving *zakat* (alms), a religious duty for Muslims. Finally, it was significant that the earthquake hit the Kashmir region, which, since the independence of Pakistan in 1947, has been very important for Pakistani national identity and imaginary. During the last 60 years, Pakistan and India have fought several wars over the disputed territory. As recently as 2002, the unresolved Kashmir conflict put these neighboring countries on the edge of a nuclear confrontation.

After the extent of the earthquake's damage was revealed, the Pakistani community in Denmark began to discuss how they could contribute to helping their needy 'brothers' and 'sisters' in Kashmir. Due to a general mistrust among Danish-Pakistanis of both Danish and Pakistani NGOs and relief agencies,[1] within a few days several collections had been organized in order to assist and support the earthquake victims. Money was collected mainly in different mosques and 'societies' that cater exclusively to Pakistanis who share a similar *zaat* (clan background) or originate from the same city, such as Lahore or Sialkot. Clothes were collected, packed, and shipped to Pakistan, and people used the Internet or SMS to donate generously to the different collections. The Pakistani embassy soon set up a fund that in a few weeks had collected $382,000, and an NGO titled Muslim Aid collected no less than 2.1 million kroner (Holm and Fabricius 2008: 91). The willingness of people to donate through such ad hoc initiatives reflected a strong sense of intimacy with and relatedness to the victims among migrants and should not be seen as individualized and impersonal relief contributions (Rehman and Kalra 2006: 313).

Danish-Pakistani doctors, as well, began discussing what they could do to help the victims and how their efforts could be set in motion. A few days after the earthquake, a group of doctors met in order to develop a strategy. First, they wanted to mobilize a larger network of Danish-Pakistani doctors who were willing and able to help. Secondly, they decided to search for sponsors to cover the cost of travel expenses and the necessary medical equipment. Thirdly, they realized that they had to make logistical plans in order to have the doctors flown into the region of the disaster. Finally, they discussed how they should handle the media so that their efforts should become visible and politically effective in placing the earthquake on the public agenda in Denmark.

After a few days, more than 40 Danish-Pakistani doctors had volunteered to help. Looking back at the event, a doctor from the first team sent to Pakistan related to me in an interview how one evening he had been sitting at home on the couch, watching images of the disaster on the television, when his wife angrily yelled at him: "You're a doctor, and yet you just sit here and watch television! Do something!" Common to everyone in the ad hoc network was a wish to take on an active role in order to make a difference.

The group that initiated the network succeeded in persuading the medical company Pfizer to donate 100,000 kroner in support of its efforts. In order to accept a gift of that amount from a corporate sponsor, the informal network was turned into a formal association. Thus, the non-profit organization Medical Doctors in Assistance to the Earthquake Victims in Pakistan (referred to hereafter as MDAEV) came into being, with the single aim of sending doctors to Kashmir. The statutory general meeting was held 12 days after the earthquake hit, but already, on the previous day, a team consisting of four doctors had been sent to

Pakistan. This was the first of what turned out to be six teams of doctors who would go to Pakistan in order to help with disaster relief.

All six teams stayed in the disaster area from 5 to 10 days. The first team arrived shortly after the disaster and worked in local hospitals or at temporary emergency clinics, treating both earthquake victims and regular patients in need of medical care. While the first couple of teams worked under primitive circumstances, the later teams faced more orderly conditions. The last teams, consisting of both doctors and physical therapists, focused mostly on rehabilitating patients. In this way, the Danish-Pakistani doctors became part of an estimated 200 medically trained overseas Pakistanis who traveled to the Kashmir region from Europe and North America in order to offer their help and assistance (Rehman and Kalra 2006: 314).

The rest of this chapter discusses the significance of the medical doctors' association and the impact of their performance on the Pakistani families, the Pakistani migrant community in Denmark, the Danish majority, and Denmark as a nation-state.

Family Objectives and Social Mobility

The first Pakistanis came to Denmark in the late 1960s, and in 1973 the Danish government put a stop to further labor-related immigration. Despite this, the immigration continued, now in the guise of family reunifications with wives and children. When Denmark joined the European Community in 1973, numerous Pakistanis relocated from the United Kingdom, motivated by better job opportunities, a generous welfare system, and the liberal legislation on family reunification that existed in Denmark at the time. Today, there are approximately 25,000 people residing in Denmark who, despite differences in having Pakistani, English, or Danish citizenship, all have a family history related to Pakistan. Most migrants, as already noted, come from the Gujrat district in rural Punjab, while the rest originate from larger cities, such as Lahore, Rawalpindi, Sialkot, and Karachi. Today, most Pakistani families are settled in Copenhagen or in the suburbs around the capital (Quraishy 1999; Rytter 2013).

The pattern of chain migration of male workers from a limited number of villages in rural Punjab—and, later on, of arranged transnational marriages within extended family networks, or *biraderi*—means that many of the older migrants now living in Denmark already knew each other when they emigrated. Since that time, Pakistani migrants have shared 40 years of immigrant life in Denmark. Whether as friends or enemies, their trajectories and family stories have criss-crossed in numerous ways. As relatives, colleagues, and neighbors, they meet in Pakistani associations or mosques, at Urdu or Qur'an lessons, at religious festivals, and on various social occasions. In recent years, increasing numbers of families have created conjugal bonds through the inter-marriages of young people in the second generation (Rytter 2012). In this close-knit migrant community, it is generally believed that everyone knows everyone else (*alle kender alle*).

Within this village-like community, people watch over each other and discuss other families' affairs. Everything from businesses, health problems, and the upbringing of children to marriage problems and wider family conflicts is discussed in these informal gossip networks. Whether or not a family is considered to have been successful and to have done well in Denmark is assessed using different criteria, such as economic, cultural, and symbolic capital (Bourdieu 1997, 2000). One parameter of success is whether the family has succeeded in becoming middle class in material terms in the sense of having a solid income, nice cars, and a large family home in the suburbs of the capital (Bajaj and Laursen 1988: 130). Another parameter concerns whether or not a family has been able to build a multi-story house in Pakistan (Ballard 2003: 45). Most important in these ongoing evaluations, however, is the cultural capital of education, that is, whether the family's children among the second generation have been able to complete higher education (Moldenhawer 2005).[2] If grown children in a family manage to stay away from criminal activity and lesser kinds of misbehavior and instead concentrate on completing an education and finding a well-paid, influential job, the family will often be given the flattering appellation of "a family that has done well" (*en familie der har klaret sig godt*) in the migrant community (Rytter 2011).

However, following the logic of community competition, education is never just education. Instead, it constitutes a hierarchy of uneven status and prestige. It is an ongoing joke among second-generation Pakistanis that their parents want them to become "a doctor, engineer, or lawyer." Becoming a medical doctor is often considered to be the highest achievement in the hierarchy—the best that you can do for yourself and your family. Both in Pakistan and within the Pakistani community in Denmark, the medical doctor is seen as a figure of esteem and status who should be approached with respect.[3]

In telling their life stories, many elders relate how they themselves left Pakistan years ago because they did not have access to a university education or could not afford the tuition fees. Instead, they have put their own (and sometimes even their parents') dreams and ambitions aside in order to emigrate and work as semi- or unskilled workers all their lives. Now it is up to their children, who have been born and raised in Denmark, to fulfill these family ambitions (cf. Østberg 2003: 172). The intense focus on education and the significance of academic achievements are evident in many migrant families and become manifest in the overwhelming interest—some might say pressure—on children's homework and study habits. Sheraz, a young medical student, briefly summarized his upbringing as follows: "Study, study, study. That was all that mattered when I went to school." This strong focus on education can, however, be extremely difficult to handle when youngsters do not have the necessary intellectual capabilities or simply have other plans for their future.[4]

When a young Danish-Pakistani man or woman finally succeeds in becoming a medical doctor, this is not only an individual career move but also an achievement that affects the entire family, improving its symbolic capital within the community. It gives new meaning to the migration process and to the loss and deprivation that first-generation parents have suffered in Denmark during four decades of hard manual labor, limited contact with their own parents and relatives in Pakistan, and the 'loss' of a homeland. It means nothing less than that the goals of parenthood, the family's legacy, and the very meaning of life are at stake in the education and school performances of the second generation.

All in all, medical doctors are ascribed a range of different positive attributes within the Pakistani community.[5] This has become especially salient in recent years, as more and more young people of the second generation study medicine and become doctors. In its own tragic way, the Kashmir earthquake provided the new elite of Danish-Pakistani doctors with an opportunity to fulfill some of the promises of their profession by using their medical training to give something back to those in need in Pakistan. The disaster enabled Danish-Pakistani doctors to create or re-create bonds of relatedness between themselves and the people and places in Pakistan that are an essential part of their common backgrounds and family histories.

One illustrative example of this process is the case of Adeel, one of the founders of MDAEV. When he was younger, he had been sent to live with his uncle in Pakistan and attend a medical school in Lahore. He was sent away so that he could focus on his studies and not be distracted by the parties, alcohol, and women that might tempt a young student in Denmark. Later, he returned and started working at one of the major hospitals in Denmark. Adeel was active in forming MDAEV and volunteered for one of the first teams to go to Kashmir. When I met him, he related that it had made his parents very proud that he had decided to clear his busy calendar and immediately travel to Pakistan to offer his help and services. Adeel's participation in the medical team proved to his parents, as well as to the rest of the Pakistani community in Denmark and his family in Pakistan, that, despite all the problems his parents had with him earlier on, the upbringing that they had given him proved successful after all. Adeel had managed to become a medical doctor just as they had wished, and now he was using his abilities to help the people of Pakistan. This made them very proud.

Community Effects

In the days following the earthquake, after the first team of Danish-Pakistani medical doctors had left for Pakistan, the number of casualties kept rising. Journalists posted ongoing reports from the area, and television broadcasts and Internet sites provided images that documented the alarming proportions of the disaster. In a speech President Musharraf directly addressed the Pakistani diaspora pleading for their help and financial support: "Allah has given you a lot and today your nation requires your support - I appeal to you, to donate generously to the President's Relief Fund for Earthquake victims. I hope you realize that this hour of crisis to your nation and come forward with a large hearth in trying to alleviate the sufferings of the people and share the burden of the Government" (quoted in Rehman and Kalra 2006: 321). In the meantime, both Pakistani and international NGOs were flocking to the area. Within the Pakistani community in Denmark, the earthquake had a series of local effects. Whereas in the beginning the general reaction to the doctors' initiative was primarily one of pride and enthusiasm, MDAEV was later criticized for various reasons. To explain this change, it is convenient to divide the period of intensive transnationalism following the earthquake into two different phases.

The first phase covers the period just after the earthquake, when everyone closed ranks and worked together. The disaster created a mutual feeling of community in which everyone suffered with the victims in Pakistan and tried to contribute in order to help them. As one of the doctors explained in an interview after the event:

> In the first period [after the earthquake] everyone wanted to help—and could help. Besides the teams of doctors who traveled to Pakistan and provided medical help in the disaster areas, this was also a time when money was collected. Organization was needed, funds were applied for, some had to talk to the media, and so on. Everyone contributed: the truck driver loaded the goods, taxi drivers drove around with messages and packages, engineers worked with the logistics … All good forces worked together. And everyone was equal within the framework of the common project: to help the earthquake victims in Pakistan.

This description resembles a study of philanthropy in the Pakistani-American diaspora, in which Adil Najam (2006) found that transnational activity was a latent resource that can be mobilized in certain critical situations, where people join forces and work together for a common cause. However, the communality of this first phase was succeeded by the splits and competition of the second phase.

Soon after the first couple of medical teams had left for Pakistan, the perception of the doctors' initiative began to change within the migrant community. This took place as the character of the disaster itself underwent change. After a few weeks, the Pakistani authorities and international NGOs had gained some control over the situation, and there was no longer the same urgent need for foreign medical professionals. Rather, the greater need was for professionals to assist with the rehabilitation of the injured and for help in reconstructing the area in general. The major, unambiguous disaster that had initially united the migrant community began to fade out of sight.

Meanwhile, a number of different relief initiatives and well-coordinated collections of money, sleeping bags, blankets, and clothes were started in Denmark. Three Danish-Pakistani brothers, who were soon referred to simply as 'the Ahmad brothers', managed to arrange a big concert in Cirkusbygningen, a well-known concert hall in the center of Copenhagen. Numerous artists performed for free, and all of the profits were donated to the earthquake victims. The Ahmad brothers received a lot of attention in the national media and ended up going to Pakistan, followed by a camera crew and television journalists who documented how they handed over more than 1 million Danish kroner that they had made from the concert. Another far-reaching initiative was undertaken by a group of Danish-Pakistani teachers, who set up a transnational NGO, Help-Education, to support the schooling of children in the disaster area.[6] But the most effective NGO at the time was Muslim Aid, also with Danish-Pakistanis in leading positions, which not only had a good reputation within the migrant community but also had the necessary local connections in Pakistan to get their help out to the disaster area.

The point in mentioning a few of the numerous initiatives within the migrant Pakistani community is not to emphasize some at the expense of others. Rather, the purpose is to illustrate the different kinds of efforts that arose during this period of intensive transnationalism and to suggest that the two phases following the earthquake were shaped by well-known community dynamics in competition for symbolic capital. In the first phase immediately after the disaster, all of the hierarchies and differences that are normally present in the Pakistani community became insignificant, but after a while, in the second phase, they returned with a vengeance. In the beginning, there was a general consensus within the migrant community that the doctors were the ones with the professional skills and background to help the victims in the best and most effective ways. This consensus ceased when the situation changed and it became apparent that other kinds of assistance were needed. In the second phase, it was legitimate to question the contributions and efforts of the doctors and to start working on other initiatives.

The many efforts to help the earthquake victims turned into yet another arena of competition for status and recognition within the Pakistani community—and this became the Achilles' heel for MDAEV. Representatives of Muslim Aid in particular questioned the way that the doctors managed the sponsor's gift that they had received from Pfizer, asking whether it was reasonable for the money to be spent on clothes and trekking equipment for the doctors instead of being given directly to the victims. Some pointed out that it would have been much more efficient to use the money to hire doctors from, for instance, Karachi and pay them to work for a longer period in the disaster area, instead of sending Danish-Pakistani doctors to the site for a few days at a time. Local doctors would have the linguistic and cultural competences, and hiring them would be a less expensive solution. Most critically, it seemed to be common knowledge in the gossip that was circulating that some of the central figures in the doctors' association were primarily interested in promoting themselves in the media at the expense of their colleagues and the common cause of helping the victims in Kashmir. This also soon became a key issue within MDAEV itself, as the doctors started accusing each other of being 'earthquake tourists', insinuating that some were primarily interested in 'the experience' of going to the disaster area and in making some impressive video recordings to show back home. As a result of various controversies, several doctors left the association and went to Pakistan on their own to help in different ways.

The point is that MDAEV soon became yet another arena of competition for symbolic capital in terms of status and recognition. This was true not only internally in the association, but also within the Pakistani community more widely, in which the MDAEV was just one among many initiatives set in motion to help the people of Kashmir in the best and most efficient ways. Many actors involved in the second phase after the earthquake had a double agenda:

to help the victims and to promote themselves within the migrant community. In this way, the impact of the Kashmir earthquake on the Pakistani community in Denmark was structured according to an already existing grammar of identity, consisting of an ongoing dialectic between equality and hierarchy (Werbner 1990: 83), as well as the continuing competition for symbolic capital in terms of status and prestige.

The Developing Dominant Cleavage

So far, I have discussed how the Kashmir earthquake changed from being a local disaster in Pakistan to becoming a global media event with numerous effects. How the disaster affected the Danish-Pakistani community is just one issue. Another is how the event influenced the relationship between the migrant community and the wider society, that is, how the disaster in Kashmir in some ways displaced the relationship between minorities and majorities in Denmark.

The reaction to MDAEV and its efforts to help was generally positive among the Danish media and public. When the first team of doctors returned from Pakistan, the doctors' association hosted a well-attended press conference at Rigshospitalet, the national hospital in Copenhagen. Afterward, the doctors received favorable press, and some were invited to participate in various radio and television shows. Nevertheless, both the doctors and the migrant community at large were frustrated that the Danish government had not made a more significant economic contribution to the earthquake victims. The frustration intensified as weather forecasts for the Kashmir region warned of the approaching winter. Now it became even more urgent to send blankets, tents, food, and medical equipment to prevent homeless earthquake victims from freezing to death during the cold winter nights.

The doctors' dissatisfaction took shape at a meeting and confrontation with Ulla Tørnæs, then minister for development cooperation in the Liberal-Conservative government. Members of MDAEV criticized the government for not using the transportable emergency hospital, which forms part of Danish preparations for national and international disasters. The lack of political will to help was interpreted as an unmistakable sign that Muslim lives in Pakistan were not considered as valuable as the lives of those Danes who had been killed when a tsunami ravaged the beach and tourist resorts of Thailand (along with the coastlines of Sri Lanka, India, and Indonesia) on 26 December 2004. Within the Pakistani community, it was also considered striking that official Danish economic assistance to Pakistan was only a quarter of the amount spent following the tsunami.

In an open letter, central figures in the MDAEV urged Prime Minister Anders Fogh Rasmussen to mention the earthquake victims and their families in his New Year's speech, to be transmitted on national television on the first day of January. The doctors drew attention to the fact that the previous year Rasmussen had spent most of his speech expressing his grief over the loss of Danish lives and extending his deeply felt commiserations to families who had been bereaved by the tsunami. Furthermore, they explicitly referred to the way that the earthquake had been handled in Norway, as follows:

> How serious the present situation is, also to people living outside Pakistan, has been recognized in other countries. For instance, the Norwegian minister of development, Erik Solheim, has proved that the official Norway knows and recognizes that many Norwegians (with a family history related to Pakistan) are personally affected by the disaster, and by doing that he has recognized the loss and grief of his fellow countrymen and thereby included them in the national community of Norwegian citizens.
>
> Signed H. L. Butt, W. Ahmad and M. Iqbal[7]

The correspondents appealed for a similar recognition of themselves as Danes and for an acknowledgment of the grief that they had suffered after losing friends and family members as a result of the earthquake. However, the prime minister ignored their request.

The experience of not being recognized as 'real Danes'[8] by officialdom in Denmark and the suspicion circulating that the lives of Pakistani Muslims were seen as less valuable than those of Protestant (or atheist) Danes once again changed the meaning and content of the disaster within the migrant community. It became yet another example of the more encompassing structural pattern dividing Danes from immigrants that has gained ground in Danish society in recent decades—a pattern in which Muslims have acquired a dubious status and are met with general suspicion.

In *Analysis of a Social Situation in Modern Zululand*, Max Gluckman ([1940] 1958) introduced the concept of a 'developing dominant cleavage' and used it to discuss the relationship between blacks and whites in Zululand during the 1930s. This analytical concept stresses the social and historical processes in which uneven distributions of power stimulate the creation of a cleavage, instead of focusing on the two groups that are separated by it. According to Gluckman, historical developments in the region, namely, colonialism, racism, and the British organization and administration of society in general, generated and strengthened a developing dominant cleavage between blacks and whites that was significant in every relationship and interaction between them (see Macmillan 1995: 51–52). A very similar cleavage is taking form in Denmark between Danes and Muslim immigrants.

Some significant changes that have taken place in Danish society over the past four decades are reflected in the life stories of older Pakistanis. In their narratives, the 1960s and 1970s are presented as a 'golden age' in which Danes accepted and welcomed immigrants. The newcomers were offered accommodations, jobs, and help in reading official documents or learning the language, and some male workers also had romantic relationships with Danish women. Today, Pakistanis generally describe the Danes as much more hostile, racist, and xenophobic (Rytter 2013). The changing perceptions of immigrants in the Danish population can also be noted in verbal categories and discourses. When Pakistanis first began to arrive, they were welcomed as *gæstearbejdere* (guest workers), but soon they became *fremmedarbejdere* (foreign workers). In public discourses, they were called *indvandrere* (immigrants) in the 1980s and *fremmede* (aliens) in the 1990s. Today, they are primarily seen and discussed as Muslims, a religious category that marks a radical difference from the lifeworlds and experiences of the Danish majority. Currently, Muslim immigrants are presented and conceived in public discourses as a potential threat to Danish values and identity (Hervik 2011; Jensen 2008; Rytter and Pedersen 2014).

In recent years, identity politics has intensified, and Muslim minorities are often constructed as a threat to Danish society and the Danish welfare state. Shortly after 9/11, the Danish Parliament adopted an anti-terrorism resolution that gave the Politiets Efterretningstjeneste (PET, Security and Intelligence Service) far-reaching power and authority to monitor potential enemies of the state. Since then, PET has on several occasions infiltrated terror cells consisting of Muslims living in Denmark, thus apparently preventing attacks from being committed in the country. Furthermore, from the start in 2001, Denmark has actively supported the US-led 'global war on terror' and sent armed forces to Afghanistan and Iraq. Finally, the heated reactions following the cartoon controversy that began in 2005 (see Kublitz, this volume) and the bombing of the Danish embassy in Pakistan in 2008 have substantiated the impression that Denmark is a nation-state at war and that the enemy is radical Islamists—maybe even Islam itself.[9]

Applied in the Danish context, the developing dominant cleavage captures the image of a social division between segments of the population along lines of race, ethnicity, and religion that sometimes becomes salient in the everyday lives of Pakistanis (and other minorities) in Danish society. The cleavage is neither tangible nor an officially sanctioned division between segments of the total Danish population. Rather, it constitutes a reservoir, a potentiality of power that can be mobilized in certain situations either by the majority, who claim as legitimate their right to decide and define specific social situations, or by the Muslim minorities, who point out that they are being treated unjustly. In general, national identity politics has intensified in recent decades and increased the dominant cleavage between 'real Danes' and Muslim immigrants, regardless of the actual citizenship of the latter.

The Danish-Pakistani medical doctors learned this lesson the hard way. Apparently, they did everything right. Their appearances in the national media showed them to be well-organized, well-articulated, and determined. Connected with Pakistan but nevertheless speaking perfect Danish, they constituted a group of immigrants who so far had been absent from the Danish debate on Muslim immigrants. The doctors contradicted the usual stereotypes of Pakistani immigrants as criminals, violent gang members, taxi drivers, or proprietors of corner shops (see Rytter 2013). Instead, they came forward and presented themselves as a group that, through education and social mobility, had risen above the crowd of 'regular' immigrants and the ongoing controversies between minorities and majorities. Within the Pakistani community they were respected for their educational achievements, while for the Danish majorities they stood out mainly as doctors, that is, as impersonal medical professionals who, regardless of personality, religion, or skin color, are expected to provide their services.

The doctors had a unique position, as they were respected and able to navigate on both sides of the cleavage. In this regard, they were special.

However, the hesitation of the Danish state to help the victims of the disaster and its failure to acknowledge publicly the Pakistani community's grief over lost friends and family members mobilized the dominant cleavage. The government's response to the earthquake became yet another example of the more encompassing structural pattern dividing Danes from immigrants that has gained ground in Danish society in recent decades, in which Muslims, as noted, have acquired a dubious status and are met with general suspicion. From the very beginning, the Danish-Pakistani medical doctors imagined that they could put the disaster on the public and political agenda and, among other things, make the government send the transportable emergency hospital to Kashmir. The doctors worked on both sides of the cleavage to fulfill these ambitions.[10] But as they failed, this was interpreted as yet another proof of how badly they, their families, and Muslims in general are treated in Denmark. The medical doctors had to realize that, despite all their efforts to contribute to Danish society by using their higher education and working as medical professionals, they were not recognized as 'real Danes' after all.

Conclusion: Social Situational Analysis, Version 2.1

Today, MDAEV no longer exists. The association had a specific purpose, and once that had been achieved, the organization simply dissolved itself. In the overall picture of the Kashmir earthquake, the Danish-Pakistani doctors played a minor role, although undoubtedly an important one to those whom they treated. It should also be emphasized that the efforts of the doctors still obtain respect when the topic comes up in my conversations with Danish-Pakistanis, regardless of profession, gender, or age.

At the outset of this chapter, I argued that the current state of globalization, being characterized by time-space compression, simultaneity, and an accelerated diffusion of uncontrolled information, presents a challenge to contemporary ethnography. Events can no longer always be characterized as they used to be. These relatively new conditions for human interaction and the creation of alternative social formations compel anthropologists to explore and theorize the relationship between locally situated events and their chaotic patterns of unpredictable global effects. Our challenge is to understand the character and scope of these types of events, showing how they create new imaginaries, hopes, and fears and how they motivate people into political action around the world. In this project, an updated 'version 2.1' of the social situational analysis approach seems to be very useful. This discussion of how the Kashmir earthquake affected the Pakistani community in Denmark should be seen as constituting a humble beginning in this endeavor.

I have shown how the disaster presented an opportunity for Danish-Pakistani doctors to fulfill some of the promises of their profession and to meet the ambitions of their families. But soon their contribution was incorporated and interpreted according to an existing logic of competition for symbolic capital within the migrant community. Finally, the period succeeding the event also taught some doctors the painful lesson of identity politics—namely, that despite their continuing efforts, they are still not recognized as 'real Danes'. The case of MDAEV illustrates how the growing dominant cleavage can be mobilized and acted on in certain historic situations. Just as Danish right-wing politicians often conjure up a picture of Muslims as dangerous, fundamentalist terrorists, it is not uncommon to be confronted with descriptions of Danes as discriminating, unjust, or racist within the Pakistani community. Sometimes these generalized images are true, and sometimes they are not.

From a transnational perspective, however, the case also seems to suggest that the Danish-Pakistani medical doctors were never really part of an international social field and reality. Their orientation was largely defined and determined by the structures governing the Danish context in which they acted. Even when they reached out to help the earthquake victims, they were often mainly preoccupied with their own performance and how it would be evaluated by real and imagined audiences of family and kin, community members, and the Danish population in general. All along, many of the doctors involved had alternative agendas, besides aiding the victims of the disaster in Pakistan.

The effects that the Kashmir earthquake occasioned among Pakistani migrants in Denmark reflect a pre-existing national and international structure, but they were also part of a process of reorientation whereby new horizons might begin to take shape. From one perspective, the intensive transnationalism that followed the earthquake was a highly innovative period in which new modes of action and imagination came into being. But from another perspective, all of these inventions were grounded in well-known categories and the already existing grammar of identity that is salient within the competitive Pakistani community. Perceived as a critical event, the Kashmir earthquake and the succeeding initiative by the medical doctor's association actually had the potential to make a difference—not only for the victims in Pakistan, but also as a way to restructure relations and dynamics between families in the migrant community and to alter stereotypical images of Muslim immigrants in the wider Danish public. Still, this potential was never realized. One important reason was that the Kashmir earthquake was subordinated to 9/11, which has turned out to be the major critical event of the century—one that continues to produce new local effects worldwide. Despite their intentions and efforts, the Danish-Pakistani medical doctors ended up confirming the image and logic of the developing dominant cleavage between the national majority and the Muslim minorities living in Denmark.

Acknowledgments

I would like to thank Morten Nielsen, Jonas Østergaard Nielsen, Bjarke Oxlund, Karen Fog Olwig, Alison Shaw, Katharine Charsley, Marta Bivand Erdal, Robert Parkin, Lotte Meinert, and Bruce Kapferer for the many generous comments and suggestions they have provided on different versions of this chapter.

Mikkel Rytter is an Associate Professor of Anthropology in the Department of Anthropology and a leader of CESAU (Center for Sociological Studies) at Aarhus University. His recent publications include *Family Upheaval: Generation, Mobility and Relatedness among Pakistani Migrants in Denmark* (2013), *Migration, Family and the Welfare State: Integrating Migrants and Refugees in Scandinavia* (2012, co-edited with Karen F. Olwig and Birgitte R. Larsen), and *Mobile Bodies, Mobile Souls: Family, Religion, and Migration in a Global World* (2011, co-edited with Karen F. Olwig).

Notes

1. For a similar observation within the Pakistani-American diaspora, see Adil Najam (2006: 145).
2. In general, Danish-Pakistanis do well in the free educational system of the Danish welfare state, as 30 percent of young men and 36 percent of young women have succeeded in finishing *en gymnasiel uddannelse* (i.e., high school or a similar level of education). Given that the equivalent figures for the average Danish peer group are 25 percent for men and 38 percent for women (Hummelgaard et al. 2002: 14), and taking into account the low educational levels or lack of education among the first generation of Pakistani immigrants, the upcoming second generation is doing quite well.
3. It is not only among Pakistanis that the position of doctor is considered prestigious. In a 2006 survey, 2,155 Danes were asked to rank 99 different occupations. The career of general practitioner came in third on the list, while hospital doctor was fourth. The first and second positions were pilot and lawyer, respectively (*Ugebrevet A4*, no. 23 [2006]: 12).
4. Billal Zahoor, chairman of the Organization of Pakistani Students and Academics, explains that Pakistani parents sometimes put considerable pressure on their children when it comes to choices regarding education and their lives as students (*Morgenavisen Jyllandsposten*, 25 February 2007).
5. Based on interviews with Danish-Pakistani medical students and doctors, I will briefly elaborate here on the range of meanings that constitute 'the doctor' as a special profession. First of all, it is well-known that only top students can enter medical school, so anyone who actually graduates deserves status and respect for being wise and intelligent. Secondly, the doctor is significant in social networks. If you know a doctor, you have access to medical help. This is especially important in Pakistan, where there is no free, efficient health care system as in Denmark. Thirdly, the doctor is a figure who knows no borders. People have experiences with doctors all over the globe, and a doctor can work anywhere in the world. In this respect, not only is being a doctor an achieved status, but it also embodies knowledge and skills that can be used everywhere—something that became very useful after the earthquake. Finally, a doctor is gifted with the power to make a difference between life and death. Within the Islamic framework, doctors have been blessed with a gift from the Creator that obliges them to help others, especially the poor and needy, without charging for their services. Since they provide help in this way, doctors are always positioned above patients and their fellow human beings.
6. In the spring of 2006, when the earthquake was no longer on the public agenda, Help-Education hosted an ambitious family show at a public school in Amager with the goal of collecting money for schoolchildren in Kashmir. Besides listening to numerous speeches, musical performances, and Qur'anic recitations, the audience, consisting of 300–400 Danish-Pakistanis, was also invited to relive the earthquake as a group of students dramatized the disaster on stage. Overall, Help-Education has taken a more long-term perspective on providing assistance than have most of the other aid initiatives.

7. See http://www.kamal.dk/fokusligenu.php?id = 90.
8. The distinction between 'real Danes' and 'not-quite-real-Danes' is significant with regard to the legislation on family reunification introduced in 2002. In order to be granted family reunification with spouses from non-European countries, a Danish citizen must fulfill a requirement of 'national attachment'. One deciding factor is family background, which means that Danes with immigrant parents, such as second-generation Danish-Pakistanis, are often denied reunification (Rytter 2010, 2012).
9. In the summer of 2001, the media reported that Danish-Pakistani Islamic fundamentalists from the transnational religious organization Idara Minhaj Ul-Quran were about to infiltrate the Social-Liberal party (Det Radikale Venstre) with the single aim of overthrowing the Danish parliamentary system and democracy. A young female candidate, Mona Sheikh, who especially appeared in the headlines, repeatedly had to explain her position on the question of the death penalty (Hervik 2002, 2011).
10. Due to their high levels of education, the doctors assumed an 'intercalary' role, a concept introduced by A. L. Epstein in his study of a strike in an African diamond mine, in which the local council of elders took up this role. The elders were respected by both the workers and the management of the mine. However, an unfortunate consequence was that neither side trusted the council, as both groups felt that they could not rely on the elders' loyalty (Hannerz 1980: 137). The same might be said about the Danish-Pakistani doctors.

References

Bajaj, Kiron, and Helle Søby Laursen. 1988. *Pakistanske Kvinder i Danmark: Deres baggrund og tilpasning til det danske samfund*. Esbjerg: Sydjysk Universitetsforlag.

Ballard, Roger. 2003. "A Case of Capital-Rich Underdevelopment: The Paradoxical Consequences of Successful Transnational Entrepreneurship from Mirpur." *Contributions to Indian Sociology* 37, no. 1–2: 25–57.

Bourdieu, Pierre. 1997. *Af praktiske grunde: Omkring teorien om menneskelig handlen*. Copenhagen: Hans Reitzels Forlag.

Bourdieu, Pierre. 2000. *Pascalian Meditations*. Cambridge: Polity Press.

Das, Veena. 1995. *Critical Events: An Anthropological Perspective on Contemporary India*. Delhi: Oxford University Press.

Evens, T. M. S., and Don Handelman, eds. 2006. *The Manchester School: Practice and Ethnographic Praxis in Anthropology*. New York: Berghahn Books.

Gluckman, Max. [1940] 1958. *Analysis of a Social Situation in Modern Zululand*. Manchester: Manchester University Press for the Rhodes-Livingstone Institute.

Gluckman, Max. 2006. "Ethnographic Data in British Social Anthropology." Pp. 13–22 in Evens and Handelman 2006. (Paper originally presented in 1959 at the Fourth World Congress of Sociology in Stresa.)

Hannerz, Ulf. 1980. *Exploring the City: Inquiries toward an Urban Anthropology*. New York: Columbia University Press.

Harvey, David. 1990. *The Condition of Postmodernity: An Enquiry into the Origins of Cultural Change*. Oxford: Blackwell.

Hervik, Peter. 2002. *Mediernes Muslimer: En antropologisk undersøgelse af mediernes dækning af religioner i Danmark*. Copenhagen: Board for Ethnic Equality.

Hervik, Peter. 2011. *The Annoying Difference: The Emergence of Danish Neonationalism, Neoracism, and Populism in the Post-1989 World*. New York: Berghahn Books.

Holm, Anne, and Anne Sophie Fabricius. 2008. "Transnationalisme på Sigt: En undersøgelse af transnational aktivitet blandt efterkommere af pakistanske indvandrere i Danmark." MA thesis, Roskilde University.

Hummelgaard, Hans, Leif Husted, Helene Skyt Nielsen, Michael Rosholm, and Nina Smith. 2002. *Uddannelse og arbejde for andengenerationsindvandrere*. Copenhagen: AKF Forlaget.

Jensen, Tina. 2008. "To Be 'Danish', Becoming 'Muslim': Contestations of National Identity?" *Journal of Ethnic and Migration Studies* 34, no. 3: 389–409.

Levitt, Peggy, and Nina Glick Schiller. 2004 "Conceptualizing Simultaneity: A Transnational Social Field Perspective on Society," *International Migration Review* 38, no. 3: 1002–1039.

Macmillan, Hugh. 1995. "Return to the Malungwana Drift: Max Gluckman, the Zulu Nation and the Common Society." *African Affairs* 94: 39–65.

Mitchell, J. Clyde. [1983] 2006. "Case and Situation Analysis." Pp. 23–42 in Evens and Handelman 2006.

Moldenhawer, Bolette. 2005. "Transnational Migrant Communities and Education Strategies Among Pakistani Youngsters in Denmark." *Journal of Ethnic and Migration Studies* 31, no. 1: 51–78.

Najam, Adil. 2006. *Portrait of a Giving Community: Philanthropy by the Pakistani-American Diaspora.* Cambridge, MA: Harvard University Press.

Østberg, Sissel. 2003. *Muslim i Norge: Religion og hverdagsliv blant unge norsk-pakistanere.* Oslo: Universitetsforlaget.

Quraishy, Bashy. 1999. *Fra Punjab til Vesterbro: Det pakistanske samfund i Danmark.* Copenhagen: Forlaget Etnisk Debatforum.

Rehman, Shams, and Virinder S. Kalra. 2006. "Transnationalism from Below: Initial Responses by British Kashmiris to the South Asia Earthquake of 2005." *Contemporary South Asia* 15, no. 3: 309–323.

Rytter, Mikkel. 2010. "'The Family of Denmark' and 'the Aliens': Kinship Images in Danish Integration Politics." *Ethnos* 75, no. 3: 301–322.

Rytter, Mikkel. 2011. "Money or Education? Improvement Strategies among Pakistani Families in Denmark." *Journal of Ethnic and Migration Studies* 37, no. 2: 197–215.

Rytter, Mikkel. 2012. "Between Preferences: Marriage and Mobility among Danish Pakistani Youth." *Journal of Royal Anthropological Institute* (n.s.) 18, no. 3: 572–590.

Rytter, Mikkel. 2013. *Family Upheaval: Generation, Mobility and Relatedness among Pakistani Migrants in Denmark.* New York: Berghahn Books.

Rytter, Mikkel, and Marianne Holm Pedersen. 2014. "A Decade of Suspicion: Islam and Muslims in Denmark after 9/11." *Ethnic and Racial Studies* 37, no. 13: 2303–2321.

Werbner, Pnina. 1990. *The Migration Process: Capital, Gifts and Offerings among British Pakistanis.* Oxford: Berg.

Chapter 6

THE CARTOON CONTROVERSY
Creating Muslims in a Danish Setting

Anja Kublitz

"Islam is peace! Islam is peace!" The slogan is being shouted tentatively in Danish and lingers above our heads before it disappears into the cold air of the main square of Copenhagen. I am in the midst of the biggest Muslim demonstration in the history of Denmark (Hansen and Hundevadt 2006: 40). Three thousand Muslims have gathered to protest against the cartoons of the Prophet Muhammad that appeared in the Danish newspaper *Jyllands-Posten*. However, rather than simply protesting, the demonstration is striving to create an alternative representation of Islam. Islam does not equal terrorism, as one of the cartoons suggested. Rather, Islam is peace.

Based on fieldwork among Palestinians living in Denmark,[1] this article presents a situational analysis of the above demonstration (cf. Gluckman [1940] 1958). I argue that the event of the cartoons, coupled with the demonstration, was a major creative situation. Not only was it instrumental in transforming the discourse on immigrants in Denmark,[2] it also created a political platform

Notes for this chapter begin on page 121.

from which Muslims could unite and form a strong opposition. In this sense, the cartoon controversy mirrors 9/11. Whereas the attack on the Twin Towers, a symbol of capitalism and the Western world, created a political platform on which Western nations could unite and initiate the 'global war on terror', the insulting of the Prophet, the main symbol of Islam, created a platform that Muslim communities could use to counter Western hegemonies.[3]

Following Max Gluckman's ([1940] 1958) *Analysis of a Social Situation in Modern Zululand*, the present chapter is organized in three parts. The first describes the actual demonstration. The second traces the national Danish discourse on Muslims and situates the cartoon controversy within a historical context. The third offers an analysis of the event. I suggest that, in order to understand the connections between phenomena of widely different scales, we need to move beyond the empirical concepts of 'local' and 'global' and study the structures that cross-cut these scales, thus making such distinctions analytically redundant.

The Event: The Demonstration

The last week of September 2005 turned out to be a bad week for the Palestinians of my acquaintance in Denmark. On Monday, Brian Mikkelsen, the Conservative minister of culture, launched the Canon of Culture[4] as part of the 'battle of culture' (*kulturkamp*) against "immigrants from Muslim countries who refuse to recognize Danish culture and European norms."[5] The rhetoric of war used by Mikkelsen prompted my Palestinian informants to rename the Canon of Culture as the 'Cannon' of Culture. On Thursday, the newspaper *Politiken* ran a story describing how a member of the Danish Parliament, Louise Frevert of the Danish People's Party,[6] compared Muslims to a fast-spreading cancer.[7] Finally, on Friday, *Jyllands-Posten* printed the 12 cartoons in an article entitled "The Face of Muhammad."[8] Later that night, the cartoons were broadcast on the Arabic satellite television channel Al Jazeera.

In the following weeks, the cartoons were a hot topic among the Palestinians. Nobody had actually read *Jyllands-Posten*, but everybody knew about the cartoons, whether through Al Jazeera, the Friday prayer in the local mosques, or chains of text messages. After a week of intense debate among my informants, the rest of the Danish media picked up the story, and shortly thereafter a call went out for a demonstration on 14 October. The message was distributed via the mosques, flyers, and text messages. According to the Palestinians, the purpose of the demonstration was threefold: to protest against what they saw as the latest offense in a continuous onslaught of public outbursts against Muslims; to counter the possibility that somebody might do something stupid (implicitly referring to local Muslims taking up violent means); and, finally, to show that Muslims are peaceful. My informants told me that the imams at Friday prayers had requested that not everyone should attend the demonstration in order to avoid making it too large. One participant in the demonstration explained: "The mosques are able to gather 10,000 people, but we are only 3,000 today." As far as I could see, the only non-Muslim ethnic Danes who participated were journalists and myself.

The demonstration began at Nørrebro Station (close to the largest mosque in Copenhagen) and continued to Rådhuspladsen, the town hall square in Copenhagen. The first two-thirds of the demonstrators consisted of men, the last third of woman and children. I spotted reporters from two Danish television channels, as well as one Swedish and two Arabic—Al Jazeera and Al Arabia. The demonstration had been registered and was escorted by the Danish police. Additionally, Muslim security guards, wearing bright yellow shirts, had been appointed to ensure that everything was in order, keeping demonstrators to one side of the road and allowing traffic to flow in the opposite direction. They also made the demonstrators stop for every red traffic light, which kept the pace rather slow. Alongside the procession, a group of people were handing out flyers in Arabic and Danish, explaining to passers-by why they were demonstrating. In keeping with this bilingual policy, all banners and signs were printed in Arabic as well as in Danish, displaying statements such as "No to the clash of civilizations, yes to the dialogue of civilizations" and "No to racism and fanaticism, yes to peace and co-existence." Along the entire route, participants were shouting the Islamic creed, "Allah la ilaha Muhammad rasulu llah" (There is no God but Allah, and Muhammad is his messenger), and "Allahu Akbar" (God is great)."

When we finally arrived at Rådhuspladsen, an imam from a local mosque gave a speech in Arabic that was translated into Danish by a Danish convert. People were encouraged to shout the slogan "Islam is peace" in both Arabic and Danish, while spontaneous outbursts of "Allahu Akbar," praising the Lord in Arabic, were downplayed. The organizers also tried to make the crowd shout "No to terror" in Danish, but without much success. The demonstration ended with a request to participate in a common prayer at the square, but only a few hundred did so, nearly all men. Afterward, I asked some of them why they had prayed, and they explained that praying is the most peaceful act one can undertake. However, some of the young Palestinians took a more critical stance. Growing up in Denmark, they had developed a double perspective (cf. Said 1994: 44), and during the demonstration they had been anticipating how indigenous Danes might perceive it. They were embarrassed by the form that the demonstration had taken, complaining that the participants had shouted in Arabic. They also distanced themselves from the common prayer, which Khadije, a young Palestinian girl, said made them appear medieval. However, the young Palestinians were pleased that the demonstration had managed to gather together so many people from different Muslim congregations and different ethnic groups.

Situating the Two Parties

Whereas Gluckman ([1940] 1958) used the opening of a bridge in Zululand to analyze the relations between a colonial white minority and a subordinated black majority, I will use the above demonstration in Copenhagen to explore a relationship that is in some ways the reverse—namely, the relations between a majority of native Danes and a minority of immigrants who have settled in Denmark. The event of the cartoons and the demonstration that followed had the effect of manifesting and constructing a set of oppositions between ethnic Danes and immigrants that are guiding the policies and social processes of settlement. Below I will briefly introduce the two positions.

On the one hand, *Jyllands-Posten* advocated freedom of speech as an absolute value that does not submit to religious feelings. This position was connected to the battle of culture that the Danish right-wing government at first launched against what it termed 'judges of taste' (*smagsdommere*), consisting of 'culture radicals' (*kulturradikale*)[9] and 'experts'. However, just five days before the printing of the cartoons, Mikkelsen declared that this battle had now been won. Instead, he opened a new frontier, aiming the Canon of Culture at immigrants from Muslim countries.

On the other hand, the Palestinians challenged this discourse by introducing an alternative interpretation of the cartoon controversy as discrimination against a minority group. All of the Palestinians whom I talked to perceived the cartoons as the last blow in a range of discriminatory measures taken against them. At the demonstration and in daily conversations, they were addressing not so much *Jyllands-Posten* as the Danish government and Danish society as a whole. However, many Palestinians also focused simultaneously on the insult to the Prophet Muhammad himself. According to this religious discourse, the Prophet is holy, and thus *Jyllands-Posten* had crossed a red line.

The two parties were situated in different times, places, and spaces. First, there were different understandings about the timing of the appearance of the cartoons. In the Muslims' view, the fact that the offensive cartoons were printed in the month of Ramadan was perceived as an additional provocation on the part of *Jyllands-Posten*. Flemming Rose, the newspaper's editor of culture, stated that he was not aware that it was Ramadan. Rather, he explained that the timing was related to several recent cases of censorship in relation to Islam. Secondly, the two parties were situated in different places. While *Jyllands-Posten* obviously communicated through its own features and reportage, the Muslims communicated through mosques, text messages, flyers, and Al Jazeera. Furthermore, ending up at the town hall square, the demonstrators assumed that they were standing in front of the *Jyllands-Posten* office building because of a huge neon billboard nearby advertising the newspaper. In reality, they were demonstrating in front of the competing daily newspaper, *Politiken*, which happens to have its offices there. Finally, the two parties were anchored within different spaces of interpretation or discourse. In order to communicate a message of peace, some Muslim participants chose to end the demonstration with a common prayer in the public square. However, partly as a result of the praying, the demonstration itself was interpreted by pedestrians passing by—and by the Danish media in general—as a demonstration *for* Islam and *against* the secular freedom of speech. Furthermore, the slogan "Islam er fred" (Islam is peace) unfortunately sounds in Danish like "Islam er vred" (Islam is angry), and, as a result, pedestrians asked some of my informants if they were about to go to war.

Tracing the Danish Discourse on Muslims

The majority of Palestinians in Denmark arrived from Lebanon in the late 1980s. While waiting to obtain asylum, they were placed in centers run by the Danish Red Cross. These centers were often situated in the countryside, where the refugees were welcomed and sometimes encouraged to host evenings in the local village halls at which they could display their culture through food, music, and small exhibitions. In interviews, my informants would highlight these events, as they had not been accustomed to anybody taking an interest in their culture. Within the refugee camps in Lebanon, Palestinian flags and other symbols had been displayed, but outside the camps people would downplay their origins. I was told that during the Lebanese civil war, Palestinians ran the risk of being shot at the roadblocks if they did not manage to hide their dialect. Hence, the young men who had just laid down their Kalashnikovs and left the war in Lebanon suddenly found themselves in the Danish countryside dancing *dabke* (the traditional Palestinian folk dance) and drawing pictures with Palestinian symbols. In other words, in the late 1980s, when the Palestinians arrived, they were perceived as a group of people defined by their ethnic origin. The first question Palestinians were asked by local Danes was, "Where are you from?" And since the Palestinians did not identify themselves as Lebanese (and were not identified by the Lebanese government as such), they would answer, "Palestine." One could say that it was the logic of the "national order of things" (Malkki 1995) that ruled at the time.

Jonathan Schwartz has traced the discourse on immigrants in Denmark. He mentions how immigrants in the late 1960s and 1970s were referred to as 'guest workers', a euphemism for the cheap labor force that Denmark was importing at the time (Schwartz 1985: 5). Expected to return 'home' after a few years, guest workers were perceived as a temporary phenomenon, and in the studies conducted at the time they were portrayed as more or less grateful *homo economicus* (Schwartz 1990: 47). In the late 1970s and 1980s, the guest workers were recategorized as 'immigrants' or 'ethnic minorities', and the people in question became objects of integration policies and studies (ibid.; see also Mørck 1998: 36). The focus in the discourse on immigrants underwent a change from the economic aspects to culture and cultural differences. Culture was viewed as a problem—an obstacle to be overcome through integration (Schwartz 1990: 47–49).[10] As reflected in the discussion on refugee centers above, Palestinian culture was also celebrated as exotic folklore. According to Yvonne Mørck (1998: 36–37), this representation continued during the 1990s. However, as part of the focus on cultural differences, the Muslim background of immigrants had already been specifically highlighted in the 1980s (ibid.). At some point during the 1990s, the immigrants were once more reconceptualized in the Danish public discourse, this time as 'Muslims' (Hervik 2002).[11]

My fieldwork confirms this development. In public places in Denmark, at schools and workplaces, or simply on the streets, Palestinians are no longer approached as immigrants and asked where they are from; rather, people assume, based on skin color, name, or dialect, that they are Muslims. Today, they are asked questions such as "What is Ramadan all about?" or "How come you don't wear a headscarf?" Whereas Schwartz (1985) identifies the metaphors 'guest' and 'host' as structuring the relationship between native Danes and guest workers, I detect a present-day 'enlightenment project' in the Danish public discourse on Muslims. If the discourse on guest workers focuses on the economy and that on immigrants focuses on culture, the discourse on Muslims focuses on mindsets. Culture is no longer conceived as the primary obstacle to integration; instead, that obstacle is now considered to be how Muslims *think*. While the discourse on culture originally highlighted traditions, that is, how the immigrants dressed or danced, the discourse on the 'Muslim mindset' indicates a belief that the immigrants' outward behavior reveals a specific set of values or ideology.[12]

This discourse can be detected in the Canon of Culture launched by Mikkelsen, as well as in the cartoons of the Prophet in *Jyllands-Posten* and in several recent public debates in Denmark on the topics of headscarves and private Muslim elementary schools, among others. However, the rest of this chapter will focus on the Canon of Culture, the cartoons of the Prophet Muhammad, and the case of Layal, a young Palestinian woman. By choosing three very different examples of statements with different senders—the minister of culture, a private newspaper, and ordinary pedestrians in a suburb of Copenhagen—I hope to show that the printing of the cartoons was not an exceptional act committed by a right-wing newspaper. Rather, my contention is that the controversy brought out a general discourse on Muslims, one that is invoked in many different settings and at many different levels in Danish society.[13]

The Canon of Culture

One of the first initiatives of the newly elected right-wing government in 2001 was to start what it referred to as a 'battle of culture' or a 'battle of values'.[14] This campaign was originally directed at what were referred to as 'judges of taste'. In his New Year's speech in 2002, Prime Minister Anders Fogh Rasmussens declared, "We believe that human beings are best choosing for themselves. We do not need experts and 'judges of taste' to decide on our behalf," adding that the government would remove all superfluous councils and advisory boards.[15] In December 2004, Mikkelsen launched the second phase of the battle of culture by introducing his idea of a national Canon of Culture. According to the minister, the purpose of the canon was to start a debate on "what it means to be Danish at a time when the nation-state is under pressure and globalization is encroaching."[16] In September 2005, just before the canon was made public, Mikkelsen elaborated on his vision at the annual national conference of the Conservative Party. As reported by the *Konservative Landsråd*, the minister announced that "the new frontier in the battle of culture" was "immigrants from Muslim countries who refuse to acknowledge Danish culture and European norms." He asserted that "a medieval Muslim culture will never become as valid as the Danish culture that grew out of the old soil between Skagen and Gedser and between Dueodde and Blåvandshuk."[17] He also stated that Danes cannot accept that "in the midst of our country a parallel society is developing in which minorities are practicing their medieval norms and undemocratic mindsets." Finally, he proceeded to give examples, such as gender segregation at public Islamic meetings and the dilemma of an author who was writing a book on Islam and who had difficulties in finding an illustrator who would agree to draw the face of Muhammad. Summing up, Mikkelsen declared, "We have to defend democracy and freedom of speech," and characterized "cultural armament" as "the best vaccine against undemocratic tendencies within the society." He ended his speech by proclaiming, "We will fight for Western values like democracy, equality, and human rights."[18]

What is most striking about the speech is that 'immigrants' have become synonymous with 'Muslims', who are again synonymous with 'Islam', and all three categories stand in an opposed and antagonistic relation to the old Danish culture that stems from the soil itself. It is also interesting that the word 'old' in relation to something Danish indicates 'authenticity', whereas 'old' in relation to immigrants or Muslims indicates 'medieval'. Furthermore, given that it is a Danish minister who is speaking, it is interesting that the value of equality is directed only at Muslim gender relations, not at ethnic relations within Danish society.

Mikkelsen's conference speech revealed a rather schematic perception of Danes and immigrants. Danes were characterized by Western values (democracy, gender equality, freedom of speech, human rights), while immigrants were characterized as being Muslim (medieval, equipped with an undemocratic mindset, and lacking freedom of speech and human rights). Although Mikkelsen situated immigrants in the Middle Ages, he also offered them a way out. If integration in the 1990s was the political instrument that would overcome cultural differences, Mikkelsen suggested a new 'cure' for treating undemocratic mindsets—the 'vaccine' of 'cultural armament'. It would be a question of educating them, of offering them knowledge, or, as the minister framed it, "of making the immigrants and their descendants familiar with Danish society, its history, and its democratic principles." Mikkelsen declared that the government had introduced free access to the National Museum and the Danish National Gallery, in addition to having created a national Canon of Culture "as a gift to all citizens in this country—including the immigrants."[19]

The Face of Muhammad

Five days later, the most widely read Danish daily newspaper, *Jyllands-Posten*, printed an article entitled "The Face of Muhammad,"[20] thus setting off what Danish public opinion has referred to as the biggest national crisis since World War II (Rothstein and Rothstein 2006: 13; Trads 2006: 9). "The Face of Muhammad" consists of a short text and 12 cartoons. Just above the text is a subtitle reading "Freedom of Speech." The article starts by summing up different examples of self-censorship in relation to Islam: the author whom Mikkelsen referred to in his speech is invoked again, as is the removal of a piece of artwork from a museum out of the "fear of Muslim reaction." The text moves on to state that "modern secular society is rejected by some Muslims. They demand an exceptional position, insisting on special consideration for their own religious feelings. This is incompatible with secular democracy and freedom of speech, where one has to put up with insults, mockery, and ridicule. It is certainly not always attractive and nice to look at, and it does not mean that religious feelings should be made fun of at any price, but that is of minor importance in the present context."[21] Finally, the text explains how *Jyllands-Posten* has called on illustrators to draw Muhammad as they see him.

Encircling the text are the 12 drawings, which can be roughly divided into three categories. The first category consists of five cartoons that are meta-comments on the task itself. One of the cartoons, for instance, shows a schoolboy named Mohammed who is pointing at a blackboard where it is written in Arabic: "The editors of *Jyllands-Posten* are a bunch of reactionary provocateurs." The second category is illustrated by two drawings that depict the Prophet in a naturalistic or symbolic way. The third category contains five cartoons that more explicitly comment on Muslims and Islam itself. Since these last cartoons are the ones that my informants would refer to, I will describe three of them. The first cartoon depicts the Prophet with a bomb in his turban and the Islamic creed printed on the bomb itself. The second shows the Prophet holding a scimitar, flanked by two women in burqas, while the third shows five stylized female figures with facial features in the shape of a crescent moon and a star. This last cartoon is accompanied by a short poem: "Prophet! You crazy bloke! Keeping women under the yoke!"

The text of the *Jyllands-Posten* article is very much in line with the rhetoric of Mikkelsen in the sense that modern secular democracy is being put in opposition to Muslims and Islam. The cartoons are more differentiated and not all of them address Muslims; some of them are pointed at the newspaper itself. However, four of the cartoons associate the Prophet with violence and/or the repression of woman. Seen as a whole, the project has a lecturing tone: Muslims must learn that in a secular democracy, religious feelings are subordinated to freedom of speech.

The Case of Layal

Finally, I will briefly describe the case of Layal to illustrate how random citizens of Denmark invoke the discourse on Muslims. Layal came to Denmark from Lebanon when she was 7 years old. Although her family has a Muslim background, she did not have a religious upbringing, and her mother does not wear a headscarf. Nonetheless, inspired by an Arabic television show hosted by the Egyptian preacher Amr Khaled, Layal decided to put on a headscarf when she was 20 years old.[22] Until then, she had been classified by those in her surroundings as 'Danish', due to her blue eyes, brown hair, and light skin color. Perceived as likable and promising, she never had any problems obtaining jobs. However, according to Layal, all that changed when she decided to wear a headscarf. At job interviews, the employees explicitly stated that the headscarf was a problem, either in relation to the customers or to her potential colleagues. She finally got a job at Amnesty International in one of their 'face-to-face' campaigns to recruit new members.

Together with two colleagues, she was sent to a Copenhagen suburb and, equipped with a portfolio, started her first day at work in a small town square. In her portfolio were three campaigns: one condemning torture, one condemning violence against women, and one advocating freedom of speech. However, when Layal approached people, they soon started discussing her instead of the campaigns. Shouting at her, a man asked how was she supposed to teach him anything about discrimination and suppression when she was obviously oppressed herself. The man was quite large, and Layal felt intimidated and unprepared for this kind of attack. Later, she approached an elderly woman, who told Layal that she would not have anything to do with a "scarf girl." The woman continued: "You should return to your homeland and try to improve things down there before you start criticizing us." Layal explained that she herself was Danish, but the woman dismissed her and her explanations. Layal told me that she did manage to sign up some people, but only by humiliating herself. Over and over, she had to explain that she was not oppressed, that her husband did not beat her up, and that Denmark was her homeland. Layal was exhausted. During the first week, one of her colleagues, who also wore a headscarf, was spat at, and their superior at Amnesty International emphasized that they should call the police if they were physically attacked. After one and a half weeks, Layal resigned. She says that she would recommend working for Amnesty International to anyone—but if a woman is wearing a headscarf, she has to be really strong.

Layal's story is interesting because it turns things upside down. Most of the young Palestinians I know are used to being distinguished as Muslims due to their skin color. However, Layal happens to have a fair complexion and was unprepared for the reactions that she experienced when she decided to wear a headscarf. Of course, she was transforming herself by starting to take up Islamic practices, but the biggest change was how other people reacted to her. From being a polite and promising young woman, she had turned into an oppressed Muslim woman. Despite this, I believe that what really sparked off the harsh responses while Layal was working for Amnesty International was not the headscarf itself, nor the fact that she was Muslim, but rather the combination of being Muslim and advocating human rights. Layal was inadvertently combining two opposing categories—the 'medieval, oppressed Muslim' (represented by the scarf) and the 'enlightened modern West' (Amnesty International, human rights)—and I suggest that it was this crossover that resulted in the condemnatory reactions. Layal was not only combining these two opposing categories but also reversing and challenging the power relations between them.

The Discourse on Muslims as an Enlightenment Project

What is most striking in the above examples is that Danes and Muslims are constituted as antagonistic oppositions in a hierarchical relationship. If we scrutinize them, a scheme of dichotomies in the Danish discourse on immigrants

TABLE 1 Dichotomies in the Danish discourse on immigrants

Ethnic Danes	Immigrants
Western	Muslim
Secularism	Islam
Modern	Medieval
Democratic	Totalitarian
Freedom of speech	Censorship
Human rights	Religious dogmas
Gender equality	Oppression of women
Peaceful	Violent

emerges, as illustrated in table 1.[23] If, for a moment, we focus on the content of the scheme, it might be worth bearing in mind Edward Said's ([1978] 1995) central thesis in *Orientalism: Western Conceptions of the Orient.* According to Said, the 'Orient' in Orientalism does not reflect the actual Orient; rather, the constructed Orient reflects the West. In other words, analyzing the content of the discourse on Muslims does not grant us insight into who Muslims are but instead illustrates how the West, including Denmark, is constructing itself. I will therefore concentrate on the left-hand column in the above scheme, which describes how Danes perceive themselves. This column lists traits and values that are all associated with the intellectual movement of the European Enlightenment, dating from the late seventeenth century to the late eighteenth century. When I refer to an 'enlightenment project', it is because the left-hand column is not just about how Danes construct themselves. It also indicates what immigrants or Muslims should strive to become.

The enlightenment discourse on Muslims is, of course, not an exact replica of the original Enlightenment but rather a contemporary, selective resampling of the values associated with the Enlightenment. In the foreword to a history textbook for Danish high-school pupils, the author comments on the 2005 proclamation of the Ministry of Education on the subject of history. He writes that the episoding of history is a rather arbitrary piece of engineering that reflects the concerns of the present as much as the past. According to him, the ministry's designation of a historical period from 1453 to 1776 reflects a contemporary interest in the relationship between Islam and the West (Thiedecke 2005: 10).[24] According to the textbook, one of the central paradigms of the Enlightenment was that human beings are born with reason and are capable of independent thinking (Kant in Thiedecke 2005: 66–67). Immanuel Kant argued that, through enlightenment, the human being, and society as such, could liberate itself from both secular and religious authorities (ibid.). In this interpretation, the Enlightenment is presented as an attempt to make society progress and to counter both absolute monarchy and the religious thinking that predominated at the time.[25] Besides Kant, the textbook introduces extracts from the writings of the philosopher John Locke, who is often credited with the idea of the separation of church and state. These two philosophers are also high-lighted in the Canon on Democracy that the Danish government launched in 2007.[26] According to the textbook and the Canon on Democracy, the concepts of democracy, equality, freedom of speech, and human rights are an outcome of the Enlightenment.[27]

An article in a recent issue of *Kritik*, a well-known Danish literary journal, is relevant here. Among the many contributions that pay tribute to the Enlightenment in this special issue is a brief critical essay by a Danish philosopher, Søren Klausen (2008), entitled "Hold Your Horses!" Commenting on the renewed interest in the Enlightenment in Danish public debate, he calls the current version "the smug Enlightenment" and accuses it of being out of touch with the original spirit of the Enlightenment in terms of self-criticism and nuances (ibid.: 30–31). According to Klausen, the contemporary discourse is character-ized by the glorification of the present, a dogmatic liberalism, and the fetishism of rights and principles (ibid.: 31). The case of Layal illustrates this in the sense that the principles of human rights seemed more important to the passers-by than the particular human being whom they were addressing. Badiou (2001: 14) writes that the ethics engrained in human rights are based on an a priori determination of evil, as a result of which "ethics prevents itself from thinking the singularity of situations as such." This is exactly what we find with regard to Layal, as well as the cartoons in *Jyllands-Posten*. In this sense, these cases demonstrate that values such as equality, human rights, and freedom of speech are not neutral concepts. Rather, they are part of a wider discourse on Muslims that is used to legitimize what Badiou describes as a "civilizing intervention" (ibid.: 13), examples of which include the canons on culture and democracy, the cartoons published by *Jyllands-Posten*, and the direct face-to-face enlight-enment of Layal. Asad (2003) urges us to study secularism, not just as an intel-lectual argument, but also as a political system that distributes and rearranges forms of suffering, recognizing some while ignoring others. Likewise, the cur-rent enlightenment discourse on Muslims tends to highlight certain kinds of inequality (in relation to gender), while simultaneously downplaying—or even creating—others (in relation to ethnicity). In the same way, it accentuates certain rights (freedom of speech) and practices indifference toward others (freedom of religion).

In attributing the values of a dark historical period to Muslims, while at the same time situating Danes within modern times, an asymmetrical set of oppositions is being constructed. Not only are Muslims assigned to an earlier evolutionary stage, but their traditions (Islam) are at the same time countered as something particularistic in relation to the universal values of the enlight-ened West (cf. Asad 2003: 169). As a consequence, the pedestrians did not see Layal as a young woman advocating human rights. Instead, she came to embody specific values attributed to a pre-modern time. Whereas the guest worker was perceived through economic relations (a kind of exchange), and immigrants were perceived through their culture (a kind of luggage that they had brought along from their 'homeland'), 'medieval mindsets' are located inside the brain of each individual Muslim. The discourse on culture was also essentializing, but the approach of invoking mindsets, which are even more difficult to change, digs one level deeper into the person. As Mikkelsen framed it in his speech, "The battle of culture will be long and tough."[28]

Finally, I suggest that, in terms of discourse, there is no one-to-one correspondence between specific human beings and the enlightenment discourse on Muslims. Not only is this discourse invoked by both secular and Christian Danes across the political divisions within Danish society, it is also invoked by Muslims themselves. Among Palestinians, it is used to criticize and distance oneself from other immigrants. One example occurred at the demonstration described above, when Khadije, a young Palestinian girl, evaluated the form of the demonstration as medieval.

Studying How the World Comes into Being: Creating Muslims in a Danish Setting

In every event, the world is created anew. While events reveal and come into being through the structures of society, they simultaneously create the self-same structures. In this sense, every event is unique and has a creative potential (cf. Kapferer 2006: 136). By using situational analysis as developed by Gluckman, it becomes possible to study and analyze this creation.

The publication of the cartoons and the subsequent demonstration were part of a range of events that not only manifested a discourse on immigrants but also transformed it. The fact that the discursive formation 'Muslim' has come to designate a mindset of specific medieval values implies that Palestinians are perceived not only as Muslims but also as a certain kind of human being, regardless of how they actually live their lives. Although the participants in the demonstration went down on their knees to pray for peace, this was interpreted by others as a hostile act. When the participants shouted "Islam is peace," it was heard as "Islam is angry." And while Layal was advocating women's rights for Amnesty International, she was perceived as a repressed woman who was unaware of her own rights.

Gerd Baumann (2004: 19) summarizes three different possible structures that are inherent in the creation of alterity. One is an Orientalist structure based on Said's work from 1978, another is a segmentary structure based on Evans-Pritchard's work from 1940, and the third is a structure of encompassment based on Dumont's studies of caste and hierarchy from 1980. Inspired by Baumann's distinctions, it is possible to trace a structural development over time in the creation of alterity in Denmark. According to Schwartz (1985, 1990), in the 1970s, guest workers were perceived and used as a cheap labor force and studied through the lens of Marxist theories on class. This approach to alterity can be identified as a structure of encompassment. As Baumann (2004: 25) puts it, "Encompassment means an act of selfing by appropriating ... selected kinds of othering." Since it is the self that does the encompassment, it always involves a hierarchy (ibid.: 26). If Danish society in the 1970s thought of itself in terms of classes, the immigrants were incorporated at the bottom of this hierarchy as workers, and then only as temporary (as guests). The discourse on culture in the 1980s and 1990s, on the other hand, followed a classic Orientalist structure, where the Other is a mirror of oneself (ibid.: 20). The Other is not just a negative reflection but is also used to mirror one's own flaws in the form of self-criticism, which is why minorities could be seen simultaneously as backward and traditional, as exotic and mystical.

What is striking about the current discourse on Muslims is that it appears as an amputated structure of Orientalism in the sense that the Other is defined only in negative terms. Whereas the culture of Muslims could be perceived as exotic or interesting, their mindsets do not have these positive connotations but are instead perceived as a threat. It was no coincidence that the Palestinians referred to the Canon of Culture as the 'Cannon' of Culture: this simply reflected the fact that the discourse on Muslims often borrows its terms from the language of warfare. Both the minister of culture and Layal herself, as well as four of the cartoons depicted in the article "The Face of Muhammad," used metaphors or symbols originating from the field of war.

Baumann (2004: 42) writes that the implosion of grammar is characterized by a return to the anti-grammar of 'we are good, so they are bad' and illustrates this structural breakdown by referring to genocide. I do not think that this is what is at stake here. I suggest that the amputated and warlike discourse reflects the fact that, in both structure and content, the discourse on Muslims in Denmark runs parallel to, and is sometimes conflated with, the discourse on terrorism. This was also obvious in the Danish debate following the printing of the cartoons. The critics asserted that *Jyllands-Posten* was discriminating against a 'religious minority',[29] while others argued that Muslims in Denmark were part of a global community that was threatening and attacking Western values.[30] In this sense, the discourse on Muslims differs from previous discourses on immigrants in Denmark. Emphasizing the Muslim background of immigrants also implies contesting whether they are a Danish minority or rather the local representatives of a global religious community that is defined as a threat to the Western world, including Denmark (cf. Asad 1997: 186).

Conclusion

The transformation of the discourse on immigrants in Denmark is part of a global shift in power relations. The attack on the Twin Towers in 2001 and the subsequent 'war on terror' have altered the perception of Muslim immigrants in particular.[31] However, the cartoon crisis did not simply reconstruct certain structures between ethnic Danes and immigrants. It succeeded in accomplishing something that until then had been impossible to achieve—uniting Muslims in Denmark, regardless of ethnic affiliations, different congregations, and differences due to class, generation, and so on.[32] By offending the main symbol of Islam, *Jyllands-Posten* engendered a discursive space within which Muslims could join together. Whereas the Danish prime minister refused to meet with representatives of other nations (i.e., Middle Eastern ambassadors and the

Palestinian representative) to discuss the controversy,[33] the Danish Muslim congregations were handed a political platform from which they could protest through demonstrations, a lawsuit against *Jyllands-Posten*, and global advocacy among Muslim leaders and institutions.

In this sense, the demonstration communicated two messages. First, it addressed the Danish nation by challenging its discourse on Muslims. In its form as well as in its content, the demonstration opposed this perception as medieval and violent, sending the message that Muslims are civilized and peaceful. It did so by choosing a democratically recognized form of protest, by obeying Danish traffic regulations, by communicating in Danish and through written and verbal statements, such as "Islam is peace," "No to racism and fanaticism, yes to peace and co-existence," and "Yes to dialogue, no to clash of civilizations," challenging the thesis of Samuel P. Huntington (1996).[34] Second, the demonstration challenged a Muslim and Middle Eastern audience simultaneously to see who would stand up for Muslims in a time of crisis. The outcome revealed the powerlessness of local national Arab leaders, but simultaneously united Muslims in Denmark and worldwide (if only for a moment).

This also explains why the 12 cartoons attracted widespread attention. The cartoon controversy became globally known because of its worldwide local potentials—that is, not because it insulted a pre-existing global Muslim community, but because it created a discursive space that any Muslim group could enter and use to counter local Arab regimes and Western hegemonies. For instance, in Palestine, Hamas won the parliamentary elections on 25 January 2006. In the following week, the Al-Aqsa Martyrs' Brigades (associated with the nationalist party Fatah), Islamic Jihad, and Hamas all organized demonstrations against the cartoons. These protests did not just address *Jyllands-Posten* or Denmark but also promoted the organizations themselves in the ongoing power struggle between nationalist and Islamic movements in Palestine. Thus, while the cartoons created a political platform on which Muslims could unite and form a dominant opposition, it is only through an exploration of the local political contexts that one can understand the timing and content of the continuous protests and attacks on Danish embassies worldwide.

Gluckman offers us a method whereby we are able to analyze the creation of the structures of the wider society by studying the micro-politics of specific events. It is exactly this methodological grasp linking events with structures that still makes situational analysis an apt method for studying the world in the twenty-first century. It has become fashionable to highlight the global state of the world. New technologies such as the Internet and cell phones are said to have created new time-space compressions that make local fieldwork redundant. Different attempts have been made to rethink fieldwork, for instance, by following the social biography of things (Kopytoff 1986) or by conducting multisited ethnography (Marcus 1995). However, I think we should be careful not to conflate the empirical and analytical levels of our observations. Multiplying periods of fieldwork locally or following people or things across nation-states does not necessarily give us a better or even a different insight into how the world is constituted. If anthropology is the study of human beings, then it does not matter, on an empirical level, whether the context is designated as global, national, or local.[35] What does matter is how on the analytical level we make sense of the world—how we are able to move beyond or at least link the actions and feelings of positioned individuals with wider social and political structures. Situational analysis provides a starting point for this.

Gluckman ([1940] 1958: 26–27) has been criticized for his concept of 'equilibrium', his emphasis on social continuity in the face of change (see van Teeffelen 1977 for a critique). However, in the present case I think Gluckman's conservative outlook is worth considering before we jump to conclusions. We should not be seduced by the global scale of the cartoon controversy into believing that it sparked a process of disruption or disorganization. A shift might have occurred on one level, but on another level nothing has really changed. To borrow a French saying, "Plus ça change, plus c'est la même chose" (cf. Sahlins in Kapferer 2006: 127). The cartoon controversy might have re-created the discourse on Muslims, and it might have generated a political platform that Muslims all over the world could use to promote their own agendas. However, it did not change the structural relationship between the Danish majority and minorities. Although the Palestinians, along with other immigrant groups in Denmark, were reconceptualized as Muslims, they continue to represent the Other.

Anja Kublitz is an Assistant Professor of Global Refugee Studies in the Department of Culture and Global Studies at Aalborg University. She has a PhD in Anthropology and has conducted 8 months of fieldwork in the Occupied Palestinian Territories and 16 months of fieldwork among Palestinians in Denmark. Her research interests are, among others, mutations of conflicts and configurations of political activists. Her recent publications include "The Ongoing Catastrophe: Erosion of Life in the Danish Camps" (forthcoming), "From Revolutionaries to Muslims: Liminal Becomings across Palestinian Generations in Denmark" (forthcoming) and "Seizing Catastrophes: The Temporality of Nakba among Palestinians in Denmark" (2013).

Notes

1. This chapter is based on one year of fieldwork among Palestinians from Lebanon who are residing in Denmark. Palestinians constitute one of the largest refugee groups in the country, and they played a prominent role in the protests against the cartoons of the Prophet.
2. For the purpose of this chapter, I will use Foucault's concept of 'discursive formation'. 'Discursive formation' designates the relationship between statements (Foucault 1972: 31). It is "the regularity of the irregular distribution of statements" (Andersen 2003: vi; see Foucault 1972: 141–148). Statements are practices that systematically form the object of which they speak, as well as the subject it enables to speak (Foucault 1972: 40–56), that is, a "statement creates discursive spaces from which something can be stated" (Andersen 2003: 11). I combine a situational analysis of the demonstration with a discursive analysis in order to show how the discourse on immigrants is manifested and transformed in the event, creating a religious opposition.

3. From December 2005 to February 2006, numerous demonstrations and other protests against the cartoons took place worldwide. More than 100 people were killed during these protests, while the cartoonists themselves received several death threats. In addition, a consumer boycott of Danish products was initiated, and the Organization of the Islamic Conference (OIC) forwarded a letter of protest to the Danish prime minister and to the Organization for Security and Co-operation in Europe (OSCE). Since then, the cartoons have been reactualized over and over again. In recent developments, the Parisian weekly *Charlie Hebdoe* was attacked on 7 January 2015, and 11 people were killed. The newspaper is known for its satirical drawings of the Prophet and had published a reprint of the Danish cartoons. On 14 February 2015, a young Danish Palestinian man opened fire at a cultural center in Copenhagen where Swedish artist Lars Vilks, who also is known for his cartoons of the Prophet, was speaking. One man was killed. The same night, the gunman killed a Jewish security guard in front of Copenhagen's main synagogue, after which he himself was shot and killed by police. For overviews of the development of the cartoon controversy, see Hansen and Hundevadt (2006), Jerichow and Rode (2006), Lindekilde et al. (2009), and Kublitz (2011).

4. The Canon of Culture is a selection of the most important Danish artifacts within seven different fields of art, for example, literature, music, and so on. This is explained in more detail in the pages that follow.

5. "Tale: Kulturkampen bliver lang og sej," *Information*, 27 September 2005. Throughout the chapter, I refer to different Danish media. *Jyllands-Posten*, *Information*, and *Politiken* are Danish daily newspapers. Ritzau is a Danish news agency. Along the political spectrum, *Jyllands-Posten* is considered right-wing, *Politiken* is closer to the Labour Party (Socialdemokratiet) and *Information* is associated with the leftist parties in Danish policy (cf. Hervik and Berg 2007: 25).

6. Established in 1995, the Danish People's Party was and is primarily known for agitating for a strict policy against immigrants and refugees. As a result of the 2001 election, it became the third largest party in Denmark.

7. "Sæt muslimer i russiske fængsler," Ritzau, 29 September 2005.

8. "Muhammeds ansigt," *Jyllands-Posten*, 30 September 2005.

9. The label *kulturradikale* refers to left-wing artists and intellectuals who dominated the cultural scene in Denmark in the 1960s.

10. See Olwig and Pærregaard (2007a) for a discussion of the concept of 'integration'.

11. For ethnographic cases involving this reconceptualization, see Johansen (2007) and Pedersen (2007).

12. This overview is admittedly rather schematic. The actual development has been much more fluid and gradual, and today, within different spheres of Danish society, all three discourses can be identified. However, I will argue that during my fieldwork the discourse on Muslims dominated.

13. I do not intend to assert that this discourse is specifically 'Danish' in any way, for I suspect that the development of the representation of immigrants in Denmark is quite similar to that in other European countries. See, for instance, Baumann (1996) for an analysis of the discourse on immigrants in London.

14. After eight years of Social Democratic rule, a right-wing government came to power in November 2001. The government was based on a coalition between Venstre (the Liberal Party of Denmark) and the Conservative Party and was supported by the Danish People's Party.

15. "Statsminister Anders Fogh Rasmussens Nytårstale 2002," Statsministeriet, http://www. stm.dk/_p_7354.html (accessed 11 November 2010).

16. "Hvad vil det sige at være dansk?" Ritzau, 8 December 2004.

17. "Kulturminister Brian Mikkelsens tale," *Konservative Landsråd*, 25 September 2005, http:// lr05.konservative.dk/modules.php?op = modload&name = News&file = article&sid = 70 (accessed 11 November 2010). The sites referred to designate the farthest corners of the country of Denmark.

18. Ibid.
19. Ibid.
20. "Muhammeds ansigt," *Jyllands-Posten*, 30 September 2005.
21. Ibid.
22. Gluckman (1963: 143) writes that the emergence of religious movements and the return to old rituals in South Africa can be seen as responses to modernity instead of cultural leftovers. Likewise, Layal's decision to wear a headscarf should be perceived as a modern token rather than as a retreat to an ancient Palestinian custom.
23. In a study of how the Danish media covered religion in 2001, a rather similar scheme is presented that opposes the Danish understanding of Christianity to Islam. The author adds that whereas Christianity is perceived as rational and associated with reason, Islam is perceived as irrational and characterized by obedience (Hervik 2002: 211).
24. With regard to the significance of this time frame, in 1453 the Muslim Ottomans conquered Constantinople, while in 1776 the United States Declaration of Independence was signed and Adam Smith's *The Wealth of Nations*, which contributed to the development of classical liberalism, was published. The year 1776 is used by the Ministry of Education to demarcate the end of the Enlightenment, although the author of the textbook chooses to include France's 1789 Declaration of the Rights of Man and of the Citizen (Thiedecke 2005: 10–11).
25. See Badiou (2001: 8) for a critique of the "immense 'return to Kant.'"
26. "Demokratikanon," Undervisnings Ministeriet, 31 May 2007, http://pub.uvm.dk/2008/demokratikanon/hel.html (accessed 11 November 2010).
27. Ralf Pittelkow (2002), a current political commentator at *Jyllands-Posten*, has written a book entitled *After September 11th: The West and Islam*. In it, he maintains that the difference between the West and the 'Islamic world' is that the former was transformed during the Enlightenment, whereas the latter never went through this transformation (ibid.: 9).
28. The discourse on Muslims also comprises legislation addressing Muslims and other immigrants, such as legislation on family reunion (Rytter 2007). In the spring of 2009, the Danish Parliament passed a law forbidding the use of political and religious symbols, including headscarves, in the Danish courts. This ban affects only judges. See http://www.womendialogue.org/magazine/headscarves-danish-workplaces.
29. See the letter from 22 former Danish ambassadors in "Danske ambassadører leverer skarp kritik af Fogh," *Politiken*, 19 December 2005, http://politiken.dk/indland/ECE132427/danske-ambassadoerer-leverer-skarp-kritik-af-fogh/.
30. See the newsletter of the Danish People's Party, dated 6 January 2006, at http://www.danskfolkeparti.dk.
31. Denmark has taken an active part in the 'war on terror', both militarily, by being engaged in the war in Afghanistan (since 2002) and the war in Iraq (since 2003), and legally, by passing a law on terror in 2002, which has resulted in several trials on terror.
32. In September 2005, the most widely read article on the Web page of one of the biggest Danish Muslim congregations was entitled "The Divisions and (Lack of) Choices of the Muslims." The article addressed the lack of unity and cooperation among Muslims and Muslim institutions in Denmark. See "Muslimernes splittelse og (fra)valg," *Det Islamiske Troessamfund i Danmark*, 20 March 2005, http://wakf.com/wakfweb/news.nsf/ByUID/ABB83C29463CDAD0C1256FCA0008356A?OpenDocument (accessed 11 November 2010).
33. In October 2005, 10 ambassadors from Middle Eastern countries and the Palestinian representative addressed a letter to Prime Minister Rasmussens, asking for a meeting concerning the cartoons. The prime minister turned down the request (Jerichow and Rode 2006: 24–25, 28).
34. Huntington (1996) proposed that, in the post–Cold War world, the cultural and religious identities of people would be the principal source of conflict.
35. The world was also 'global' at the time of Gluckman's fieldwork ([1940] 1958: 62): "Since Zululand is a territorial section of the world system, its developments are determined by structural relations in the whole system."

References

Andersen, Niels Å. 2003. *Discursive Analytical Strategies: Understanding Foucault, Koselleck, Laclau, Luhmann*. Bristol: Policy Press.

Asad, Talal. 1997. "Europe against Islam: Islam in Europe." *Muslim World* 87, no. 2: 183–195.

Asad, Talal. 2003. *Formations of the Secular: Christianity, Islam, Modernity*. Stanford, CA: Stanford University Press.

Badiou, Alain. 2001. *Ethics: An Essay on the Understanding of Evil*. London: Verso.

Baumann, Gerd. 1996. *Contesting Culture: Discourses of Identity in Multi-ethnic London*. Cambridge: Cambridge University Press.

Baumann, Gerd. 2004. "Grammars of Identity/Alterity: A Structural Approach." Pp. 18–52 in *Grammars of Identity/Alterity: A Structural Approach*, eds. G. Bauman and A. Gingrich. New York and Oxford: Berghahn Books.

Foucault, Michel. 1972. *The Archaeology of Knowledge and the Discourse on Language*. New York: Pantheon Books.

Gluckman, Max. [1940] 1958. *Analysis of a Social Situation in Modern Zululand*. Manchester: Manchester University Press for the Rhodes-Livingstone Institute.

Gluckman, Max. 1963. *Order and Rebellion in Tribal Africa*. London: Cohen & West.

Hansen, John, and Kim Hundevadt. 2006. *Provoen og profeten: Muhammedkrisen bag kulisserne*. Aarhus: Jyllands-Postens Forlag.

Hervik, Peter. 2002. *Mediernes Muslimer: En antropologisk undersøgelse af mediernes dækning af religioner i Danmark*. Copenhagen: Nævnet for Etnisk Ligestilling.

Hervik, Peter, and Clarissa Berg. 2007. "Denmark: A Political Struggle in Danish Journalism." Pp. 25–39 in *Reading the Mohammed Cartoons Controversy: An International Analysis of Press Discourses on Free Speech and Political Spin*, ed. Risto Kunelius, Elizabeth Eide, Oliver Hahn, and Roland Schroeder. Working Papers in International Journalism. Berlin: Projektverlag.

Huntington, Samuel P. 1996. *The Clash of Civilizations and the Remaking of World Order*. New York: Simon and Schuster.

Jerichow, Anders, and Mille Rode, eds. 2006. *Profet-affæren: Et PEN-dossier om 12 Muhammed-tegninger—og hvad der siden hændte ... Dokumenter og argumenter*. Copenhagen: Danske PEN.

Johansen, Katrine S. 2007. "Kategorisering i psykiatrien." Pp. 155–172 in Olwig and Pærregaard 2007b.

Kapferer, Bruce. 2006. "Situations, Crisis, and the Anthropology of the Concrete: The Contribution of Max Gluckman." Pp. 118–155 in *The Manchester School: Practice and Ethnographic Praxis in Anthropology*, ed. T. M. S Evens and Don Handelman. New York: Berghahn Books.

Klausen, Søren H. 2008. "Klap hesten! Forsvar for en ydmyg oplysning." *Kritik* 188: 29–43.

Kopytoff, Igor. 1986. "The Cultural Biography of Things: Commoditization as a Process." Pp. 64–91 in *The Social Life of Things: Commodities in Cultural Perspective*, ed. Arjun Appadurai. Cambridge: Cambridge University Press.

Kublitz, Anja. 2011. "The Mutable Conflict: A Study of How the Palestinian-Israeli Conflict Is Actualized among Palestinians in Denmark." PhD diss., University of Copenhagen.

Lindekilde, Lasse, Per Mouritsen, and Ricard Zapata-Barrero. 2009. "The Muhammad Cartoons Controversy in Comparative Perspective." *Ethnicities* 9, no. 3: 291–313.

Malkki, Liisa. 1995. *Purity and Exile: Violence, Memory, and National Cosmology among Hutu Refugees in Tanzania*. Chicago: University of Chicago Press.

Marcus, George. 1995. "Ethnography in/of the World System: The Emergence of Multi-sited Ethnography." *Annual Review of Anthropology* 24: 95–117.

Mørck, Yvonne. 1998. *Bindestregsdanskere: Fortællinger om køn, generationer og etnicitet*. Frederiksberg: Forlaget Sociologi.

Olwig, Karen F., and Karsten Pærregaard. 2007a. "Integration: Antropologiske perspektiver." Pp. 9–36 in Olwig and Pærregaard 2007b.

Olwig, Karen F., eds. 2007b. *Integration: Antropologiske perspektiver*. Copenhagen: Museum Tusculanums Forlag.

Pedersen, Marianne H. 2007. "Umm Zainaps rejse." Pp. 191–210 in Olwig and Pærregaard 2007b.

Pittelkow, Ralf. 2006. *Efter 11. September: Vesten og Islam*. Copenhagen: Lindhardt & Ringhof.

Rothstein, Klaus, and Michael Rothstein. 2006. *Bomben i turbanen*. Copenhagen: Tiderne Skifter.

Rytter, Mikkel. 2007. "'Familien Danmark' og 'de fremmede': Slægtskabsbilleder I dansk integrationspolitik." Pp. 63–86 in Olwig and Pærregaard 2007b.

Said, Edward. [1978] 1995. *Orientalism: Western Conceptions of the Orient*. London: Penguin Books.

Said, Edward. 1994. *Representations of the Intellectual*. London: Vintage.

Schwartz, Jonathan M. 1985. *Reluctant Hosts: Denmark's Reception of Guest Workers*. Kultursociologiske Skrifter No. 21. Copenhagen: Akademisk Forlag.

Schwartz, Jonathan M. 1990. "On the Representation of Immigrants in Denmark: A Retrospective." Pp. 42–52 in *Every Cloud Has a Silver Lining: Lectures on Everyday Life, Cultural Production and Race*, ed. Flemming Røgilds. Copenhagen: Akademisk Forlag.

Thiedecke, Johnny. 2005. *Europa i opbrud 1453–1799: Renæssance, reformationer, oplysningstid og kolonisation*. Copenhagen: Pantheon.

Trads, David. 2006. *Islam i flammer: Danskerne og det muslimske oprør*. Copenhagen: Høst & Søns Forlag.

van Teeffelen, Toine. 1977. *Anthropologists on Israel: A Case Study in the Sociology of Knowledge*. Amsterdam: University of Amsterdam.

Chapter 7

STUDYING HUMAN RESOURCE MANAGEMENT
Beyond Corporate Consensus and Colonial Conflicts

Jakob Krause-Jensen

Value/'vælju:/n **1 (a)** [C, U] worth of something in terms of money or other goods for which it can be exchanged ... **2** [U] quality of being useful or worthwhile or important ... **3 values** [pl] moral or professional standards of behaviour; principles: artistic, legal, scientific values ...

— *Oxford Advanced Learners Dictionary*

When I think about my previous job trying to make life easier for Zambian peasants living on approximately DKK 10, it is a little strange for me to be here selling DKK 50,000 televisions.

— *Anthropologist about his work at Bang & Olufsen*

In this chapter I intend to explore the usefulness of the Manchester School in a context that is as different from Max Gluckman's colonial Africa as one could imagine—the world of a private Danish company that produces very expensive

Notes for this chapter begin on page 137.

home electronics (televisions, sound systems, telephones) for the global elite. I will argue that the fundamental legacy of the Manchester School, that is, its sensitivity to complexity and difference and its commitment to developing theories and methods to grasp them, is very helpful when it comes to the study of modern corporations. I also want to suggest, however, that corporate complexity in a 'value-based' organization is of another kind than the conflicts in colonial coke towns. This different reality calls for the development of other supplementary concepts and theoretical takes in order to be adequately grasped.

Value-Based Organizations and the Legacy of the Manchester School

Organizations are social formations whose raison d'être is to perform specific purposes and achieve distinct objectives. They are defined by goal-oriented, instrumental rationality. If looked upon as a process, organization can be described as a continuous effort to impose order for strategic ends. This is clearly also true of business organizations: at the most general level, these sociotopes are characterized by an attempt to align individual aspirations with organizational goals. As an anthropologist I am interested in the fact that many corporations use one of anthropology's key concepts, 'culture', for these purposes. How is it that in the heartland of instrumental, utilitarian rationality, among business organizations that are normally considered to be the frontrunners in processes of disenchantment, we find notions of vision, mission, passion, commitment, culture, and value? How should we understand "the facts-and-figures-oriented corporation's turn toward its soft cultural underbelly" (Marcus 1998: 2)? And how do employees work with and react to these ideas?

Bang & Olufsen, a company that develops and manufactures audiovisual products that are world famous for their distinctive design, was a good place to explore these issues. At the time of my fieldwork in 1999, the company had just defined a new set of values and was arguably the most prominent and publicized example of value-based management in Denmark. This chapter is based on six months of participant observation in Bang & Olufsen, where I worked as a human resource consultant, participating in daily routines, work tasks, and assignments—including seminars, where the company's values were addressed and communicated. During my participation in these social situations, it became clear that working with values was full of ambiguity and lurking contradiction—somewhat like walking a tightrope.

It is a long way from colonial Africa to corporate Denmark, but as I will emphasize in the following, the Manchester approach—including its steady gaze at social situations—has been an important source of inspiration. It is true that the circumstances underpinning this analysis are different from the spectacular political events that are the paradigmatic objects of study in the Manchester tradition (Gluckman [1940] 1958; Kapferer 1995; Lindgren 2006). The societal setting of this study is not a 'social drama' in Turner's sense (1974); it does not even represent an emergent, conjunctive moment in corporate history. It is a 'meeting' in the narrow, pedestrian, bureaucratic meaning of the term. It is a "miniscule type of social setting," one of those "small areas of negotiation" for which Gluckman showed little interest or enthusiasm (Handelman 2006: 106). Furthermore, the clear-cut conflicts implied in the jurisprudential root metaphor of Gluckman's 'extended case' analysis do not characterize the encounters with which I am dealing. On the contrary, these social situations could best be described by their lack of clarity or rather by their systematic ambiguity.

Looked at from a great height, organizations—with their well-defined mandates and precise boundaries—resemble the long-lost, isolated pacific paradise of anthropological inquiry in the structural-functionalist paradigm. This is a mirage, of course, and Gluckman's warning always to be aware of the distinction between the "idealized self-perception of a people of their culture and the more messy realities of historically shifting processes of cultural formation and practice" (Kapferer 2006: 125) is obviously relevant in a business environment, where 'the natives' use notions of culture extensively. What Gluckman (1967: xxiii) wrote in his introduction to *The Craft of Social Anthropology* is still good advice in a corporate environment characterized by flux and rapid change: "[A]s we appreciate more fully that customs and values are to some extent independent of one another, discrepant, conflicting, contradictory, we shall have to evolve concepts to deal with social life which are less rigid and which can cope with lack of interdependence as well as the existence of interdependence, with the haphazard as well as the systematic."

As implied in the entitled *The Craft of Social Anthropology*, another and related legacy from Manchester is a pragmatic view of theory-as-tool. This is not meant to be a narrow fetishization of method; rather, it is a view of theory necessitated by the acknowledgment of the relative indeterminacy and fuzziness of social reality. Concepts should be regarded not as one-size-fits-all systems but as particular equipment suited and developed to solve specific problems that we might encounter along the way. They are instruments of perception that, in Gluckman's words, enable you to "[f]ollow your nose wherever it leads you" (Handelman 2006: 94) and to make sense of your encounters.

The Fundamental Values of Bang & Olufsen

Bang & Olufsen A/S is located in Struer, a town of 20,000 inhabitants in the windswept northwestern periphery of Denmark. The firm is by far the largest industrial workplace here. Since the mid-1990s, the aim of management has been to turn Bang & Olufsen into a value-based corporation. The company's assets no longer refer solely to the bottom line but instead describe some fundamental orientations and attitudes that are not connected to economics in any immediate way. Central to the value-based corporation is the idea that there should be a consistency in how the organization operates, a continuity between what the firm develops and sells and the beliefs and practices of its employees. Thus, in 1997, a process was started to identify a new set of company values that would cover the entire corporation. This platform of ideas was intended to inspire not only designers and product developers but also other company staff who did not live in Struer and who were not directly involved with the product. For a period of six months, a group of internal and external people appointed by management met regularly to brainstorm. They gave each other small assignments to research and investigate particular aspects and issues and finally came up with a report that specified three concepts and briefly stated the reasoning behind each one. A video was produced that explained the values, which were subsequently communicated to managers, key white-collar employees, and retailers through a range of 'value seminars' arranged by the company's Human Resource (HR) Department. The three fundamental values were identified as 'poetry', 'synthesis', and 'excellence'. It was made emphatically clear that these values were not 'invented' or 'produced' but rather 'discovered' or 'recognized'.

When the process of identifying a corporation's values is described in archaeological rather than architectural terms—as a question of discovering (*finde*) an essence rather than a matter of constructing (*opfinde*) a new baseline for company practice—it is a practical example of an attempt to derive an 'ought' from an 'is': obviously, the uncovering of the values is intended to have practical ramifications and normative consequences, or there would be no reason to spend time and money on the effort. It was the explicit intention of the group, however, that the values should *not* be normative in a narrowly prescriptive sense. As Egon, a former HR manager and one of the participants in the group, later told me: "We have the Ten Commandments. That must be enough!"

The question of whether and how the values and the vision actually informed the practices of employees and guided them in their work is difficult (if not impossible) to answer. Gluckman (2006: 20) urged us not to use empirical material just as "apt illustrations," but to include more of the rugged, 'dirty' case material itself in the analysis. This also implies that we should be careful not to assume a simple relationship between verbalized norms and actions (Holy and Stuchlik 1983: 7). This is no less true when it comes to values that are even more remote from practice than norms—figures of speech rather than models for action. As the Norwegian anthropologist Fredrik Barth (1993: 35) observes, "Behind the best-laid plans of mice and men loom nebulous objectives and unresolved alternatives. It is not that values cannot be found—it seems rather as if one finds a surfeit of them: too many, too discrepant, too often disconnected with any field of effective choice, or applied as ways of speaking rather than action, and sometimes, but not always, increasingly vacuous and irrelevant the wider their scope and the more fundamental their pretensions."

Effective collaboration does not depend on belief in a common set of ultimate values. It is a fact that many, if not the majority, of the employees below the managerial level and outside the Human Resources and Marketing Departments did not know that the firm's three values had been identified as poetry, synthesis, and excellence. The abstract nature of the values and the official claim that employees "live them without thinking about them" (as put by one HR consultant) seem to render meaningless, from any point of view, an empirical investigation of the extent to which the values are reflected in the practices of the employees. However, this does not mean that the discourse on values and vision should be dismissed as free-floating rhetoric, devoid of practical consequence. Values and vision are powerful corporate concerns, and even if they do not have the assumed direct effect on corporate action—and even if they reflect mostly managerial fantasies—they became keywords in the company's cosmology, legitimating particular corporate strategies and priorities and the allocation of corporate resources. Thus, in 1999, it was decided to double the marketing budget from DKK 50 million to DKK 100 million per year. The new strategic emphasis on communication and human resources—the areas whose primary concern was the articulation and implementation of the values in organizational development and external communication—was emphasized by the fact that a new HR senior manager was appointed and that the company's CEO, Anders Knutsen, took direct responsibility in these two areas. But why spend money on the effort? What is the value of values?

The Value of Values

I believe that the current popularity of the notion of values in business management owes something to semantics. In this respect, some comparative insight might be gained by looking at values in the functionalist perspective of a former pupil in the Manchester School, Victor Turner, and his analysis of Ndembu ritual. Arguing that ritual symbols are 'multi-vocal', that they are systematically vague or open-ended in the sense that they condense and combine the normative with the physiological, Turner (1974: 55) states: "The drama of ritual action ... causes an exchange between these poles in which the biological referents are ennobled and the normative referents are charged with emotional significance." A clue to the current popularity of the discourse of value in managerial programs has to do with the fact that the concept of value contains a similar ambiguity. The value of value lies in its ability—on an abstract level—to resolve a potential contradiction between the 'hard' bottom line and 'soft' human concerns. Apparently, it offers a prospect of 'having your cake and eating it too', as Thomas Peters and Robert Waterman summed up culture management over 25 years ago.[1]

Majken Schultz, a professor at the Copenhagen Business School who at some point supervised the value process at Bang & Olufsen, argues that the foundation of value-based management differs radically from company to company. The emphasis can range from a strong focus on ethics to a concern with the company's position on the market: "But disregarding the content of the value base, the aim is the same in all cases: to earn money and create value for the stockholders. Because of the new knowledge accounting, ethical accounting, and environmental accounting, etc., the stockholders have really acknowledged the immaterial values. The stakeholders are profitable" (*Børsen*, 5 March 1999).

As this quotation suggests, the word 'value' harbors a double meaning. It describes "that which is worthy of esteem for its own sake; that which has intrinsic worth"; yet it also denotes "the material or monetary worth of something"

(*Oxford English Dictionary*). The word thus establishes an immediate translatability between, on the one hand, the bedrock bottom-line objectives of the economic enterprise (i.e., the need to generate profit) and, on the other, our most profound personal orientations and deepest moral imperatives—that which is *not* for sale.[2] Thus, the word 'value', through its reference to both the material and the immaterial, helps to ennoble the material pole and to render the moral one strategically significant. A similar duality is contained in the concept 'human resources', which has connotations that are simultaneously passive/objectifying (humans as resources) and active/subjectifying (resourceful humans).

As with the workings of Turner's ritual symbols,[3] continuously oscillating between the normative or societal and the emotional or individual aspects, through the abstract concepts of 'value' and 'human resources', ideally "a milieu is created in which a society's members cannot see any fundamental conflict between themselves as individuals and society. There is set up, in their minds, a symbiotic interpenetration of individual and society" (Turner 1974: 56). Human resource management works in a field of tension between corporate goals and those of the individual.

How Did the Human Resource Consultants Manage?

A major part of my fieldwork at Bang & Olufsen took place in the Human Resource Department. This department was intended to have a key role in defining and communicating the firm's values to the rest of the company. When I visited Bang & Olufsen for the first time and explained my project to the HR manager, I used the word 'exclusive' to describe the company's products. After hearing the word, he frowned, stood up, and, with a joking gesture, opened his office door. "The meeting is over. Bang & Olufsen is not exclusive. It is *excellent*," he said with a twinkle in his eye. The HR manager's relaxed attitude seemed to mock the hair-splitting preoccupation with the meaning of the concepts that went into the official definition of the three values. At the same time, of course, he demonstrated that he was familiar with canonical interpretations.

I soon discovered that the half-joking attitude toward the fundamental values was characteristic of the way that HR employees referred to the words, perhaps to counterbalance the high-flown semantics and elevated level of abstraction that made their everyday use awkward. A straight-faced reference to the concepts in normal work contexts would seem ridiculously pretentious and out of place. Erving Goffman's (1969) concept of 'role distance' is helpful for understanding the humorous detachment expressed vis-à-vis the values: "[The concept] was introduced to refer to actions which effectively convey some disdainful detachment of the performer to the role he is performing" (ibid.: 63). It is "a wedge between the individual and his role, between doing and being. This 'effectively' expressed pointed separateness between the individual and his putative role, I shall call 'role distance'" (ibid.: 61). Thus, according to Goffman, we will always find that the individual tries to keep a certain distance between him- or herself and what others think he or she ought to identify with (Goffman 1967: 234). In his ethnography of corporate ideology, Israeli ethnographer Gideon Kunda (1992: 221) puts it even more accurately when he elaborates on the dialectic between individual and organization: "[T]he central experience of membership is not only that which the ideology seeks to instill, but also the experience of struggle with it." During an interview, one HR manager expressed his critical views with surprising boldness:

> Many of the words used in this world are so inflated, hyped up, and exaggerated (*gummiagtige, forskruede og overpumpede*) that often you don't know what you are talking about. You find that here as well. It's often a load of bullshit that some smartass in the United States invented to earn a lot of money. It really does sound pretty smart—'the learning organization', and all that. But when you go deeper into Peter Senge, it's all pretty banal. Organizations are sometimes very self-centered, and there are periods when it has been too much. Bang & Olufsen doesn't believe that there is anything in the world but the vision, and everybody should know that. But the truth is that Mrs. Hansen in Humlum [a small town near Struer] doesn't give a damn *what* Bang & Olufsen's vision is.

Jan, another HR consultant, also had a very relaxed and tongue-in-cheek attitude toward official corporate ideology. In meetings with other employees and among colleagues in HR, he would sometimes refer to the values and the official corporate material (for which he himself was partly responsible) as 'gobbledygook' and 'corporate bullshit'. But rather than making himself untrustworthy in other people's eyes, his humor and relaxed attitude seemed to point to his personal integrity and inspired trust among his colleagues. Such expressions of role distance seemed to indicate that he had his feet on the ground and was not completely consumed by corporate abstractions.

Outside the Human Resource Department, the 'three dirty words' were rarely mentioned. In more tightly defined, specific contexts, such as departmental seminars, assemblies, and pep talks, the values were often invoked as a framework into which particular departmental concerns and strategies were to be incorporated. One such situation was a seminar held at a conference center in Rønbjerg, a 90-minute drive from Struer. Its purpose was to help the Information Technology (IT) Department—which had a turbulent past and was facing a difficult future (Y2K)—to become an 'integrated part' of Bang & Olufsen's success.

Talking Values

At the seminar, the official program started with an introduction by Kim Glasgård, the departmental manager. This pep talk was scheduled as 'the Chief's' 'State-of-the-Tribe' speech to his 'Indians'. Kim spoke fluently and without a manuscript. Contextualizing the IT Department as part of the overall company, he started by reminding everyone of the ambitious goals (i.e., mission) contained in the business plan: "The mission is measurable. We have a target: a 10 percent increase in turnover per year, a 15 percent increase in profits per year, 100 new B1 shops."[4] After having lined up the well-known figures from the business plan, he introduced the 'three dirty words', that is, the fundamental values of the company: poetry, synthesis, and excellence. As he spoke the words, he glanced in the direction of Aksel (a human resource consultant) and myself. Compared to the facts and figures rationality of the first part of his presentation, he was evidently now on less secure ground: "Most of us probably think that it sounds a bit longhaired ... I think it is necessary to translate the 'three dirty words'. So I want to give you my personal understanding of the three words. As I see it, synthesis is the same as 'cooperation'. Poetry I understand as 'dialogue', and I understand excellence to be 'quality'."

Although the chief's speech to his tribe was meant to be a monologue, Magnus, a 'hot-liner'[5] known in the department as a loudmouth (*brokrøv*), intervened from the back of the room: "To translate 'excellence' as 'quality'— isn't that aiming a little low?" Kim, seeming slightly baffled by the interruption and the subsequent critique, insisted on his version, but Magnus persisted: "As I understand it, quality is about making things that don't break. Excellence is about surprising people, exceeding their expectations—and we don't have many opportunities for doing that in the IT Department! Well, not where I sit anyway." Some giggled quietly, while others looked down at their coffee cups, not quite sure how to react. Obviously irritated by the persistence of the questions, Kim said: "I think quality covers it nicely, but I don't want to be a preacher on those values. What matters is that we locate and dig up the golden eggs in our department." Someone else from the audience backed up Magnus's interpretation by arguing that McDonald's was a firm known for quality but definitely not excellence. Aksel, the HR consultant, interrupted, reorienting the audience to the frame by humorously suggesting that the "philosophical debate" be postponed, and asked Kim to continue his speech.

The incident had been embarrassing to us as HR middlemen. According to official corporate ideology, Magnus was clearly right. It is quite obvious from corporate orthodoxy that the word 'excellence' has a meaning that, although vague by nature, clearly differentiates it from the more pedestrian word 'quality'. Aksel told me afterward that he had chosen not to insist on canonical readings, opting instead to leave the matter undecided. In order to assist with the rest of the two-day program, he had judged it necessary to help Kim out and try to back up his legitimacy as a leader as much as possible.

On previous occasions and in interviews with managers, I had witnessed a similar uneasiness about the values; one manager told me that he did not know "what to do with the values." It is not difficult to understand why Kim had thought it necessary to interpret and flesh out the company's abstract values in order to fit the needs of a department that is generally concerned with the implementation of large, predefined IT systems. The focus was on keeping the department running as smoothly as possible (*driftsopgaver*), since its "primary task was to be invisible," as one senior manager put it. Kim's interpretation of the values was not a result of intellectual deficiency or an inability to comprehend the ideas behind the concepts. For the past year, the IT Department had been struggling to meet the deadlines for the company-wide introduction of the SAP management program.[6] It was difficult, then, for these employees to imagine themselves as being an integral part of Bang & Olufsen's success.[7] For the values to be rendered meaningful at all in a work environment characterized by tight schedules, high levels of stress, and 'firefighting', the words 'poetry' and 'excellence' called for radical reinterpretations. When he continued his speech, Kim mentioned the hard work and extreme pressure that the department had experienced:

> We have worked very hard, and it hasn't been without problems, and many of you may ask how the IT Department can become a part of Bang & Olufsen's success. Well, we already are! Torben Petersen [the senior manager responsible for the IT Department] has said that the best our department can hope for is to avoid getting a spanking (*undgå at få smæk*). I don't agree! But we have to wait a little before we get to the development tasks (*udviklingsopgaverne*). When I presented the visions of the IT Department to senior management, they said: "Well, that is only what is expected of you (*pligtegenskaber*). Where are the visions?" I answered by using an image—the stand for the Christmas tree. The operations (*driften*), the infrastructure, the basic systems—everything else has to function before we can put on the star!

Kim then rounded off his speech on a note of cheerful optimism: "I think we can be proud. We might not quite be there yet, but we have become so much better at delivering the goods ... Do you remember September last year? We have come a long way—with SAP, for instance. This is very well done, guys!" This final salute provoked another remark from the back of the room: "If I was a customer, I would return the product and ask to have my money back!" Pointedly ignoring the origin of the sarcasm, Kim said, with a note of irritation in his voice, "Unfortunately, that is *not* a possibility."

The next point on the agenda was 'customer feedback'. Following the IT manager's opening speech, two 'representatives from neighboring tribes'—that is, two managers from other departments who were prime recipients of the services of the IT Department—were to give their views on the service they had received. Søren Larsen from the Finance Department, a rising star in the corporate hierarchy,[8] immaculately dressed in a dark suit, white shirt, and well-polished black shoes, started off candidly. In a soft and mellow voice, he used his allotted 10 minutes to recount a seemingly endless list of complaints about the level of service he and his department had experienced. The next 'customer', Torkild Mølholm, a project manager for a retail management system, was then invited to give his feedback. He stood up and, with a disarming smile and an unshakable authority that seemed indicative of managerial habitus, added to the list of laments, concluding his talk with a small gift-giving ceremony. He presented the IT Department with a shovel, describing the present with a few words that revealed its ambivalent meaning: "You can use a shovel for digging trenches and holes for hiding. But the shovel can also be a useful working tool when you want to discover gold."

Framing this part of the seminar as customer feedback rather than a debate or discussion meant that the communication rules that usually guide interaction were temporarily set aside. Under normal circumstances, such very direct attacks, some of them bordering on insults, would have provoked counterattacks.

Hidden beneath a thin veil of humor, the shovel, for instance, was easily under-stood as an insult: the words 'shovel' and 'spade' in Danish are slang for a stupid person. Later, Aksel told me that for a moment he was afraid that such a massive critique would have swept people off their feet, killed their motivation, and destroyed the purpose of the seminar. But everybody in the room seemed to be aware of the implicit rule governing such feedback. Everyone seemed to acknowledge that this was not supposed to be a discussion. This framing was symbolically emphasized by the word 'customer', as in a market-based uni-verse, the customer is the ultimate object of respect. Customer feedback was an occasion for listening only: the customer is king.

After this session, it was time for a break before the second part of the program, in which participants were to define and find solutions to specific work-related issues. During this interval, Erik, another 'hot-liner' who had been taking part in the preparation of the seminar, discussed the values with a small group of employees. He invited Aksel and myself to join the group and asked how the seminar was connected to the company's stated values. The small group was standing by the whiteboard with the three values written on it. Aksel explained how he understood the connection and emphasized that the whole point about value-based management was to try to avoid manuals and ready-made solutions in the form of 'how-to' books. Erik then looked at the board and said that management ought to have come up with words that were easier to understand. Aksel took a red marker and wrote the word 'DIALOGUE' across the three values. He then added, with a smile: "Don't treat the values as rules you have to obey and learn by heart, but as occasions to reflect about the place you work, Bang & Olufsen. I don't want to preach the values. If you are inspired or moved, then everything is fine. If not, you shouldn't worry much about it."

The Predicament of the Middleman

Keeping the two sides of the value concept in mind, the HR consultants could well be described as cultural entrepreneurs. Barth's (1966: 18) classic defini-tion of the entrepreneur is suggestive: "Innovation for an entrepreneur must involve the initiation of transactions which *make commensurable some forms of value* which were previously not directly connected" (emphasis added). As is clear from the above, communicating the values was not an easy task. The HR consultants found themselves in a middleman position in more than one sense: they were at the same time authors, transmitters, and receivers of corpo-rate culture discourse. An important part of the job of the HR consultant was to help bridge what are normally seen as distinct spheres, trying to accommodate potentially contradictory demands. As Jan told me: "Taking pleasure in your work is crucial. Take that away and you take away an important condition. But there seems to be a contradiction. [The targets in the business plan mean that] we have to run faster, and at the same time the company is asking us to reflect more and enter into dialogue and all that. Surely these conditions can be solved at a higher level, I hope."

Being a 'self-managing employee', it was necessary to live within and try to deal productively with these contradictions. Thus, in the Human Resource Department, close to the center of corporate power, the freedom and vulnerability ensuing from cultural ambiguity and social volatility were particularly clear. To some HR employees, the notion of the self-managing employee was both a cultural ideal to be communicated and a concrete and hard social reality, since they, as internal consultants, were dependent on marketing and selling their services to other departments. The freedom to define their own job, the benefits of being afforded corporate resources, and the challenge and creativity involved in working with strategic development were outbalanced and overshadowed by the precariousness of working in the exposed position of strategic HR—a liability that was also indicated by the pace and extent to which people in the department were fired or chose to move.[9]

At a more general level, the situation just described also testifies to other consequences of working with value-based management. According to official understandings, the values were fundamental in the sense that they were embedded in the deeper deposits of corporate history. But as values are excavated, objectified, and communicated by the culture experts, they become symbolic stakes in a social field—forces that exert pressures and pulls, attraction and repulsion, or just indifference. The stated intention behind the value work was to go 'back to basics', but many felt that the process had instead lost touch with reality. The use of high-flying rhetoric generated resentment, although this was mostly backstage and in private contexts. Indeed, it appeared that the more comprehensive the values—that is, the more abstract and unspecific they seemed—the more people questioned their value. Thus, the identification of the values, which was meant to unite the employees, came to symbolize and engender a split between the administrative staff and other parts of the company.

Conclusion

The legacy of the Manchester School was both to broaden the horizon and to focus our attention. One of the important overall lessons from Manchester engagements with colonial Africa was to make us careful not to fall into the ready-made abstractions of 'a culture' and 'a society'. In the wake of this realization, the Manchester School developed methods—network theory, situational analysis, extended case study strategies—that were not predicated on assumptions of value consensus. Following in this tradition, we should acknowledge that cultural orders are always the result of a power struggle among contending interests, a conflict that often takes us beyond the local community. This sensitivity to social process and cultural difference is sound advice in a corporate environment, where value consensus is continuously stressed and unproblematic boundaries implied in descriptions of corporate culture, learning organizations, and so forth.

Considering the sensitivity to empirical particularity that is the hallmark of the Manchester School in general, and a background to the development of situational analysis in particular, it would not be true to the Manchester legacy simply to transpose its ideas across all territories and time spans and apply them uncritically in other empirical contexts. Clearly, the human resource policies of Bang & Olufsen, whose middle-class middlemen were involved in the ambiguous process of value-based management, are different from colonial connections and categorical classifications in coke towns in urban Central Africa. To grasp adequately the experience of these people and the situations in which they were involved, I had to resort to notions such as role distance and theory-as-tool (see Krause-Jensen 2010). Whereas the situations of the Manchester School were ones of conflict and clear differences, in Bang & Olufsen's Human Resource Department I found myself in situations characterized by complicity, irony, and ambiguity—situations that called for additional 'tools' in order to be comprehended. In the words of literary theorist Kenneth Burke (1962: xx): "[W]hat we want is not terms that avoid ambiguity, but terms that clearly reveal the strategic spots where ambiguities necessarily arise."

Jakob Krause-Jensen is an anthropologist and Associate Professor at the Danish School of Education, Aarhus University. His research focuses on how ethnographic methods and anthropological theory can be used to understand organizations and the life within them in critical and creative ways. His book *Flexible Firm* (2010) uses classical anthropology to shed light on value-based management. His most recent research explores the social and cultural consequences of importing management notions such as 'lean management' from the business world into public sector institutions.

Notes

1. Peters and Waterman (1982) authored the management bestseller of all times, *In Search of Excellence*. This volume inaugurated the managerial interest in 'meaning' and 'culture'.
2. Thus, when the notion of values is used in a business context in the extended sense of the term, the suspicion of insincerity and cynicism is immediate. As exemplified in the quote from Schultz, commercial value often becomes the ultimate value, thereby devaluing and fundamentally undermining the very meaning of the moral values and, in so doing, converting their 'absolute worth' to pragmatic vocabulary: "We care for the environment because that's what the customers want!" "We treat our employees well because that way we might gain leverage over our competitors!"
3. Of course, in other respects the company's three highly abstract values—poetry, synthesis, and excellence—are as far from Turner's concrete, ritual objects as one can imagine.
4. 'B1 shops' refer to specially designed retail outlets for Bang & Olufsen products.
5. 'Hot-liners' are staff who work to solve the immediate day-to-day computer problems that employees might have.
6. SAP is an acronym for Systeme, Anwendungen und Produkte in der Datenverarbeitung, a software company based in Germany that offers large-scale programs for managing economy and planning. During the previous year, Bang & Olufsen had introduced the SAP program company-wide.
7. In subsequent discussions, one of the general problems of the IT Department repeatedly surfaced. Not only were the majority of employees concerned mostly with supporting and servicing other departments, but these service tasks were far removed from the products themselves. To many of the employees, this was a source of frustration.

8. Larsen had been selected to participate in the Young Talents Program, a management development plan for a small group of young leaders between 20 and 30 years of age considered to have 'senior management potential'.
9. It is revealing to compare the Human Resource Department with the Department of Ethnography and Anthropology at Aarhus University. At the time of fieldwork, Bang & Olufsen's Human Resource Department employed 17 and 19 people, respectively. During the year I was in regular contact with the department, one-third of its employees either moved voluntarily or went to other departments or companies. When I returned on a visit five years later, not one of the 17 people I used to work with was still there. In a university department the situation is different: once people get a position, they very rarely move.

References

Barth, Fredrik. 1966. "Models of Social Organization." Royal Anthropological Institute, Occasional Paper No. 23. Glasgow: University Press.

Barth, Fredrik. 1993. "Are Values Real? The Enigma of Naturalism in the Anthropological Imputation of Values." Pp. 31–46 in *The Origin of Values*, ed. M. Hechter, L. Nadel, and E. Michod Richard. New York: Aldine de Gruyter.

Burke, Kenneth. 1962. *A Grammar of Motives, and A Rhetoric of Motives*. Cleveland, OH: World Publishing.

Evens, T. M. S., and Don Handelman, eds. 2006. *The Manchester School: Practice and Ethnographic Praxis in Anthropology*. New York: Berghahn Books.

Gluckman, Max. [1940] 1958. *Analysis of a Social Situation in Modern Zululand*. Manchester: Manchester University Press for the Rhodes-Livingstone Institute.

Gluckman, Max. 1967. "Introduction." Pp. xv–xxiv in *The Craft of Social Anthropology*, ed. A. L. Epstein. London: Tavistock.

Gluckman, Max. 2006. "Ethnographic Data in British Social Anthropology." Pp. 13–22 in Evens and Handelman 2006. (Paper originally presented in 1959 at the Fourth World Congress of Sociology in Stresa.)

Gluckman, Max. 1967. *Anstalt og Menneske*. Viborg, Denmark: Paludans Fiolbibliotek.

Gluckman, Max. 1969. "Role Distance." Pp. 39–103 in *Where the Action Is*. London: Allen Lane.

Handelman, Don. 2006. "The Extended Case: Interactional Foundations and Prospective Dimensions." Pp. 94–117 in Evens and Handelman 2006.

Holy, Ladislov, and Milan Stuchlik. 1983. *Actions, Norms and Representations: Foundations of Anthropological Inquiry*. Cambridge: Cambridge University Press.

Kapferer, Bruce. 1995. "Bureaucratic Erasure: Identity, Resistance and Violence—Aborigines and a Discourse of Autonomy in a North Queensland Town." Pp. 69–90 in *Worlds Apart: Modernity through the Prism of the Local*, ed. D. Miller. London: Routledge.

Kapferer, Bruce. 2006. "Situations, Crisis, and the Anthropology of the Concrete: The Contribution of Max Gluckman." Pp. 118–155 in Evens and Handelman 2006.

Krause-Jensen, Jakob. 2010. *Flexible Firm: The Design of Culture at Bang & Olufsen*. New York: Berghahn Books.

Kunda, Gideon. 1992. *Engineering Culture: Control and Commitment in a High-Tech Corporation*. Philadelphia: Temple University Press.

Lindgren, Björn. 2006. "The Politics of Ethnicity as an Extended Case: Thoughts on a Chiefly Succession Crisis." Pp. 272–291 in Evens and Handelman 2006.

Marcus, George E., ed. 1998. *Corporate Futures: The Diffusion of the Culturally Sensitive Corporate Form*. Chicago: University of Chicago Press.

Peters, Thomas J., and Robert H. Waterman, Jr. 1982. *In Search of Excellence: Lessons from America's Best-Run Companies*. New York: Harper & Row.

Turner, Victor. 1974. *Dramas, Fields, and Metaphors: Symbolic Action in Human Society*. Ithaca, NY: Cornell University Press.

Chapter 8

FIGURATIONS OF THE FUTURE
On the Form and Temporality of Protests among
Left Radical Activists in Europe

Stine Krøijer

The present chapter analyzes the relationship between what we conventionally think of as the present and the future in the context of a protest event during NATO's sixtieth anniversary summit in Strasbourg in 2009. During the rally, a collective body of protesters emerged in a situation that resulted in approximately 300 left radical activists[1] being 'kettled', police jargon for the temporary confinement of protestors at a demonstration, on a bridge near the French-German border. The situation reveals how the body becomes a site of qualitative transformation that I conceptualize as a bodily figuration of the future.

During the past decade, Europe has been the scene of recurrent protests against the global economic and political elite at World Bank, European

Union, NATO, and G8/G20 summits. These are well planned and tightly scheduled events when it comes to the official summit participants and organizers (as well as the police), and this applies as well to protesters who appear on the streets to call attention to the injustices committed in the name of civilization and progress. In this sense, summit events—and the protests in particular—have much in common with elaborate performative rituals (Juris 2008; cf. Turner 1982, 1987). During the protests, different techniques, such as masks, colors, music, and performative styles, are employed to engage participants and to engender particular effects among participants and audiences (Mitchell 2006). I therefore think of performances as acts in themselves that organize time and space, that is, activists' temporal incarnations of another future.

In describing events during a day of protests—particularly the moment of bodily and violent confrontation between activists and the police at the Grand Pont near the Bridge of Europe that connects France and Germany—I have been inspired by the situational analysis of the Manchester School and its acute attention to conflict and change (Gluckman [1940] 1958; van Velsen 1967). Victor Turner's work on rituals and performances is of particular relevance here; Turner (1982: 29–32) developed an anthropological concept of performance through his attention to liminoid phenomena in 'modern' societies while simultaneously preserving a dialogue with classical studies of ritual and liminality (see also Mitchell 2006: 384; Sjørslev 2007: 15–16). In earlier work, Turner (1967, 1968) had stressed the integrative function of ritual in agreement with Gluckman, and in so doing he also reproduced Emile Durkheim's basic thesis about the function of symbols in rituals, namely, that rituals first and foremost reaffirm the sentiments upon which a group is based (cf. Durkheim [1912] 1954: 216).[2] Turner epitomized this notion in the concept of communitas (1982: 44). Yet later, he came to highlight the transformative and potential quality of the liminal or liminoid phase in rituals and social drama that, as he put it, "can generate and store a plurality of alternative models for living, from utopias to programs" (ibid.: 33; cf. Kapferer 2006: 137). Turner's allusion to the existence of other such immanent models or worlds that may appear during a ritual or performance goes to the heart of what is at stake here.

I preserve the concept of performance, along with the particular attention to form that it entails, but in approaching the protest event, I aim at stripping it of its Durkheimian constructivist legacy in order to draw attention instead to the effects of the protest event (cf. Kapferer 2005). What interests me with regard to the collective body in the 'kettle' is not communitas or affective solidarity but rather synchronicity and bodily affect (cf. Massumi 2002). In attending to the collective body, I seek to dissolve the linear ontology of time underlying the ritual process, even in Turner's version, by pointing to the body's indeterminacy and openness to an otherwise in the here and now. In the following, I shall explore the dynamic at the bridge in Strasbourg, a situation that forms part of a two-year period of fieldwork (2007–2009) among left radical activists in Northern Europe.

'Kettled' in Strasbourg

The atmosphere is tense at the evening spokes council meeting[3] after the morning's confrontations with the police at the entrance to the protest camp. The clashes got underway after a group of demonstrators left the camp, which is located 6 kilometers south of the center of Strasbourg, to protest against the killing of a participant at the London G20 summit a few days earlier. Barricades have been built in the street and set on fire by activists, who have all changed into black clothes and covered their faces with hoods or bandanas, while the approaching police have been met by several more or less coordinated waves of stones and bottles.

The meeting is supposed to discuss the organization of a 'black bloc'[4] in conjunction with the large demonstration organized by members of the European Peace Movement to be held the following day, but now the idea of a 'diversity of tactics' is put to the test. Half a year earlier, visiting activists from all over Europe had hammered out an action concept at a secret meeting during which it was agreed to respect all tactical preferences and to avoid public condemnation of other groups in the context of the protests that are due to start tomorrow. Now, hundreds of people have crowded into the large red-and-blue circus tent used for meetings in the camp. Activists sit on stacks of hay on the ground, and the tent buzzes with the urge to discuss the day's events.

Alvin from the Block NATO coalition, who is organizing a civil disobedience action to blockade the access roads to the summit venue, speaks first. He informs the assembled that the police plan to seal off the whole inner city, and he argues that people wanting to take part in the blockade the following morning should leave within a few hours and try to sleep somewhere in the city's center. Another option would be to walk to the city in smaller groups in the early hours of the morning. He also urges people not to get into a confrontation with the police the following day.

Several activists around me are visibly bothered, including two of my key interlocutors, Natalie and Nicola, whom I have followed for the past month in their preparations for the protests, and Alvin's words are clearly lost on the gathering. Before entering the tent, Natalie had told me that there will be riots. In her view, people are "pissed off" due to the violent death of the protester in London, by the fact that their protest in Strasbourg is being relegated to an industrial zone outside the city's center, and because approximately 5,000 protesters have been held at the French-German border and denied entrance into France. For days there have been whispers about "alternative targets." Natalie interrupts Alvin by shouting, "That's all very fine, but the police have informed us that they will not let us leave the camp until 11 AM when the summit has already started." I never find out if this is actually true, or whether it is just one of the many rumors that has been circulating all week. Nicola, a young architect and a member of the French Anarchist Federation, who is sitting next to me in the hay, whispers, "I love this. Now you have to think for yourself."

Those who want to participate in the black bloc decide to leave in the early hours of the morning. I am inclined to follow them, but I am concerned about both my own safety and that of the four undergraduate students whom I have taken along to make a study of the construction of the camp and its imaginary effects. Outside the tent, people are having talks in smaller groups. Military helicopters have been circling over our heads for days, and some activists are worried that the police might finally decide to raid the camp during the night. Nicola and I decide to drive my students and a group from Revolt France, who will act as street medics the following day, into the city's center in his car. We agree that we can probably find a place to have a few hours rest at Molodoi, a self-managed social center that also serves as a point of convergence during the summit. We grope around for our sleeping bags and a few other personal belongings in the dark and finally take off to find Nicola's car. Before leaving, Nicola remembers to remove a metal truncheon from his trunk and hide it in some nearby shrubbery.

The streets of Strasbourg lie dark and empty. Since yesterday, they have been deserted. Shops, schools, and other institutions have been closed, and all public transportation has been canceled. Special summit passes have been issued for the local inhabitants, allowing them to move to and from their homes. The first trip into the city goes well, but on our second trip from the camp we start getting nervous. We have a creeping feeling that we are being followed, although we tell each other that we have done nothing wrong. Police officers are posted on the street corners, and in a moment of absent-mindedness, Nicola drives the wrong way down a one-way street. We are pulled over. The police search the car, the trunk, and us. In the trunk, they find Nicola's bike helmet, his skater safety gear, and his notebook. The highest-ranking officer starts turning over its pages with a display of great interest. "So, you are an organizer," he says to Nicola. Nicola denies it, but he is taken into custody. The rest of us are left on the street, and we walk to Molodoi while my notebook burns in my pocket. Luckily, Nicola and I remembered to exchange personal data before we left the camp, and after waiting anxiously for an hour and a half, I call up the legal team[5] to inform them of Nicola's arrest. An hour later, he is back. He says that he is "OK" except for having "his head screwed up by all their questions." We drink tea before tiptoeing into the upstairs room where sleeping activists cover every inch of the floor.

We get up before 7 AM and quickly head to the meeting point for the blockade. We walk along the quays surrounding Strasbourg's inner city, which is also the perimeter of the 'red zone' that is off limits to protesters. We observe the police who have taken guard on the bridges. When we reach the Quai des Alpes, we see the first groups of the black bloc arriving from the camp. Tear gas already fills the air, and clashes with the police get underway as the groups try to find a crossing point. We watch in silence for a while and then decide to move on. We head north and pass the official meeting point of the blockade, which has already been abandoned. We turn west toward the center, following the trail of another gathering (the 'pink bloc') and the scent of tear gas until we reach the blockade at the intersection of Avenue des Vosges and Avenue de la Paix (Peace Avenue). We are stopped and searched repeatedly. These measures are intended to help the police identify the 'unwanted elements' moving through the public space, and everybody walking on the streets has to undergo repeated identity checks and bag searches.

The pink bloc, which is related to the queer movement, is a colorful gathering mainly organized around a large samba band. The men and women typically dress in pink, wear elaborate hairdos and hats, and engage in street theatre and drum beating. There is also a contingent of German clowns, each wearing a hilarious mix of army and clown costumes. They march and drill in front of the police line, mimicking the officers' movements, which adds an element of comic suspense to the situation. The police watch with their visors up, but only half an hour earlier they had tried to chase the pink bloc protesters from the street. The participants have inhaled some tear gas in their effort to hold the blockade, but whether they have prevented the delegates to the NATO summit from reaching the conference center at the Palais de la Musique et des Congrès in time is still uncertain.

We take turns dancing and resting, and Nicola attends to a few people who are feeling queasy from the tear gas. Much to my surprise, I run into both Swedes and Greeks whom I had met during the 2008 European Social Forum in Malmö, and as the situation has calmed down, we have time for a chat. Using a megaphone, Alvin announces that the summit has been delayed for an hour due to the blockade, but my Greek companion seriously doubts this. "The blockade has not been sufficiently effective," he says. "There are plenty of places to get through. The delay was probably caused by Berlusconi going to the restroom." In light of the peaceful attitude of the police, it is clear that we no longer pose a threat to the smooth running of the official summit, so at a spokes council meeting that follows Alvin's announcement, it is decided to pull up stakes and head toward the large demonstration organized by the European Peace Movement (which also includes a black bloc) that is due to start within the hour.

First, however, Nicola and I prepare to join the confrontations in the harbor area close to the French-German border. We make a detour back to Molodoi to stock up on medical supplies. When we leave, our bags are stuffed with bandaging, cotton wool for broken noses, a few medicines, and six or seven bottles of Maalox, a wonder treatment for heartburn and tear gas. We are both eager to return to the action, and I try to ignore my growing fatigue due to lack of sleep. From a distance we see black smoke rising from the Bridge of Europe, normally the busiest border between France and Germany. Close by, the NATO leaders took part in 'a diplomatic footstep'—that is, an official photo session—a few hours earlier, and now the border post has been set on fire by protesters. Nicola is wearing his bike helmet and skater safety gear. It is a warm day, and he looks at me smiling. "The border is burning," he says. "Let's go to war."

We follow the directions of the smoke and the sound of the helicopters until we reach Grand Pont, a long bridge connecting the inner city with the harbor area, which is about 1.5 kilometers from the burning border post. On the way to the bridge, we are stopped repeatedly by police officers searching our bags and questioning us about our whereabouts, intentions, and organizational affiliation. As we reach Grand Pont, a large water cannon and a dozen police vans take up positions in the middle of the bridge. Cement blocks covered with plastic and barbed wire have been placed across the street. Nicola approaches a police officer and asks to be let through in order to provide medical aid to some of the activists on the other side. In a polite but firm voice, the officer informs us that it will not be possible.

At the foot of the bridge, we meet up with some 300 activists from the pink bloc, who had all participated in the failed attempt to blockade the NATO summit. Some people are taking a rest or looking for food and water, while others are eager to cross the bridge, either to join a large demonstration convened by the European Peace Movement or to participate in clashes with the police, which have been underway since around 7 AM. A row of police cars leaves the bridge, and after a spokes council meeting, the assembled protestors decide to make an attempt to 'open' the bridge.

As we walk up the bridge, three rows of riot police, protected by anti-riot helmets and shields and tactical knee, arm, and chest pads, obstruct our retreat. For a minute I consider jumping down the steep slope on the side of the bridge to avoid what seems to be an imminent arrest, but I am discouraged by the way a couple of protesters are severely beaten and kicked back into the group when they try to make an escape. The police line moves forward quickly and, aided by portable fences, pushes the samba band and everybody else ahead, while the drummers struggle to keep time. We are squeezed together in what I later learn is called a 'kettle'—police jargon for the temporary confining of protestors. The scent of tear gas reaches us from the other side of the bridge, where around a thousand activists are hurling stones at the police. In our kettle on the bridge, the samba band continues to play against a background of silence. The refrain "This is what democracy looks like!" is shouted repeatedly. When it was played at the blockade in the morning, I thought it referred to our control of the street. Now, however, it sounds more like a reference to police repression. I talk briefly to Svante, a familiar face from the European Social Forum in Malmö who is a member of a Swedish anti-militarist group. He explains that he had slept under a bridge that night in order to participate in the blockade. His affinity group had been planning to head back to the camp. "Now we don't know how it will end up," he says with a pale smile.

We are compressed further, and the temperature rises in the kettle. People raise their hands to show their peaceful intentions. I become acutely aware that if someone panics or loses her or his temper, the situation may turn into violent confrontations, resulting in mass arrests. When the first line is pressed back by the police, it instantly produces a collective wave among the protestors that rolls back and forth, with the rhythmic drumming of the samba band giving us a shared pulse. We have become one body acting together: a movement in one part instantly exerts an influence on the rest. I am filled with a strong sense of strength and solidarity, mixed with fear. Nobody moves or talks. The air is full of a vibrant tension, and I observe the jaw muscle of the nearest police officer turning white as he fixes his gaze somewhere above my head. I wonder what kind of being is hiding beneath the armor. It is a long, terrifying moment of possibility in which I mostly feel our own collective breathing.

After some 15 minutes, the riot police withdraw without a word, and we are allowed to walk away. People start talking again. We hug and laugh, and some even start dancing in the street. When I question him, Nicola says that he has mixed feelings of both strength and relief. Around us, people are laughing, and I share the outburst of joy. The elation is tinged with anger and a rare sense of power, which seems rather odd, given that we did not have the upper hand in the situation. I observe the large water cannon pulling away. Someone pops open a red fire hydrant to allow everybody a sip of water. The water pours out onto the warm asphalt, and Svante, who had stood next to me in the kettle, remarks how happy he is that we were able to "keep calm and control the situation." A middle-aged German man joins in to tell us that he had spent several hours in his car that morning to reach the protest and now "had experienced what he came for." He rambles on, but I turn away to find out what our next move will be.

After the moment of joyful celebration, we hold another spokes council meeting at Rue du Grand Pont. About half of the group, including half the samba band, decide to return to the camp, while the rest of us want to proceed to the remainder of the demonstration-cum-riot. Several clowns from the pink bloc remove their make-up and costumes. The next day, while driving me to the railway station, one of the clowns from Freiburg explains: "I lost the clown in the kettle. I used to run with the black bloc but started clowning about four years ago. Clowning is a good way to go into a confrontation, I think. But I got so angry [in the kettle] that I could not continue clowning and handle the situation in a humorous manner. After all the tension, I just felt angry and had to strip off the clown."

In the otherwise deserted harbor area, the demonstration has fallen apart, and people drift around aimlessly. Simultaneously, the violent clash between militant protesters, joined by youngsters from the *banlieues*,[6] and the riot police continues near the Bridge of Europe. The confrontation takes place at a distance and follows a slow pace. Small, dispersed groups of activists take turns throwing stones and Molotov cocktails at police officers on foot, who keep their distance and respond with tear gas, concussion grenades, and eventually a few stones. The activists are ritually clothed in black, with gas masks, helmets, and padding in striking similarity to the police. Even their bodily movements, when attacking and hiding behind their shields, are similar— coordinated yet without central coordination, as is, I think, the idea about the need 'to take action' to change the course of events.

At the Bridge of Europe, activists have set fire to the border post and a nearby Ibis hotel. Two participants explain that police officers have been stationed at the border post, while others seem to think that it has been used for rejected asylum seekers. In either case, the target is considered legitimate. One of my student assistants, who did not wish to take part in the blockade, had been present at the bridge by mistake, and in the evening she describes how small groups of youngsters ran around the burning buildings, shouting with joy and giving each other the thumbs up. Locals from the nearby *banlieue* joined in, she explained, plundering a couple of smashed-up gas stations. The black bloc riots and the property destruction are the incidents that will be reported in the mainstream media during the days that follows. "No Borders," reads the graffiti scrawled on the burned-out border control post.

In the late afternoon, people start walking back toward the camp, while others change their clothes to appear like 'regular citizens', which might allow them to pass through the police checkpoints into the city's center. Nicola, myself, and a few others walk toward the center, but to reach Molodoi and Nicola's car we have to pass over one of the bridges, which the police are still heavily guarding. We are repeatedly turned away, although we try to appear as inoffensive as possible. "Try not looking them in the eyes," Nicola advises. I remember thinking that there is apparently no agreement between the activists and the police about when the party is over. I have trouble walking due to large blisters on both my feet, and we are all soon overwhelmed by fatigue. At the fourth bridge, we change our tactic. One of my female student assistants and I walk up the bridge first. We approach the police directly and kindly ask them to let us through. They check our passports and question Nicola, but it works. Once we are well on the other side, Nicola mumbles, "So, they are humans after all. I told him [the police officer] that I was tired, and he said that he was too."

When we are back in the car, Nicola describes the day as a great success. "You can't expect that we can accomplish everything in one day," he says, "but we managed to control the street and to create disorder in their planning." "What do you mean by 'everything'?" I ask. "Well, you know, that the revolution doesn't come in one day," Nicola replies. We continue in silence, lost in our own thoughts. Later in the evening in Molodoi, while we are eating and waiting for some transport back to the camp, Nicola rests his forehead on the tabletop and starts to cry. "I was just not strong enough," he repeats. I am overwhelmed by a deep sadness that will stay with me for weeks, without being able to pinpoint the reason why.

Bodily Affect and Becoming Otherwise

The situation that I have described poses more questions than I will be able to answer here, but the moment at the bridge begs further analysis. What was the nature of the compressed body of protesters on the bridge? How did the activists come to associate strength and control with a situation in which the police clearly had the upper hand? What is the relationship between body and time as revealed by this incident?

There is little doubt that the actions of protesting and engaging in bodily confrontation with the police give rise to what we usually think of as strong emotions. I have described how being kettled in Strasbourg evoked not only anxiety and even fear, but also a sense of mutual solidarity, control, and strength. An obvious model for understanding these emotions is that of the ritual process, as people close to the movement have argued (see Jordan 2002; Juris 2008). Protests, and particularly the moment of confrontation, has been associated with the liminal or liminoid phase of rituals. According to Turner (1982), it is characteristic of this phase that strong feelings are evoked.[7] Yet I am reluctant to understand the ritual, and thus the protests, as a social construction of personal feelings, as is argued in much anthropology of emotions (Lutz and White 1986;

Wulff 2007). Rather, what seems to be at stake here has to do with the intensity and compression of the body/ies at the bridge.

I have described the physical compression of protesters at the bridge in Strasbourg as a collective body with joint breathing, the movement of one part instantly impinging on the rest and the rhythm of the samba band becoming the collective pulse. In my view, the compression and intensity of the situation gave rise to a bodily synchronicity, that is, a bodily belonging to the same moment in time. The experience of becoming a synchronic body occurs frequently at protests, but it may take a variety of forms, as when activists walk in tight rows with their arms locked together during a demonstration. Dressed similarly in black clothes, they thereby become indiscernible from one another. Becoming a synchronic body can also occur when free-form actions, such as the riots in Strasbourg, obtain a swarming effect, which implies a synchronicity between dispersed elements. An outside force may produce a similar effect: the emergence of a synchronic body often seems to arise in situations in which bodies are confined in narrow spaces or become physically compressed. This was particularly salient when several hundred activists were kettled by the police in Strasbourg.

In the notes to his translation of *A Thousand Plateaus*, Massumi offers a Deleuzian concept of affect. He argues that affect is "prepersonal intensity corresponding to the passage from one experiential state of the body to another and implying an augmentation or diminution in that body's capacity to act" (Massumi in Deleuze and Guattari 1987: xvii). Hence, affect is an experience of intensity, a moment of unformed potentiality that cannot be captured in language (Massumi 2002: 30). In my view, this can enable us to grasp the contradiction between the immobility experienced in the kettle and the increased sense of power and strength. The moment at the bridge entailed a change in the experiential state of the body; simultaneously, it was a change in bodily form and state of vitality. I think of these moments as a state of 'active time' in which some of the ideals that activists struggle for temporarily become real and concrete, a bodily otherwise in the here and now of the confrontation. The body temporarily becomes the source of an otherwise in the plane of immanence (cf. Deleuze and Guattari 187: 266–267).

These moments of active time that correspond to the emergence of a synchronic body can be contrasted with several other moments in the case above, namely, when we had the experience of being followed and watched by the police during our nightly drive, when Nicola was taken into custody, and when he cried from his lack of strength to face up to the situation. In these situations, in which activists are singled out and individualized, they describe themselves as overwhelmed by sadness, resignation, and paranoia. In sum, the life of an activist oscillates between various temporal modes of being, namely, between active time and 'dead time', both of which hinge on the body (Krøijer 2015; Krøijer and Sjørslev 2011).

Active time is prevalent in situations, such as the one at the Strasbourg bridge, when activists come to exist in a state of differentiated or precipitated synchrony. In this context, what we think of as experiences of solidarity, horizontality, strength, and freedom are embedded within this time. In the case of street protests, it is the bodily confrontation between activists and the police (in its various forms) that works as the point of transition between active time and dead time. I think of these as different bodily perspectives along the lines suggested by Viveiros de Castro (1998, 2004) in his theorization of Amerindian perspectivism.

In his work on Amerindian cosmology, Viveiros de Castro redefines the categories of nature and culture and criticizes the use of Western naturalism, which is founded on the idea of a shared nature and multiple cultures, to describe non-Western cosmologies. Based on his study of the way humans, animals, and spirits see each other among the Arawete in Brazil, Viveiros de Castro (1998) argues that all of these categories share an anthropomorphic essence (culture), but that they show themselves in different 'clothes', that is, different bodily appearances (natures). Thus, Western multiculturalism is replaced with Amazonian multi-naturalism, implying a spiritual unity and a corporal diversity. The result is a cosmology of multiple bodily viewpoints. The existence of multiple points of view does not mean that the same world is being apprehended from different angles, but "that all beings see the world the same way—what changes is the world they see" (ibid.: 477).

Obviously, a European activist cosmology is different from that of indigenous Amazonians, but the bodily ability to take a certain point of view is analogous. It is the body that makes the difference. If we transpose Amazonian multi-naturalism to Western thinking about time, it should be possible to reconsider the antinomy between the present and the future, between immanence and transcendence, which is inherent in much thinking about social change. It is often taken for granted that time is linear and fluid—that it is a single, shared 'clock time', which we may in turn perceive differently (Gell 1992; Hodges 2008). My point is that Turner's ritual model suffers from a linear ontology of time that describes the ritual as a unified and linear process around which order and disorder, rule and exception, the everyday and the festive are temporally reversed. In this light, I find it unsuitable for grasping the multiple ontologies of time that intersect during a protest event.

In the present context, it is the skillful performance that makes the temporal bodily perspective appear. This capacity to move between different temporal perspectives—namely, dead time and active time—depends, for example, on the ability of protestors to take a certain bodily point of view during confrontations with the police. In the case of the kettle, the compressed body/ies is/are put together as one composite entity and become, in the words of Viveiros de Castro (1998: 482), "the site of a differentiating perspective."

Conclusion: Figurations of the Future

In this chapter I have argued that a skillful protest performance has an effect on time. I have found that paying attention to the body and the question of time in confrontations between left radical activists and the police is decisive for understanding the form that political actions take among left radical activists.

The bodily confrontation is key here because it has an effect on time: it is the body that splits time when it is confronted with an obstacle (in this instance, the police). However, the synchronic body can be characterized neither as entirely immanent nor as a perfectly transcendent force. I have therefore argued that the materiality of the body matters.[8] Through the study of these intensified moments of potentiality, or quasi-events, that took place in the shadow of the formal summit event, I have shown how the body engenders time (cf. Povinelli 2011). The confrontation implies not multiple epistemologies of time but various temporal perspectives, which is what I refer to as 'figurations of the future'.

The kettled body of protesters works as a figuration of the future, which stands in a simultaneous relationship to what we conventionally think of as the present and the future, by materializing the otherwise in the here and now. This figuration is not a pre-figuration—that is, it is not an anticipation or fore-shadowing of a future to come (Maeckelbergh 2009). Instead, it is a giving of bodily form to the indeterminable.[9]

In sum, what my ethnography suggests is that time is not one flow from the past through the present to the future, but that it is non-chronological and that multiple times are simultaneous or co-existent (cf. Foucault 1986: 24–26; Hodges 2008: 409; Tonkin 1992: 72–75).[10] Like the different natures that shamans and spirits may assume in Amazonian societies, I argue that, by way of bodily alterity, activists acquire different temporal perspectives. What we conventionally think of as the future is not bound to the present, nor can it be extrapolated from it; rather, it exists only as a kind of latent active time (cf. Grosz 2005: 110; Miyazaki 2004: 70). In the present context, it is the performative confrontation that makes the future appear.

Stine Krøijer is an Assistant Professor in the Department of Anthropology at the University of Copenhagen. Her new book on left radical activism, *Figurations of the Future*, is forthcoming in 2015. She has co-edited a special issue of *Social Analysis* on the anthropology in and of Scandinavia. Currently, she is working on a new research project, titled "The Political Life of Trees," which focuses on human interaction with trees in the Ecuadorian Amazon and among environmental activists, as well as the forms of politics and political potentiality emerging from this interaction.

Notes

1. 'Left radical activists' is an umbrella term used by activists in Northern Europe to denote people of an anarchist, autonomist, and syndicalist bent. The term largely covers groups that can also be identified as the radical strain of the global justice movement (Graeber 2009; Maeckelbergh 2009).
2. Turner (1982: 20) characterized his work as 'comparative symbology', which refers to the interpretation of symbols but also to the study of expressions by means of symbols. Turner had earlier adopted a processual view of the rite of passage from Arnold van Gennep, which stated that the ritual process was divided into three phases: separation,

transition (a state of social limbo out of secular time that generates a strong sense of communitas among the participants), and reincorporation (Turner 1982: 24; see also Turner 1987: 34). Focusing explicitly on the forms of religious life, Durkheim ([1912] 1954) asserted that the true function of the rites performed by Australian clans was not, as they themselves understood it, to increase their totem species but to produce socially useful effects. According to Durkheim, during the rite the Australians experience a strong enthusiasm and, as a consequence, are "transported to another level of reality," which makes them feel outside and above normal moral life (ibid.: 216, 226).

3. A spokes council is an assembly of affinity groups working by consensus (Graeber 2002: 70–71). Affinity groups are small assemblages of activists who know and trust each other. Usually, people travel together to events or actions, but affinity groups can also be formed on a more ad hoc basis around specific goals during an action. Within the affinity group, a decision is made about what kinds of activities the group will participate in and with what means. Moreover, the group members look after each other during and after confrontations with the police. Each group sends a delegate to spokes council meetings, which are held several times throughout an action or blockade to reach a consensus on tactical issues.

4. The term 'black bloc' denotes a particular tactic employed by left radical activists during demonstrations. This protest action, developed by German left radicals in the 1980s, involves demonstrators wearing black clothes and masks and forming a tight block by locking arms. In the activists' own words, this is done to avoid identification and arrests and to give the demonstration a militant expression. The tactic sometimes includes vandalism and street riots (cf. Graeber 2009; Katsiaficas 2006).

5. During summit protests, activists rely on an organizational infrastructure that includes voluntary medical teams, trauma support units, and a legal team, which checks up on arrested activists, in addition to the event planners, those who are involved in the camp's organization (e.g., the kitchen and clean-up crews), the press group, and the information team.

6. A *banlieue* is a residential area on the outer edge of a city. In France, the term is used more frequently to describe areas of low-income apartments and social housing.

7. The words 'feeling' and 'emotion' are often used interchangeably. Following Massumi (2002), I take feeling to be personal and biographical, whereas emotions are social (e.g., collective expressions of feelings or their social construction). Affects are pre-personal and non-conscious experiences of (bodily) intensity.

8. Looking for politics in the body is not a new thing. Inspired by theories of feminism and philosophy, anthropologists have, over the past 40 years, interrogated nature-culture and mind-body dualities and have pointed to the social and discursive production of sex, gender, and bodies (see Lock 1993: 135; Povinelli 2006; Vilaça 2005; Wolputte 2004). According to Povinelli (2006), however, the much-needed critique of the Western metaphysics of substance has led to an unfortunate side effect—the abandonment of the material aspects of the body. Nonetheless, the attention that I give to the materiality of the body in the present context does not prevent it from being considered highly unstable (cf. Vilaça 2005).

9. For a further discussion on this topic, see Krøijer (2015).

10. In a short article titled "Of Other Spaces," Michel Foucault (1986) describes the present epoch as one of the simultaneity of spaces. He talks of 'heterotopias' as real places but also as 'counter-sites' or effectively enacted utopias that have the property of standing in relation to all other spaces "in such a way as to suspect, neutralize, or invert the set of relations that they happen to designate, mirror, or reflect" (ibid.: 24). According to Foucault, it is a principle of the heterotopia that it juxtaposes several spaces in a single real place (the example being the Persian carpets that are reproductions of gardens, and gardens as the rug onto which the whole world is enacted). Moreover, heterotopias are linked to "slices in time," that is, to heterochronicity (ibid.: 26), which implies the emergence of several simultaneous modes of being in time.

References

Deleuze, Gilles, and Félix Guattari. 1987. *A Thousand Plateaus: Capitalism and Schizophrenia*. Minneapolis: University of Minnesota Press.
Durkheim, Emile. [1912] 1954. *The Elementary Forms of Religious Life*. New York: Free Press.
Foucault, Michel. 1986. "Of Other Spaces." *Diacritics* 16: 22–37.
Gell, Alfred. 1992. *The Anthropology of Time: Cultural Constructions of Temporal Maps and Images*. Oxford: Berg.
Gluckman, Max. [1940] 1958. *Analysis of a Social Situation in Modern Zululand*. Manchester: Manchester University Press for the Rhodes-Livingstone Institute.
Graeber, David. 2002. "The New Anarchists." *New Left Review* 13: 61–73.
Graeber, David. 2009. *Direct Action: An Ethnography*. Edinburgh: AK Press.
Grosz, Elizabeth. 2005. *Time Travels: Feminism, Nature, Power*. Durham, NC: Duke University Press.
Hodges, Matt. 2008. "Rethinking Time's Arrow: Bergson, Deleuze and the Anthropology of Time." *Anthropological Theory* 8, no. 4: 399–429.
Jordan, John. 2002. "The Art of Necessity: The Subversive Imagination of Anti-road Protest and Reclaim the Streets." Pp. 347–357 in *The Cultural Resistance Reader*, ed. Stephen Duncombe. London: Verso.
Juris, Jeffrey S. 2008. *Networking Futures: The Movement against Corporate Globalization*. Durham, NC: Duke University Press.
Kapferer, Bruce. 2005. "Sorcery and the Beautiful: A Discourse on the Aesthetic of Ritual." Pp. 129–160 in *Aesthetics in Performance: Formations of Symbolic Construction and Experience*, ed. Angela Hobart and Bruce Kapferer. New York: Berghahn Books.
Kapferer, Bruce. 2006. "Situations, Crisis, and the Anthropology of the Concrete: The Contribution of Max Gluckman." Pp. 118–155 in *The Manchester School: Practice and Ethnographic Praxis in Anthropology*, ed. T. M. S. Evens and Don Handelman. New York: Berghahn Books.
Katsiaficas, Georgy. 2006. *The Subversion of Politics: European Autonomous Social Movements and the Decolonization of Everyday Life*. Oakland, CA: AK Press.
Krøijer, Stine. 2015. *Figurations of the Future: Forms and Temporalities of Left Radical Politics in Northern Europe*. New York: Berghahn Books.
Krøijer, Stine, and Inger Sjørslev. 2011. "Autonomy and the Spaciousness of the Social: The Concern for Sociality in the Conflict between Ungdomshuset and Faderhuset in Denmark." *Social Analysis* 55, no. 2: 84–105.
Lock, Margaret. 1993. "Cultivating the Body: Anthropology and Epistemologies of Bodily Practice and Knowledge." *Annual Review of Anthropology* 22: 133–155.
Lutz, Catherine, and Geoffrey White. 1986. "The Anthropology of Emotions." *Annual Review of Anthropology* 15: 405–436.
Maeckelbergh, Marianne. 2009. *The Will of the Many: How the Alterglobalisation Movement is Changing the Face of Democracy*. New York: Pluto Press.
Massumi, Brian. 2002. *Parables for the Virtual*. Durham, NC: Duke University Press.
Mitchell, Jon P. 2006. "Performance." Pp. 384–401 in *Handbook of Material Culture*, ed. Chris Tilley, Webb Keane, Susanne Küchler, Mike Rowlands, and Patricia Spyer. London: Sage.
Miyazaki, Hirokazu. 2004. *The Method of Hope: Anthropology, Philosophy, and Fijian Knowledge*. Stanford, CA: Stanford University Press.
Povinelli, Elizabeth A. 2006. *The Empire of Love: Toward a Theory of Intimacy, Genealogy, and Carnality*. Durham, NC: Duke University Press.
Povinelli, Elizabeth A. 2011. *The Economies of Abandonment*. Durham, NC: Duke University Press.
Sjørslev, Inger. 2007. "Ritual, performance og socialitet: En introduktion." Pp. 9–23 in *Scener for samvær: Ritualer, performance og socialitet*, ed. Inger Sjørslev. Aarhus: Aarhus Universitetsforlag.

Tonkin, Elizabeth. 1992. *Narrating Our Pasts: The Social Construction of Oral History.* Cambridge: Cambridge University Press.

Turner, Victor. 1967. *The Forest of Symbols: Aspects of Ndembu Ritual.* Ithaca, NY: Cornell University Press.

Turner, Victor. 1968. *Schism and Continuity in an African Society.* Manchester: Manchester University Press.

Turner, Victor. 1982. *From Ritual to Theatre: The Human Seriousness of Play.* New York: PAJ Publications.

Turner, Victor. 1987. *The Anthropology of Performance.* New York: PAJ Publications.

van Velsen, Jaap. 1967. "The Extended-Case Method and Situational Analysis." Pp. 129–149 in *The Craft of Social Anthropology,* ed. A. L. Epstein. London: Tavistock.

Vilaça, Aparecida. 2005. "Chronically Unstable Bodies: Reflections on Amazonian Corporalities." *Journal of the Royal Anthropological Institute* 11, no. 3: 445–464.

Viveiros de Castro, Eduardo. 1998. "Cosmological Deixis and Amerindian Perspectivism." *Journal of the Royal Anthropological Institute* 4, no. 3: 469–488.

Viveiros de Castro, Eduardo. 2004. "Exchanging Perspectives: The Transformation of Objects into Subjects in Amerindian Ontologies." *Common Knowledge* 10, no. 3: 463–484.

Wolputte, Steven Van. 2004. "Hang on to Your Self: Of Bodies, Embodiment, and Selves." *Annual Review of Anthropology* 33: 251–269.

Wulff, Helena. 2007. "Introduction: The Cultural Study of Emotions, Mood and Meaning." Pp. 1–18 in *The Emotions: A Cultural Reader,* ed. Helena Wulff. Oxford: Berg.

Chapter 9

MIMESIS OF THE STATE
From Natural Disaster to Urban Citizenship
on the Outskirts of Maputo, Mozambique

Morten Nielsen

In her analysis of 'temporal ruptures', Ann Game (1997: 117) describes the effects of catastrophes on everyday understandings of time: "The movement of living involves ruptures and disruptions to the future which thus disrupt time as we commonly understand it as consisting of a past-present-future." Rather than seeing time as a constant linear progression, in moments of temporal rupture we are brought "face to face with contingency." In other words, temporal ruptures open toward a world of possible futures that co-exist in the brief moments when linear time is dissolved (ibid.).

In this chapter, I explore the effects of a particular temporal rupture with a special emphasis on the potential production of 'possible futures', indicating novel temporal trajectories toward hitherto uncharted terrains. This will be done through an extensive situational analysis of the socio-economic and cultural

Notes for this chapter begin on page 168.

effects of the devastating floods that hit Mozambique in 2000. From January to March, more than 700 people died and over 550,000 lost their homes due to the heavy rains (Christie and Hanlon 2001: 37). In Maputo, the country's capital, the municipality faced the serious challenge of finding shelter for the afflicted families. After a series of intense political debates, it was decided that Mulwene, a peri-urban *bairro* (neighborhood) on the outskirts of the city, was the appropriate place to resettle what was initially thought to be 100 families from one urban *bairro*, an optimistic figure that soon proved to be a gross underestimate. At the end of 2000, a census taken at the conclusion of the resettlement process showed that 2,040 families from a total of eight different *bairros* had been resettled in Mulwene.[1] From the outset, state and municipal agencies declared that Mulwene was to be transformed into a *bairro modelo* (model neighborhood) with all the attributes of a modern urban neighborhood. However, given overall administrative weaknesses resulting from failed social-ist schemes after Mozambican independence in 1975, followed by the more recent adoption of neo-liberal economic policies, Mozambique has proved completely incapable of realizing such ambitious visions. Thus, newcomers currently access land informally through local chiefs and civil servants who are bribed to parcel out plots irrespective of any legal basis to the property. Not-withstanding the failures of the Mozambican state in creating a *bairro modelo*, residents are taking this ambitious project into their own hands. Thus, where the state was incapable of urbanizing the area in accordance with predefined 'fixed urban norms', residents are using these as a basis for house-building projects despite the apparent illegality of their occupancy. As I will show, resi-dents ultimately secure their occupancy as this 'mimesis of the state' positions them in a momentarily powerful position in relation to state agencies that are threatening them with forced resettlement. The copy, so to speak, has exposed the fragility of the original.

Before entering the local socio-cultural universe in Mulwene, however, I begin by outlining an analytical approach to the interlinkages between hous-ing strategies in Mulwene and the broader processes surrounding the flooding. This takes us back to the work of researchers associated with the Rhodes-Livingstone Institute (RLI) on social change and, subsequently, to more recent discussions centering on the work of Gilles Deleuze.

Back to the Rhodes-Livingstone Institute

At the outset, the analytical aim of the RLI researchers[2] was to capture a hetero-geneous colonial environment in British Central Africa defined by conflicting belief systems and shifting modes of behavior (Gluckman [1940] 1958: 10). Based on a broad reading of historical Marxism, and in stark opposition to Malinowski's dominant idea of 'culture contact',[3] RLI researchers proposed to see Africans and Europeans as members of a single system that was racially diverse and economically and socially interdependent (ibid.; see also Mitchell 1956: 30).[4] As Gluckman argued, it was only by insisting on seeing the society as a whole that people's modes of behavior could be properly understood as cultural variations conditioned by the particular situations in which interactions occurred (Macmillan 1995: 48). The decisive process to be analyzed was consequently social change, not oppositions between mutually incompatible systems (Gluckman 1949). In short, not only particular cultural practices but also broader normative understandings should be studied as processual rather than structural phenomena.

In order to capture the complexity and ambiguities inherent in socio-economic processes, the RLI researchers made use of the concept of 'situational analysis' (Gluckman [1940] 1958; Mitchell 1983). Rather than seeing local occurrences as merely 'apt illustrations' of fixed social configurations, the RLI researchers' meticulous analyses of particular situations revealed the tension-ridden and always emergent character of the relationship between individual acts and broader socio-economic and political structures (Long 1992: 162). Through the use of situational analysis, it was thus possible to unfold both the vagueness of enacted norms and the heterogeneous ways that they were being manipulated by agents pursuing different objectives (van Velsen 1967: 146).

Although it might be argued that the work of the RLI researchers invariably got caught up in the structural functionalist paradigm of their time,[5] it is now possible to elaborate on their ground-breaking studies in the light of more recent philosophical and anthropological work. By doing this, I suggest, it becomes possible to see how situational analysis also enables broader understandings of the still unrealized potentials inherent in particular events. In a sense, we are thus returning to the opening idea of coming face to face with contingency through temporal ruptures (Game 1997).

Events as Potentialities

For Max Gluckman, the notion of the 'situation' referred to a "total context of crisis, not just contradictory and conflicting processes but a particular tension or turning, a point of potentiality and of multiple possibility," as Bruce Kapferer (2005: 89) sees it. According to Kapferer, when everything is in process, it makes no sense to try to determine whether a situation aspires to be an apt illustration or not since "[e]verything is in some way or another different and potentially unique" (ibid.: 100). Perceived from this analytical perspective, there is always a certain emergent potentiality to the situation that reaches beyond its immediate temporal perimeters. In order to grasp fully the significance of these potentialities, I briefly turn to the concept of the 'event' in the work of the French philosopher Gilles Deleuze.

In Deleuze's (1997: 5) view, an event is neither a decisive rupture nor a new beginning. Rather, it is essentially the introduction of change and variation into already existing structures. As James Williams (2008: 1) argues, it is "a change in waves" resonating through the environment that causes series of elements to interact in novel ways.[6] In such instances, the occurrence of the change is predicated on its capacity to affect many interconnected processes that gradually alter their structure as a consequence of the introduced variation. Any element, whether temporal or spatial, has certain properties that can be determined (DeLanda 2006: 10, 20). A given occurrence can be fixed to a precise temporal moment, while a physical object, such as a hammer, has a certain texture and weight. At the same time, different elements also exhibit particular capacities to interact and become affected by other elements. Given the appropriate association with a particular temporal occurrence, a tool might come to manifest a particular idea or ideology. It is precisely such associations that the event affords. As Deleuze (2006) argues, the introduction of variation in a structural configuration instantiates a constant enfolding, unfolding, and refolding of matter, time, and space (cf. Fraser 2006: 131), whereby constellations of heterogeneous elements come together in "areas of more and less clarity and obscurity" (Williams 2003: 76). According to George Mead (1959: 52), we might therefore see the event as "the occurrence of something which is more than the processes that have led up to it and which, by its change, continuance, or disappearance, adds to later passages a content they would not otherwise have possessed." This "creative excess" (Ansell Pearson 2002: 70) that the event exhibits finds its impetus in the virtual nature of interlinked elements.

According to the *Concise Oxford Dictionary*, the word 'virtual' is defined as "that which is almost or nearly as described, but not completely or according to strict definition."[7] Its lack of physicality notwithstanding, Deleuze (2004: 260) emphasizes that the virtual is fully real, as it is constantly being actualized through events.[8] An apt example of a strictly virtual phenomenon might be risks as analyzed by Ulrich Beck (1986, 1998). Although risks are held to pertain to the future, they have such a huge influence on our present that they come to exist 'in practice'. Beck (1998: 11) thus argues that "risks are a kind of virtual, yet real, reality." Virtuality is consequently the capacity of each element to be actualized as a singular, concrete object when connected with other elements. It is, in other words, the latent potentialities inherent in individual elements that, by themselves, are "confused, inchoate, and undetermined" (Ansell Pearson 2002: 104), as such constituting an unrepresentable composite of overlapping tendencies. The virtual potentialities of individual elements are thus known only by their effects, that is, as particular realizations arising with the event (Hallward 2006: 41). In order to grasp this process, Deleuze (2004: 264, emphasis added) suggests that we see the event as "a task to be performed or a *problem* to be solved." As the event connects hitherto detached virtual elements, it comes to orient series of processes by imposing a certain degree of systematicity in the ways that agents relate to the problems arising out of the event (Boundas 1996: 88). The event, seen as a problem, thus expresses a particular tendency that "orientates, conditions and engenders solutions" (Deleuze 2004: 264).[9]

In the following, I approach the flooding that hit Mozambique in 2000 as a 'Deleuzian event' and will consequently explore how it 'reverberated' with its socio-economic environment in particular ways whereby hitherto detached elements were connected. Through a detailed situational analysis, I explore how the process produced imageries of alternative futures in the vicinity of the state.[10]

The Emergence of a 'Model Neighborhood'

Until 2000, Mulwene was inhabited only by *nativos* (natives),[11] living off the produce of small-scale agricultural farming, and a group of newcomers building houses in the southern part of the area.[12] In 2000, the situation changed almost overnight when flooding victims were resettled in the area. When the victims first came to Mulwene, they were installed in military tents in a section of the *bairro* later known as Matendene.[13] Other than a few scattered huts and houses belonging to local *nativos*, this section of Mulwene was uninhabited and thus lacked basic infrastructure in the form of public roads, electricity, and a functioning water system. Given the obvious opportunity to create an urban neighborhood from scratch, the Maputo municipality soon decided that Mulwene should be a 'model neighborhood' (*bairro modelo*), with all the "requirements that constitute adequate habitation,"[14] that is, parceling should follow a fixed set of urban norms according to which individual plots had to be 15x30 meters, with houses located 3 meters from the boundary lines to the street (Nielsen 2008, 2011). Before long, Matendene had indeed been parceled out in evenly sized plots that were allocated to the homeless flood victims, many of whom were installed in small cement houses built by international donor organizations working in collaboration with the Maputo municipality. Furthermore, realizing that the rapid influx of people necessitated a strengthened administrative framework, Mulwene was established as a municipal neighborhood in 2001.[15] Soon afterward, it was constituted as an operational municipal entity and subdivided into 56 quarters, each consisting of approximately 80 to 120 households headed by individual *chefes de quarteirões* (quarter chiefs) and subordinate block chiefs. Although initially projected for only 100 families (in addition to the *nativos* and newcomers already living in the area), a census carried out by the neighborhood administration in 2005 showed that there were 30,813 residents occupying an area of 6.8 square kilometers.[16]

During my first months in Mulwene, I was continually struck by the homogeneity of the area, with its evenly structured blocks, each consisting of sixteen 15x30 meter plots that were laid out in a uniform grid and separated by straight, 10 meter-wide roads. I supposed that the physical environment reflected the Maputo municipality's initially stated ideal of creating a *bairro modelo* that adhered to a set of fixed urban norms.[17] I was therefore quite surprised to learn that the greater part of the *bairro* had never been parceled out by the formal administrative authorities (see fig. 1). As I would come to find out, the structured appearance emerged through overlapping processes of informal parceling carried out by municipal land surveyors and architects, acting either on their own or in collaboration with local chiefs, with the intention of selling individual plots to needy newcomers in the initial post-resettlement process (Nielsen 2007b).[18] Indeed, as transport facilities and basic infrastructure were gradually improved, people who were in no position to obtain land closer to the city center took advantage of the opportunity to acquire a plot in the emerging *bairro*. Through informal transactions with either local leaders or *nativos*,[19] these newcomers were able to buy plots in Mulwene that, although

FIGURE 1 Overview of the officially parceled sections in Mulwene

informally parceled out by corrupt civil servants, nevertheless imitated the fixed urban norms associated with the *bairro modelo*.

Given the initially high-profile political ambitions of creating a formally structured area where legitimate residents would acquire legal use rights to evenly parceled-out plots, the difference between ideal and reality in Mulwene is striking in a peculiar way. Although the physical landscape appears to be ordered in accordance with an overall urban plan, this is clearly not the case. In order to understand the particular co-existence of urban ideals and actual parceling practices, we first turn to a brief discussion about urban governance in Maputo before unpacking a unique case of parceling in Mulwene.

Muddled Ideals

In considering access to land in Maputo (whether formal or informal), the importance of *parcelamento* (parceling out) cannot be underestimated, for it is not until a plot is parceled out and allocated a registration number that occupancy is officially recognized. As I discovered, however, urban planning initiatives in peri-urban areas of Maputo generally lack a legal basis. Although operational land laws and regulations stipulate that individual processes of *parcelamento* need to be rooted in comprehensive urban plans,[20] these are rarely drawn up, as neither state nor municipal agencies have the financial or human capital to realize such ambitious initiatives. During conversations with municipal civil servants, architects, and land surveyors, I discovered that planning initiatives in peri-urban areas were guided mostly by what is known locally as 'ad hoc administration' (*gestão ad hoc*), with the goal of securing a minimum of 'urban order'. As I was told by a former department head of the Direcção Municipal de Construção e Urbanização (DMCU, Municipal Department for Construction and Urbanization), the municipality was not at all interested in how a person gained access to a plot. The only decisive factor was whether the occupancy was at odds with ongoing projects: if not, the occupant remained. In most instances, then, *parcelamento* constituted a practical means of achieving what can best be defined as the pragmatic legitimation of illegal occupancy.

The current weaknesses of urban governance structures need to be seen in their historical context. At independence in 1975, the ruling socialist party, the Frente de Libertação de Moçambique (Frelimo), inherited what was already a poorly equipped and badly functioning bureaucratic system. With no attempt being made to strengthen administrative capacities, the government's short-comings dramatically increased in the following decades (Alexander 1997: 2). These weaknesses were particularly aggravated starting in the late 1980s, when Mozambique, sponsored by the International Monetary Fund (IMF), made its 'turn toward the West' and agreed to implement a series of structural adjust-ment programs (Devereux and Palmero 1999: 3). At the time, the country had been brought to its knees by a severe 14-year civil war between Frelimo and the Resistência Nacional Moçambicana (Renamo).[21] When Mozambique was then hit by the worst drought in decades, the need for urgent aid was evident. Before giving its financial support, however, the IMF made it a condition that government spending had to be drastically reduced, and salaries were cut by two-thirds (Hanlon 2002: 7). As a consequence, civil servants, including archi-tects and land surveyors, began to moonlight in order to secure a viable level of subsistence for themselves. Today, the effects of a weak state apparatus are apparent everywhere. Dilapidated public buildings are occupied by civil ser-vants who lack the necessary qualifications to manage a state administration that is incapable of carrying out even the simplest tasks and services (Nielsen 2007a). Illicit activities are endemic in all sectors to such an extent that we might speak of an 'inversion of values', as it is frequently considered immoral *not* to steal from the state, given that one's primary responsibility is to support one's own family (Hanlon 1996: 2).

Urban management in Maputo is a particularly salient reflection of this devel-opment. Despite rapid population growth in the years following independence,[22] the neglect of the urban population that transpired during the colonial period was reproduced. Of all the houses built from 1980 to 1997, only 7 percent were supplied by state or private sector agencies (Jenkins 1999: 23–24). Without a functioning system of urban governance, people have found alternative ways of accessing land. According to Paul Jenkins (2000a: 214; 2000b: 145), 75 percent of land acquisition occurs informally, that is, through local leaders or civil servants illegally parceling out plots that are later sold informally.

In sum, as an effect of overall weak administrative capacities at both the state and municipal levels, informal occupancy is pragmatically legitimized, provided that it is not at odds with ongoing projects. As we shall see next, the overall ambition of simply creating ad hoc administration has particular consequences when it occurs in a setting initially imagined as a *bairro modelo*. Indeed, the lack of formality with regard to the parceling-out process and the acquisition of individual plots notwithstanding, for the residents of Mulwene, a cement house in a 15x30 meter parceled-out plot has come to constitute a viable way of becoming legitimate members of both the local community and the wider society.

The Commercial Zone

I first heard about the parceling out of the commercial zone on 25 April 2005 while accompanying Magalhães, the *secretário de barrio* (neighborhood leader) in Mulwene, and Samuel, the land chief, to a meeting with Marta Simango, a local resident, regarding a particular dispute over land. When we got to her plot, the elegantly dressed Simango was already waiting with Boavida Wate, a former *chefe de quarteirão*. According to Simango, she acquired a plot prior to the 2000 floods when the area had still not been parceled out. After the parceling-out, she was allocated a 15x30 meter plot, but as she did not close it off with *espinhosa* (thorny bushes), her neighbor Magaia usurped parts of it, which he attached to his own plot and closed off with *espinhosa* before selling the entire property to an unidentified buyer. Wate then intervened: "The problem started when we opened the streets. This *senhora* was caught by the street, so we had to cut off some of her land and some of old Massango's land." "So, you know what parts you cut off from her plot, then?" Samuel wanted to know. "Yes," Wate confirmed. "And it is this smaller plot, which, according to Simango, is too small because it is not like it used to be." Simango interrupted: "Well, it's not exactly like that. I know that I can't get a plot like the one I used to have. It's just that the one I have now is really small (*pequeno mesmo*)." She turned to Wate, "And it was Magaia who was caught by the street, not me!"

Simango's plot was located in a section of Mulwene known as the 'Teachers' Zone' because it had been formally parceled out by the Ministry of Education and allocated to needy primary school teachers in the late 1990s. As can be seen from figure 2, when DMCU allocated the area for the Teachers' Zone, they also envisaged the creation of three *zonas de comércio* (commercial zones) intended for local residents to establish small shops.[23] However, fulfilling this objective was impeded from the outset. When DMCU made the first blueprint of the Teachers' Zone, the area was already partially inhabited by *nativos*, and as the neighborhood was gradually parceled out after the flooding in 2000,

FIGURE 2 Original DMCU blueprint of the Teachers' Zone

more and more newcomers acquired land in the zones through local quarter chiefs and former plot owners. Thus, by the end of 2000, the commercial zones had been totally occupied.

For people living in the Teachers' Zone (but outside the commercial zones), the process turned out to be beneficial, as it brought *parcelamento* to their area, which ensured their ongoing occupation of it. In other words, irrespective of whether or not they were in fact teachers, residents in the area were allocated 15x30 meter plots. For people living within the commercial zones, the situation was somewhat different. Obviously, they were prevented from being allocated formally parceled 15x30 meter plots, as their area was not intended for housing. When the area was parceled out as the Teachers' Zone, their status was transformed from informal residence to illegal squatting, with the implicit threat of being forcibly resettled to the remotest part of Mulwene. Without a doubt, this would have had serious consequences for people's ability to maintain a viable household income. Not only would they have to start new and costly house-building projects, but the doubling of transport costs to go to the city center would have ruined most household economies. No wonder, then, that residents living in the commercial zones were eager to find a way to remain where they were.

Marta Simango was one of the unfortunate newcomers who had acquired a plot in the commercial zone from Obadias, a now deceased *nativo*. In contrast to other residents in the area, however, she had not immediately occupied her plot.[24] After acquiring the land in 1995, she moved to Tete with her husband. Until her return to Maputo in 2004, she had allowed her uncle, Américo Gomes, to live in the plot in a two-room *casa de caniço* (reed hut). During her absence, however, the overall spatial configuration of the commercial zone had changed radically.

Although the Teachers' Zone was not directly part of the resettlement area for flood victims, the increased influx of people also affected housing dynamics in this section of the neighborhood. As previously described, given the opportunity to acquire relatively cheap land in an urban region with improved infrastructure and housing conditions, more people moved into the area and started building houses in accordance with the fixed urban norms associated with the *bairro modelo*. However, within the commercial zone, residents continued to inhabit irregular pieces of land that lacked the orderly structure of the surrounding areas. Moreover, due to the fear of forced relocation, piles of cement blocks continued to lie unused on the plots of prospective but still inactive house-builders.

During the first months of 2001, residents in the commercial zone grew increasingly frustrated, as the situation was becoming more untenable. Headed by Magaia, Américo, Belmira, and Massango, who had all lived locally for some years, a first attempt was made to restructure the area so that the parceling out would adhere to general urban norms. According to the agents involved, this *comissão de parcelamento* (parceling committee), as it was soon called, placed wooden plot markers in the ground throughout the area so that it followed the road traversing the Teachers' Zone. However, when it reached the far end of the area, it was clear that not all the current residents would be allocated plots if 15x30 meters was going to be the norm, since there was simply not enough land for this. Realizing the potential for an increase in disputes between residents, members of the commission therefore turned to Boavida Wate, the former *chefe de quarteirão* in the area, and Munguambe, who currently held the position in Quarter 18 and who had functioned as Wate's informally appointed notary when the latter had been *chefe de quarteirão*. Although initially skeptical, Wate agreed to lead a second parceling-out process. "Wate told them that we were not the DMCU," Munguambe later explained. "We agreed to do it, but we emphasized that it wasn't *parcelamento*. Actually, the initial intention was to make 15x30 meter plots, but we realized that problems would arise, because if we made them 15x30 meters, there wouldn't be enough space for everyone. In the end, we made plots of approximately 14x20 meters."

"It was at the time of the flooding," Wate remembered, when we finally sat down to discuss the parceling out of the commercial zone. "That's why we managed to open the streets." As Wate told me, the parceling out of the neighboring areas made people realize the need for similar urban norms within the commercial zone as well. This assumption was confirmed by Leonardo, the land chief in the neighboring Quarter 19: "The residents agreed to help Wate and Munguambe take the measurements, because in here there was a confusion of houses. So they said, 'We're a family' and began to subdivide the area so that all plots became equal." I asked Magaia, who was part of the commission working with Wate and Munguambe, how they had decided to use 15x30 meters as the dimensions. He replied: "We liked (*gostar*) using 15x30 meters because it's the norm for a land plot here in Mozambique." This opinion was widely shared among residents in the commercial zone. Sobusa, Magaia's neighbor, summed up the overall view: "This zone is very beautiful now, whereas before it only had narrow paths (*becos*). Now, there are streets, street lights … But back then it was different. The snakes (*cobras*) managed to invade the area in all kinds of ways. But now, as we are already accustomed to the *aldeias* (villages),[25] a lot of old things have changed. Now, I see more advantages in comparison to the life of the old ones (*antigos*)."

The overall agreement on the advantages of parceling notwithstanding, the conversion of the irregular pieces of land within the commercial zone into properly parceled-out plots mimicking the surrounding areas was anything but easy. According to the current residents, all landowners had to cede parts of their land, especially those who lost land to the street traversing the area. In this regard, Marta Simango and her neighbor Magaia were particularly unfortunate, as their plots were almost entirely taken for the street. As neither had erected cement houses, they were relocated to significantly smaller 14x20 meter plots. It was at this point that Simango erred by not fencing off her property with *espinhosa*, as is the norm among residents in Mulwene.

Inverse Governmentality

In order to understand the relatively unproblematic overall acceptance of the initial decision to parcel out the commercial zone, we must see it in the context of the increasing possibilities for those involved to become legitimate urban residents by building houses that adhered to the norms associated with the *bairro modelo*. Although several residents had already built small, one-room cement houses in the area, the *chefes de quarteirões* refused to allocate the land occupation cards (*fichas de ocupação de terreno*)—which documented the names and ages of all the inhabitants of the individual plots—to residents with cement houses, as this would represent the formal acceptance of their illegal occupancy. However, with the parceling out of the (still illegally occupied) commercial zone, local quarter chiefs accepted the building of cement houses and consequently allocated land occupation cards both to residents already living in the area and to newcomers starting house-building projects.

As was made clear above, urban norms of 15x30 meter plots with cement houses 3 meters from the boundaries were the aesthetic norm that both leaders and residents aspired to achieve. Hence, when later praising the work of the parceling committee in allocating a parceled plot to a resident who had previously lived on a diminutive triangular plot of less than 30 meters, Magalhães, the neighborhood leader, argued, "This is not Chamanculo [an urban neighborhood], you know. In Chamanculo, the triangle would be a huge area—but certainly not here! We don't allow anyone to live in a plot like that because here plots are 15x30 meters or even 20x25 meters … So a plot which is not even 10x10 meters … not even 10x5 meters … we don't allow people to live like that." In other words, according to Magalhães, the stated aspirations to create a *bairro modelo*, as realized by the parceling committee, were perceived as a complete contrast to the disorganized neighborhood of Chamanculo. According to local residents such as Sobusa, the result of the parceling out was a "beautiful zone" without unwanted invasions of capricious beings, including the dangerous *cobras*.

In her analysis of low-income model communities in Cape Town, South Africa, Fiona Ross (2005) brilliantly unpacks the intricate ways in which residents conceptualize linkages between new housing forms and ideals about becoming 'decent people'. Although they considered it to be an essential feature of what it is to be human, residents felt that decency (*ordentlikheid*) was being eroded by environmental factors. Whereas attractive gardens were a sign of *ordentlikheid*, it was generally assumed that slum conditions gave rise to "indecent behaviour" (ibid.: 639–640). What Ross's study shows, in other words, are the intricate interlinkages between housing forms and "moral structures" (ibid.: 636) that emerge when residents attempt to concretize sanctioned social forms. Hence, *ordentlikheid* crystallized the "approved forms of sociality as these are made apparent in appearances and interaction: both in recognition by others and in self-projection" (ibid.: 640).

Like the peri-urban community described by Ross, then, residents in the commercial zone were collectively attempting to make manifest similarly approbated social forms, which implied a partial imitation of the state. By building a house according to fixed urban norms introduced with the flooding in 2000, residents were therefore not merely copying the state; they were, so to speak, partially becoming the state by appropriating certain key aesthetic elements associated with state-authored urban planning. It is therefore clear that parceling and house building within the commercial zone did not openly contain the potential for contesting existing social orders. Rather than transforming social structures, these processes aimed to secure a stable position for the house-builders within the urban fabric by becoming partially visible through the appropriation of state-defined urban norms. In order to elucidate this partial visibility, let me turn briefly to the relationship between local house-builders in the commercial zone and outside forces, such as central state agencies.

During colonial rule, the African population was allowed to occupy urban land only on a temporary basis, so permanent housing was considered illegal by definition (Bryceson and Potts 2006: 15). However, as African migrants began to see the city as a place of more promising opportunities (Jenkins 2006: 125), the need for durable housing increased. According to my friends in Mulwene, residents in these areas therefore built cement houses inside the more unstable huts made of clay and reed. When they reached the roof, the surrounding hut was demolished and corrugated iron sheets were rapidly put in place for the roof of the hitherto concealed building. Realizing that a cement house had been erected, the local chief fined the house-builder, but the latter was nevertheless allowed to continue to reside there, given the 'urban look' of the new house.

In light of the discussion so far, we might argue that these previous housing practices were, to some extent, being reproduced by residents in the commercial zone. In both instances, possibilities emerging from the building process afforded house-builders a unique position from which to avoid further involvement with official agencies, given the aesthetic norms used for parceling and house construction. Indeed, as was the case during colonial rule, the parameters for accessing land could continue to be defined in terms of kinship-based or communitarian normative codes because building practices began to occur in accordance with urban norms defined by the Portuguese rulers. Similarly, in Mulwene, the apparent illegality of residents' occupancy was pragmatically legitimized because they built according to the fixed urban norms associated with the *bairro modelo*. Following James Ferguson (2006: 157), we might argue that these processes reflect a form of alterity that refuses to be other. Rather than distancing itself from the locus of power, it seeks to be (partially) visibly recognized, given the imagined affordances emanating from such a position (Nielsen 2010).

Surely, house building in the commercial zone was neither a condition for nor a rejection of urban governmentality, that is, institutional attempts to reform not only socio-economic environments but also peoples' desires and expectations, so that the operations of both are in conformity (Coquery-Vidrovitch 1991; Foucault 1991; cf. Li 2007; Osborne and Rose 1999; Outtes 1994; Rose and Miller 1992: 188; Scott 1998).[26] Rather, we might perhaps argue that parceling and house building in the commercial zone reflected a form of 'inverse governmentality' in which local agents actually strove to be partially met by the ordering gaze of power. In confronting the state with an imitation of those urban norms that the state was incapable of actualizing and subsequently feeding them back into the formal urban governance system, the activities of the house-builders created the ordering gaze of power by which they ought to be illuminated. The gaze radiated, as it were, back from the object toward the source. Let me briefly expand on this assumption.

Several recent academic works on peri-urban housing in sub-Saharan Africa focus on insurgent struggles waged by poor residents for improved urban rights (Bryant 2008; Cain 2007; Gatabaki-Kamau and Karirah-Gitau 2004; Gibson 2008; Miraftab and Willis 2005; Mitlin and Satterthwaite 2004; Mosoetsa 2005; Pithouse 2008; Skuse and Cousins 2007). Without neglecting to analyze intra-group disputes arising out of socio-political processes of asserting rights to the city, these works might be said to highlight the productive powers of collective oppositions. An example is Richard Pithouse's (2008: 85) study of the Durban-based shack dwellers' movement, Abahlali baseMjondolo, which "democratized the governance of settlements" through its collective opposition to forced evictions.

As is clearly apparent, the circumstances in Mulwene are radically different from these situations of overt opposition. Like some adept spiritual experts in the northern regions of Mozambique, who are capable of manipulating competing ethereal forces in both the visible and invisible realms (West 2001, 2005), residents in the commercial zone attempted to balance forces in their surrounding world without aspiring to circumvent existing structures of power. Still, as we saw above, local acts of house building might reverberate in different ways that end up strengthening the position of the residents without the need for overt opposition. Rather, in a peculiarly inverse way, the realization of alleged state-derived norms potentially becomes the covert medium of opposition that forces state and municipal agencies to acknowledge the continuing occupancy of otherwise illegal squatters (Nielsen 2011). Lacking any aspirations to circumvent the existing political governance system, this approach nonetheless challenged current distributions of rights to residents in peri-urban areas such as Mulwene. By appropriating urban norms and thus partially becoming the state, residents in the area were able to advance their claims to become legitimate residents like those in surrounding areas.[27]

The effects of these covert oppositional practices become manifest when one explores the current urban planning tools used in Mulwene. As can be seen on the recently updated map of the Teachers' Zone (fig. 3), the block that was previously parceled out as six formal plots has now been extended into the commercial zone by the addition of six additional plots. Needless to say, this does not indicate a full formalization of the whole area. Indeed, the map was probably drawn up by a DMCU architect who is not even aware that the parceling out has occurred. It does, however, suggest that the parceling out of the commercial zone successfully transformed the status and localization of residents in the area.

Conclusion: One Situation, Multiple Futures

Through an analysis of the interlinkages between the flooding that hit Mozambique in 2000 and the subsequent resettlement process in the neighborhood of Mulwene, I have tried to show how particular events come to reverberate with

FIGURE 3 Updated blueprint of the Teachers' Zone

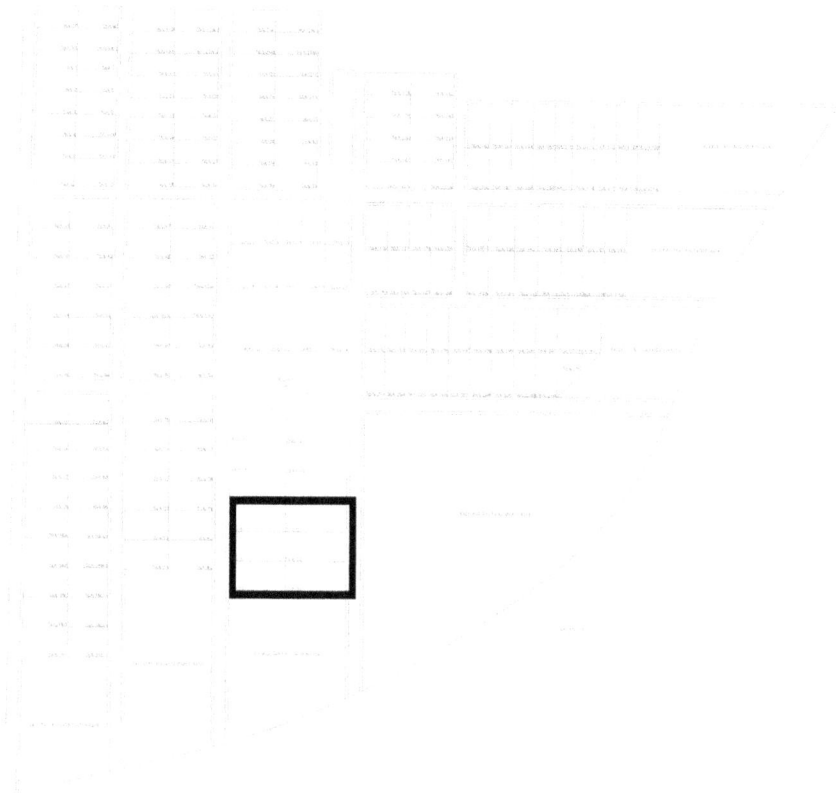

Note: The black square indicates where the additional six blocks have been parceled out within the commercial zone.

their surrounding socio-political environment so that hitherto detached elements become connected in novel ways. As we have seen, despite the informality of their status, residents in the commercial zone have been able to secure occupancy through the application of fixed urban norms associated with the initial aspirations of state agencies to create a *bairro modelo* in Mulwene. Indeed, in confronting the state with an imitation of those urban norms that it is incapable of realizing, the imitation acquires the status of the original; thus, residents pre-empt legitimate occupancy by, so to speak, becoming the state (Nielsen 2014).

I have also sought to outline the virtual and therefore, in a sense, unrealized potentials linked with the parceling-out process in the commercial zone. As an effect of the post-flooding process, residents connected the political aspirations to create a *bairro modelo* with their own attempts to secure legitimate positions in the neighborhood, irrespective of the apparent illegality of their occupancy.

In other words, the flooding (as an event) came to constitute a generative moment that gave rise to new and potentially accessible futures in which residents have been reconfigured as legitimate citizens within the urban fabric.

Researchers associated with the Rhodes-Livingstone Institute have shown us how the subjects of our inquiries are always "engaged within the changing forces of history" (Kapferer 2005: 89). Now, more than 50 years after the RLI's heyday, we are perhaps equipped to grasp properly the full magnitude of these crucial insights, which, at the time, were enfolded in an overly rigid structural functionalism. In this chapter, I have thus tried to show how a contemporary elaboration of work emanating from the Manchester School makes possible a more nuanced understanding of the potentials inherent in temporal ruptures such as natural disasters in Mozambique.[28]

Morten Nielsen is an Associate Professor at Aarhus University. His first major fieldwork project was in Recife, Brazil (2000–2001) among community leaders in poor urban neighborhoods. Since 2004, he has been working in Mozambique doing ethnographic research in peri-urban areas of Maputo as well as in rural areas of Cabo del Gado, the northernmost region. Based on his fieldwork in Brazil and Mozambique, he has published on issues such as urban aesthetics, time and temporality, materiality, relational ontologies, and political cosmologies. In 2013, he commenced a new research project on land rights and 'collapsed futures' in the Scottish highlands and islands. He is currently completing a book manuscript with Morten A. Pedersen and Mikkel Bunkenborg, University of Copenhagen, based on a comparative ethnographic research project on Chinese infrastructural interventions in Mozambique and Mongolia. His monograph *Bricks of Time: Inverse Governmentality through Informal House-Building Projects in Maputo, Mozambique* is forthcoming.

Notes

1. *Relatório anual ano 2001* (6 March 2002). Document in municipal archive in Mulwene.
2. In 1937, the RLI was set up in Livingstone, in what was then Northern Rhodesia, and it continued as such until 1964, when it was transformed into the Institute for Social Research of the new University of Zambia in connection with the founding of independent Zambia (Hannerz 1980: 119). The most prominent RLI researcher was undoubtedly Max Gluckman, the director at the institute from 1942–1947 (Colson 1977: 47). After a two-year lectureship at Oxford, Gluckman became the first holder of the chair of social anthropology at the University of Manchester in 1949 (Brown 1979: 539). Gluckman retained great influence over the development and research personnel of the RLI during the next 15 years. Given his huge influence, later generations have referred to RLI researchers as members of the Manchester School (known as such after Gluckman's move to Manchester in 1949).
3. Gluckman argued that Malinowski's idea of culture contact buttressed a policy of racial segregation (Schumaker 2001: 79). It obscured the fact that colonialism in Africa was not a matter of one culture influencing another; rather, "it was a matter of the forced incorporation of Africans into a wholly new social and economic system" (Ferguson 1999: 26).
4. In "The Seven-Year Research Plan of the Rhodes-Livingstone Institute of Social Studies in British Central Africa," Gluckman (1945: 9) stated the overall assumption that would

guide future empirical research: "(T)here is a Central African Society of heterogeneous culture-groups of Europeans and Africans, with a defined social structure and norms of behaviour, though it has many conflicts and maladjustments."

5. As an apt illustration, we might take Turner's (1957) seminal monograph, *Schism and Continuity in an African Society*. Although emphasizing the normative variations inherent in the situations being studied, it nevertheless reflects an overall emphasis on the reproduction of existing socio-cultural structures. This is, I suggest, apparent even from the way that the monograph is structured.

6. Apt examples of Deleuzian events could be "a set of animals altering course due to climatic change, or politically disinterested citizens woken from apathy by events, or the slow silting of a river strangling a port and its estuary into decay" (Williams 2008: 2).

7. Everyday examples of the virtual might be dreams or vivid memories, which are real without displaying immediate tangible compositions.

8. Paraphrasing Proust, Deleuze (2004: 260) thus claims that the virtual is "real without being actual, ideal without being abstract."

9. It is important to emphasize, however, that the problem is never completely actualized in a given solution. We might speak of the problem of communication prior to any language structure or the problem of political community as expressed in the idea of a social contract, both of which continue to produce series of dissimilar solutions. Following Paul Patton (1997: 15), we might therefore argue that "[s]pecification is necessary for the production of particular solutions, but the problem-event is not thereby dissolved or exhausted since there always remains the possibility of other specifications and other solutions." As it were, the event continues to assert its 'creative excess', as agents produce momentary solutions to the virtual problem.

10. This chapter is based on 13 months of fieldwork in Mulwene on the outskirts of Maputo, from September 2004 to August 2005, and again from mid-October 2006 to mid-November 2006. Whereas during the first period I lived for part of the time in Mulwene and part of the time in the city center with my family, I lived entirely in Mulwene during the second period of fieldwork. Throughout my stay in Mulwene, I focused on making extended case studies of particular disputes over land, which then guided my choice of informants and methodological approaches. Hence, in order to understand the historical trajectories of the disputes, my assistant Cândido Jeque and I undertook extensive archival research in Mulwene and at the administration offices in Urban District 5. These crucial insights were augmented through lengthy and ongoing interviews with all of the parties involved and as a result of participant observation, for example, at meetings and various informal gatherings. Finally, we carried out a household survey with all the household heads in a *quarteirão* (quarter) in Mulwene (a total of 131 interviews).

11. *Nativo* is the locally used designation for a resident who is believed to have been born in Mulwene.

12. Given the scarce habitation of the area, it served as the only remaining 'urban expansion zone' for which the Maputo municipality envisaged wide-ranging urban planning initiatives. According to the 1985 urban structure plan for Maputo, urban expansion zones are peripheral areas of the city where no formal occupation was envisaged until 2010 (Secretaria de Estado do Planeamento Físico 1985).

13. Matendene is the proper name used to describe the section of Mulwene where flooding victims were resettled. The word is essentially a mixture of Portuguese and xiChangana (xiTsonga), the language spoken by the Tsonga people. With the plural xiChangana prefix 'ma' attached to 'tendas' (Portuguese for 'tents'), Matendene means 'the area of the tents'.

14. *República de Moçambique: 1 Draft do Projecto de Reassentamento das Populações em Mulwene* (April 2000). Document in municipal archive, Mulwene.

15. *Município de Maputo, Resolucão No. 36/2001* (29 August 2001).

16. *Breve historial do Bairro Mulwene* (26 May 2005). Document in municipal archive, Mulwene.

17. When comparing Mulwene to peri-urban neighborhoods in Mozambique and other sub-Saharan states, the differences are striking. The new *bairro* is in many ways the antithesis of the many unplanned communities on the outskirts of African cities, which lack everything from basic infrastructure and sanitation to functional housing mechanisms.

18. With the nationalization of land at independence in 1975, monetary transactions in land were formally banned (Garvey 1998).

19. *Nativos* who were forced to cede their *machambas* (cultivated fields) to the flood victims were subsequently compensated with 15x30 meter plots for each family member above the age of 18. In many instances, these plots were later sold to the newcomers.

20. These stipulations are described particularly in Article 3 of the Territorial Ordering Regulations and in Article 19 of the Land Law Regulations accompanying the 1997 Land Law.

21. Primarily defined by its opposition to Frelimo, Renamo was initially a rebel movement. However, after the peace treaty in 1992, it was transformed into a political party (Carbone 2005; Vines 1996) that was supported first by Rhodesia and later South Africa.

22. In 1980, five years after independence, the population of Maputo numbered 775,000. This constituted a 97 percent increase over 10 years (Jenkins 2000a: 209). The city's rapid growth was caused primarily by the civil war, as well as by the lack of resources for family agriculture in the rural areas (Jenkins 2006: 119).

23. In fact, although most of the blocks shown on the blueprint have been parceled out, the commercial zones make up a much larger area than that indicated on the map. Thus, the middle block, which, on the map, is tied to six parceled-out plots, actually constitutes eight 15x30 meter plots.

24. Letter from Marta Isabel Simango to the administrative structure in Mulwene (27 April 2005). Document in municipal archive in Mulwene.

25. Sobusa is referring here to the communal villages (*aldeias communais*) created by the Frelimo government during the 'villagization' process, which also functioned as secure safe havens during the civil war between Frelimo and Renamo (Dinerman 2006: 51, 56; Egerö 1990).

26. According to Foucault (1991: 100), this particular form of governance emerges when the "population comes to appear above all else as the ultimate end of government … it is the population itself on which government will act either directly through large-scale campaigns, or indirectly through techniques that will make possible, without the full awareness of the people, the stimulation of birth rates, the directing of the flow of population into certain regions of activities, etc."

27. Since the first parceling out, several residents have submitted requests for legal building permits, irrespective of the initial illegality of their residence.

28. Although I emphasize the temporal potentials of the flooding, it is not my intention to disregard its devastating consequences for thousands of Mozambicans. Still, in order to perceive current realities as the effects of intricately interwoven forces of different scales, it is important to understand how emerging temporal and ideational horizons are interlinked with broader socio-political processes and thereby produce new potentials.

References

Alexander, Jocelyn. 1997. "The Local State in Post-war Mozambique: Political Practice and Ideas about Authority." *Africa* 67, no. 1: 1–26.

Ansell Pearson, Keith. 2002. *Philosophy and the Adventure of the Virtual*. London: Routledge.

Beck, Ulrich. 1986. *Risk Society: Towards a New Modernity*. London: Sage Publications.

Beck, Ulrich. 1998. "Politics of Risk Society." Pp. 9–22 in *The Politics of Risk Society*, ed. J. Franklin. Cambridge: Polity Press.

Boundas, Constantin V. 1996. "Deleuze-Bergson: An Ontology of the Virtual." Pp. 81–106 in *Deleuze: A Critical Reader*, ed. Paul Patton. Oxford: Blackwell Publishers.

Brown, Richard. 1979. "Passages in the Life of a White Anthropologist: Max Gluckman in Northern Rhodesia." *Journal of African History* 20, no. 4: 525–541.

Bryant, Jacob. 2008. "Towards Delivery and Dignity Community Struggle from Kennedy Road." *Asian and African Studies* 43, no. 1: 41–61.

Bryceson, Deborah Fahy, and Deborah Potts, eds. 2006. *African Urban Economies: Viability, Vitality or Vitiation?* Basingstoke: Palgrave Macmillan.

Cain, Allan. 2007. "Housing Microfinance in Post-conflict Angola: Overcoming Socioeconomic Exclusion through Land Tenure and Access to Credit." *Environment and Urbanization* 19, no. 2: 361–390.

Carbone, Giovanni M. 2005. "Continuidade na renovação? Ten Years of Multiparty Politics in Mozambique: Roots, Evolution and Stabilisation of the Frelimo-Renamo Party System." *Journal of Modern African Studies* 43, no. 3: 417–442.

Christie, Frances, and Joseph Hanlon. 2001. *Mozambique and the Great Flood of 2000*. Oxford: International African Institute, in association with James Currey.

Colson, Elizabeth. 1977. "The Institute under Max Gluckman, 1942–47." *African Social Research* 24: 285–296.

Coquery-Vidrovitch, Catherine. 1991. "The Process of Urbanization in Africa." *African Studies Review* 34, no. 3: 1–98.

DeLanda, Manuel. 2006. *A New Philosophy of Society: Assemblage Theory and Social Complexity*. London: Continuum.

Deleuze, Gilles. 1997. "Immanence: A Life." *Theory, Culture and Society* 14, no. 2: 3–7.

Deleuze, Gilles. 2004. *Difference and Repetition*. Trans. Paul Patton. London: Continuum.

Deleuze, Gilles. 2006. *The Fold: Leibniz and the Baroque*. Trans. Tom Conley. London: Continuum.

Devereux, Stephen, and Alessandro Palmero. 1999. *Mozambique Country Report. Creating a Framework for Reducing Poverty: Institutional and Process Issues in National Poverty Policy*. Maputo, Institute of Development Studies, University of Sussex.

Dinerman, Alice. 2006. *Revolution, Counter-Revolution and Revisionism in Postcolonial Africa: The Case of Mozambique, 1975–1994*. Oxon: Routledge.

Egerö, Bertil. 1990. *Mozambique: A Dream Undone. The Political Economy of Democracy, 1975–84*. Uppsala: Scandinavian Institute of African Studies.

Ferguson, James. 1999. *Expectations of Modernity: Myths and Meanings of Urban Life on the Zambian Copperbelt*. Berkeley: University of California Press.

Ferguson, James. 2006. *Global Shadows: Africa in the Neoliberal World Order*. Durham, NC: Duke University Press.

Foucault, Michel. 1991. "Governmentality." Pp. 87–104 in *The Foucault Effect: Studies in Governmentality*, ed. G. Burchell, C. Gordon, and P. Miller. Chicago: University of Chicago Press.

Fraser, Mariam. 2006. "Event." *Theory, Culture and Society* 23, no. 1–2: 129–133.

Game, Ann. 1997. "Time Unhinged." *Time and Society* 6, no. 2–3: 115–129.

Garvey, Jennifer. 1998. "The Nature of Rights in Land under Mozambique's Reform Land Law: An Analysis." Unpublished manuscript.

Gatabaki-Kamau, Rose, and Sarah Karirah-Gitau. 2004. "Actors and Interests: The Development of an Informal Settlement in Nairobi, Kenya." Pp. 158–175 in *Reconsidering Informality: Perspectives from Urban Africa*, ed. K. T. Hansen and M. Vaa. Uppsala: Nordiska Afrikainstitutet.

Gibson, Nigel C. 2008. "A New Politics of the Poor Emerges from South Africa's Shantytowns." *Asian and African Studies* 32, no. 1: 5–17.

Gluckman, Max. [1940] 1958. *Analysis of a Social Situation in Modern Zululand*. Rhodes-Livingstone Papers No. 28. Manchester: Manchester University Press for the Rhodes-Livingstone Institute. (Published originally in *Bantu Studies* 14: 1–30.)

Gluckman, Max. 1945. "The Seven-Year Research Plan of the Rhodes-Livingstone Institute of Social Studies in British Central Africa." *Rhodes-Livingstone Journal* 4: 1–32.

Gluckman, Max. 1949. "Malinowski's Sociological Theories." Rhodes-Livingstone Papers No. 16. Livingstone, Northern Rhodesia: Rhodes-Livingstone Institute.

Hallward, Peter. 2006. *Out of This World: Deleuze and the Philosophy of Creation*. London: Verso.

Hanlon, Joseph. 1996. *Peace without Profit: How the IMF Blocks Rebuilding in Mozambique*. Oxford: James Currey.

Hanlon, Joseph. 2002. "Are Donors to Mozambique Promoting Corruption?" Paper presented at the conference, "Towards a New Political Economy of Development." Sheffield, 3–4 July 2002.

Hannerz, Ulf. 1980. *Exploring the City: Inquiries toward an Urban Anthropology*. New York: Columbia University Press.

Jenkins, Paul. 1999. "Mozambique: Housing and Land Markets in Maputo." Research Paper No. 72. Edinburgh, Edinburgh College of Art/Heriot-Watt University, School of Planning and Housing.

Jenkins, Paul. 2000a. "City Profile Maputo." *Cities* 17, no. 3: 207–218.

Jenkins, Paul. 2000b. "Urban Management, Urban Poverty and Urban Governance: Planning and Land Management in Maputo." *Environment and Urbanization* 12, no. 1: 137–152.

Jenkins, Paul. 2006. "Image of the City in Mozambique: Civilization, Parasite, Engine of Growth or Place of Opportunity?" Pp. 107–130 in Bryceson and Potts 2006.

Kapferer, Bruce. 2005. "Situations, Crisis and the Anthropology of the Concrete: The Contribution of Max Gluckman." *Social Analysis* 49, no. 3: 85–122.

Li, Tania Murray. 2007. *The Will to Improve: Governmentality, Development, and the Practice of Politics*. Durham, NC: Duke University Press.

Long, Andrew. 1992. "Goods, Knowledge and Beer: The Methodological Significance of Situational Analysis." Pp. 147–170 in *Battlefields of Knowledge: The Interlocking of Theory and Practice in Social Research and Development*, ed. N. L. A. Long. London: Routledge.

Macmillan, Hugh. 1995. "Return to the Malungwana Drift: Max Gluckman, the Zulu Nation and the Common Society." *African Affairs* 94, no. 374: 39–65.

Mead, George Herbert. 1959. *The Philosophy of the Present*. La Salle, IL: Open Court.

Miraftab, Faranak, and Shana Willis. 2005. "Insurgency and Spaces of Active Citizenship: The Story of Western Cape Anti-eviction Campaign in South Africa." *Journal of Planning Education and Research* 25, no. 2: 200–217.

Mitchell, J. Clyde. 1956. *The Kalela Dance*. Rhodes-Livingstone Paper No. 27. Manchester: Manchester University Press for the Rhodes-Livingstone Institute.

Mitchell, J. Clyde. 1983. "Case and Situational Analysis." Pp. 165–186 in *Case Study Method*, ed. R. Gomm, M. Hammersley, and P. Foster. London: Sage Publications.

Mitlin, Diana, and David Satterthwaite. 2004. *Empowering Squatter Citizen: Local Government, Civil Society and Urban Poverty Reduction*. London: Earthscan.

Mosoetsa, Sarah. 2005. "Compromised Communities and Re-emerging Civic Engagement in Mpumalanga Township, Durban, KwaZulu-Natal." *Journal of Southern African Studies* 31, no. 4: 857–873.

Nielsen, Morten. 2007a. "Filling in the Blanks: The Potency of Fragmented Imageries of the State." *Review of African Political Economy* 34, no. 114: 695–708.

Nielsen, Morten. 2007b. "Shifting Registers of Leadership: An Ethnographic Critique of the Unequivocal Legitimization of Community Authorities." Pp. 159–176 in *State Recognition of Local Authorities and Public Participation: Experiences, Obstacles and Possibilities in Mozambique*, ed. Lars Buur, Helene M. Kyed, and Terezinha da Silva. Maputo: Ministry of Justice/ Center for Legal and Judicial Training.

Nielsen, Morten. 2008. "In the Vicinity of the State: House Construction, Personhood, and the State in Maputo, Mozambique." PhD diss., University of Copenhagen.

Nielsen, Morten. 2010. "Contrapuntal Cosmopolitanism: Distantiation as Social Relatedness among House-Builders in Maputo, Mozambique." *Social Anthropology* 18, no. 4: 396–402.

Nielsen, Morten. 2011. "Inverse Governmentality: The Paradoxical Production of Peri-Urban Planning in Maputo, Mozambique." *Critique of Anthropology* 31, no. 4: 329–358.

Nielsen, Morten. 2014. "A Wedge of Time: Futures in the Present and Presents without Futures in Maputo, Mozambique." *Journal of the Royal Anthropological Institute* 20, no. S1: 166–182.

Osborne, Thomas, and Nikolas Rose. 1999. "Governing Cities: Notes on the Spatilisation of Virtue." *Environment and Planning D* 17: 737–760.

Outtes, Joel. 1994. "Disciplining Society through the City: The Genesis of City Planning in Brazil and Argentina, 1902–1945." *Bulletin of Latin American Research* 22, no. 2: 137–164.

Patton, Paul. 1997. "The World Seen from Within: Deleuze and the Philosophy of Events." *Theory and Event* 1, no. 1: 1–21.

Pithouse, Richard. 2008. "A Politics of the Poor: Shack Dwellers' Struggles in Durban." *Asian and African Studies* 43, no. 1: 63–94.

Rose, Nikolas, and Peter Miller. 1992. "Political Power beyond the State: Problematics of Government." *British Journal of Sociology* 43, no. 2: 173–206.

Ross, Fiona C. 2005. "Model Communities and Respectable Residents? Home and Housing in a Low-Income Residential Estate in the Western Cape, South Africa." *Journal of Southern African Studies* 31, no. 3: 631–648.

Schumaker, Lyn. 2001. *Africanizing Anthropology: Fieldwork, Networks, and the Making of Cultural Knowledge in Central Africa*. Durham, NC: Duke University Press.

Scott, James. 1998. *Seeing Like a State: How Certain Schemes to Improve the Human Condition Have Failed*. New Haven, CT: Yale University Press.

Secretaria de Estado do Planeamento Físico (Secretary of State for Physical Planning). 1985. *Cidade de Maputo: Plano de Estrutura*. Maputo: National Institute for Physical Planning, Department of Urban Planning.

Skuse, Andrew, and Thomas Cousins. 2007. "Spaces of Resistance: Informal Settlement, Communication and Community Organisation in a Cape Town Township." *Urban Studies* 44, no. 5–6: 979–995.

Turner, Victor. 1957. *Schism and Continuity in an African Society: A Study of Ndembu Village Life*. Manchester: Manchester University Press for Rhodes-Livingstone Institute.

van Velsen, Jaap. 1967. "The Extended-Case Method and Situational Analysis." Pp. 129–149 in *The Craft of Social Anthropology*, ed. A. L. Epstein. London: Tavistock.

Vines, Alex. 1996. *Renamo: From Terrorism to Democracy in Mozambique?* London: James Currey.

West, Harry G. 2001. "Sorcery of Construction and Socialist Modernization: Ways of Understanding Power in Postcolonial Mozambique." *American Ethnologist* 28, no. 1: 119–150.

West, Harry G. 2005. *Kupilikula: Governance and the Invisible Realm in Mozambique*. Chicago: University of Chicago Press.

Williams, James. 2003. *Gilles Deleuze's* Difference and Repetition: *A Critical Introduction and Guide*. Edinburgh: Edinburgh University Press.

Williams, James. 2008. *Gilles Deleuze's* Logic of Sense: *A Critical Introduction and Guide*. Edinburgh: Edinburgh University Press.

ABOUT THE EDITORS

Lotte Meinert is a Professor of Anthropology at the Department of Culture and Society at Aarhus University, Denmark, and currently a Visiting Scholar in the Anthropology Department at Johns Hopkins University in the US. Recent selected publications include "Tricky Trust: Distrust as a Point of Departure and Trust as a Social Achievement in Uganda" (2015), "Connections" and "Clientship" (2014, co-authored with Godfrey E. Siu, Phoebe Kajubi, and Susan R. Whyte), *Ethnographies of Global Youth: Time Objectified* (2014, co-edited with Anne L. Dalsgaard, Martin D. Frederiksen, and Susanne Højlund), "Creating the New Times: Reburials after War in Northern Uganda" (2013, co-authored with Susan R. Whyte) *Hopes in Friction: Schooling, Health, and Everyday Life in Uganda* (2009). Since 2008 she had been leading research capacity-building programs between universities in Denmark and Uganda: "Changing Human Security: Recovery from Armed Conflict in Northern Uganda" and "Governing Transition in Northern Uganda: Trust and Land." With Jens Seeberg, she is the project leader of Epicenter: Center for Cultural Epidemics. Since 1994, she has carried out extended periods of fieldwork in Uganda.

Bruce Kapferer is a Fellow of the Australian Academy of Social Sciences and is currently Professor of Social Anthropology at the University of Bergen, Norway. He was affiliated with the Rhodes-Livingstone Institute (1963–1966) and was later appointed to the Department of Social Anthropology at the University of Manchester (1966–1973). He was subsequently Foundation Professor of Anthropology at the University of Adelaide and later at James Cook University, as well as Professor and Chair at University College London. He has held research fellowships at the Center for Behavioral Sciences, Palo Alto, the Netherlands Institute for Advanced Studies, and the National Humanities Center, North Carolina. His published books include *A Celebration of Demons* (1983), *Legends of People, Myths of State* (1988), *The Feast of the Sorcerer* (1997), and *2001 and Counting: Kubrick, Nietzsche, and Anthropology* (2014). He has edited *Beyond Rationalism* (2002) and has co-edited, with Angela Hobart, *Aesthetics in Performance* (2005) and, with Bjørn Bertelsen, *Crisis of the State* (2009). He was formerly joint editor of *Anthropological Theory* (2012–2015) and is chief editor of *Social Analysis*. He was Director of the Challenging the State project, supported by the Norwegian Research Foundation, and is currently Director of an egalitarianism project funded by the EU under the ERC Advanced Grant Scheme. This involves an international team of researchers inquiring into historical and current egalitarian/inegalitarian social and political processes.

INDEX

Collier, John, 52
Collier, Malcolm, 52
Colson, Elizabeth, 168n2
community: Buddhist, 74n8; European, 87, 94; global religious, 119–120; local, 136, 160; Pakistani migrant, 90–103; peri-urban, 164; political, 169n9; religious, 32, 35–36, 39; social, 9, 49; student, 54
compression (bodily), 147. *See also* time-space compression
Conde, Cecilia, 86
confrontation: absence of, 41; between activists and police, 140–141, 143–149, 150n3; nuclear, 93; political, 56, 99
Coquery-Vidrovitch, Catherine, 165
Cousins, Thomas, 166
customer feedback, 134–135

Das, Veena, 5, 13, 21, 90
Dawson, Marcelle C., 49, 53, 55
de Bruijn, Mirjam, 83, 87n1
Deeb, Lara, 35
Delanda, Manuel, 18, 156
Deleuze, Gilles, 2, 3, 10, 15–18, 20, 22, 24n4, 25n16, 25nn18–19, 30, 147, 154–156, 169n8
demonstration: political, 21, 107–110, 118, 120, 121n2, 122n3, 139, 141, 143–145, 147, 150n4; ritual, 24n3; student, 53–54; and violence, 41
Denmark, 21, 61, 87, 90–97, 99, 103, 104n5, 107–112, 114–116, 118–121, 121n1, 122n6, 122n9, 122nn13–14, 122n17, 123nn31–32, 127–128
development projects, 77, 80, 82, 84–86
Devereux, Stephen, 159
D'haen, Sarah, 77
Dinerman, Alice, 170n25
Diouf, Awa, 87n1
discourse: on corporate culture, 21–22, 135; on development, 86; on empowerment of women, 85; on event analysis, 17; on immigrants (public/national), 100–101, 107–108, 110–112, 114–119, 121n2, 122n12–13, 123n28; on values and vision, 130
dominant cleavage, 19, 48, 60, 99–103
drought, 21, 76–77, 79–80, 86, 159
Durkheim, Emile, 5, 7, 24n7, 140, 149n2

education, 36–37, 41, 49, 52–55, 57, 81, 95–97, 101–102, 104n2, 104n4, 104n6, 105n10, 116, 123n24, 137, 160
Egerö, Bertil, 170n25

Elmqvist, Bodil, 87n1
enlightenment project, 112, 115–118
Enlightenment, the, 116, 117, 123n24, 123n27
Evans-Pritchard, Edward E., 8, 118
Evens, T. M. S., 17, 23n1, 48–49, 77
event: as apt illustration, 2, 48, 60, 86, 129, 155, 169n5; as atypical, 2–4; as case, 1; Deleuzian, 15–16, 19–20, 22, 155–156, 169n6; Gluckman and Sahlins compared, 13–15; as potentiality, 155–156; summit, 140, 149
extended case analysis, 9, 16, 49, 60, 128, 136, 169n10

Fabricius, Anne Sophie, 90, 93
family, 31, 33, 35–37, 40, 42, 45n14, 54, 65, 83–85, 92, 94–96, 100, 102–104, 104n6, 105n8, 114, 123n28, 159, 163, 169n10, 170n19, 170n22
fatwa, 38–39
Ferguson, James, 25n12, 25n15, 165, 168n3
Fibiger, Thomas, 4, 19–20, 33, 44
figuration, 139, 148–149
flagellation, 30, 38
Foucault, Michel, 121n2, 149, 150n10, 165, 170n26
Francke, Rend R., 31, 33
Fraser, Mariam, 156
freedom: and active time, 148; movements, 54; religious, 34, 39, 117; and self-managing employees, 136; of speech, 35, 110, 113–117
Fuller, Graham, 31, 33
future: bodily figuration of, 139–140, 148–149; and climate change, 86; Deleuze on events and future, 16, 20; and education, 95; and freedom, 35–36; of gender relations, 86; of a human resource department, 132; of landscapes, 69; political, 50, 58–59; potential/alternative, 16, 22, 25n18, 156, 166, 168; and risks, 156; ruptures and disruptions of, 153

Game, Ann, 153, 155
Garvey, Jennifer, 170n18
Gatabaki-Kamau, Rose, 166
Gayley, Holly, 74n5
Geertz, Clifford, 1, 5, 14, 24n6
Gell, Alfred, 148
gender, 21, 60, 76, 80, 82–86, 102, 113, 116–117, 150n8
Gengler, Justin, 33
Gibson, Nigel C., 166
Giesen, Bernhard, 13

www.ingramcontent.com/pod-product-compliance
Lightning Source LLC
Chambersburg PA
CBHW060041030426
42334CB00019B/2429